JEAN PETERS

HOLLYWOOD LEGENDS SERIES
CARL ROLLYSON, GENERAL EDITOR

JEAN PETERS

Hollywood's Mystery Girl

MICHELANGELO CAPUA

University Press of Mississippi • Jackson

The University Press of Mississippi is the scholarly publishing agency of
the Mississippi Institutions of Higher Learning: Alcorn State University,
Delta State University, Jackson State University, Mississippi State University,
Mississippi University for Women, Mississippi Valley State University,
University of Mississippi, and University of Southern Mississippi.

www.upress.state.ms.us

The University Press of Mississippi is a member
of the Association of University Presses.

All photographs are from the author's collection.

Library of Congress Cataloging-in-Publication Data

Names: Capua, Michelangelo, 1966– author.
Title: Jean Peters : Hollywood's mystery girl / Michelangelo Capua.
Other titles: Hollywood legends series.
Description: Jackson : University Press of Mississippi, 2024. | Series:
Hollywood legends series | Includes bibliographical references and
index.
Identifiers: LCCN 2023048931 (print) | LCCN 2023048932 (ebook) | ISBN
9781496850263 (hardback) | ISBN 9781496850270 (epub) | ISBN
9781496850287 (epub) | ISBN 9781496850294 (pdf) | ISBN 9781496850300
(pdf)
Subjects: LCSH: Peters, Jean, 1926–2000. | Motion picture actors and
actresses—United States—Biography.
Classification: LCC PN2287.P4 C37 2024 (print) | LCC PN2287.P4 (ebook) |
DDC 791.4302/809273 [B]—dc23/eng/20231031
LC record available at https://lccn.loc.gov/2023048931
LC ebook record available at https://lccn.loc.gov/2023048932

British Library Cataloging-in-Publication Data available

CONTENTS

JEAN PETERS

Introduction

FROM 1947 TO 1955, JEAN PETERS APPEARED IN NINETEEN FILMS OPPOSITE Hollywood's leading men such as Tyrone Power, Marlon Brando, Burt Lancaster, Spencer Tracy, Richard Widmark, and Robert Wagner, as well as international stars including Louis Jourdan and Rossano Brazzi. It wasn't just her acting ability that caught the eye of producers and directors; her screen presence was electrifying, with 20th Century Fox production head Buddy Adler noting, "Jean Peters was an excellent actress. She had a great deal of fire that she kept under control, and you could feel it."

People who knew "Pete," as friends and colleagues called her, remarked on her authenticity and down-to-earth qualities. Unlike most film stars of the day, Jean Peters remained levelheaded and was never seduced by fame. Off-camera, her style was informal and ordinary, her face was makeup-less, and she wore clothes that she'd often sewn herself. She had grown up on a farm, was no stranger to manual work, and could wield an ax like the best of them. She'd always been a trousers type of girl, and these rustic qualities never left her.

Vast candy-colored mansions were eschewed for plain rented houses, flash cars were passed over in favor of simple rides, and she never embraced the Hollywood lifestyle. This behavior, at a time when ordinary people were engulfed in post-war austerity and Hollywood was regarded as the height of glamour, contributed to her being described by influential newspaper columnist Louella Parsons as a "Hollywood mystery girl." Parsons, whose well-read gossip column could launch or sink careers, could not understand why Jean refused to discuss her love life or embrace the much-coveted lifestyle of a true star. From that moment on, Jean Peters was marked as an enigma.

She became a challenge for reporters who constantly tried to discover tidbits about her personal life. When rumors started circulating that billionaire business magnate Howard Hughes—a mystery in his own right—had fallen hard for Jean and that she was in love with him too, the media went crazy. However, while Jean would talk about her career (she was delighted that she played so many different characters and was never typecast), her dressmaking abilities, and her passion for baseball, her love life remained off-limits.

Her penchant for dressing simply off-screen meant she was rarely noticed and could live an ordinary life. "I am not recognized half the time," she told reporters. When fans did recognize her, they would ask, "Are you Jean Peters?" and she would frown and ask in a puzzled voice, "Who's Jean Peters?" leaving them to walk off bewildered.

Howard Hughes would become Jean's second husband in 1957. After this, she retired from Hollywood and public life for eighteen years. They divorced in 1971, and from then on, she was simply Mrs. Hughes. Despite the many lucrative offers she received from publishers to write a memoir about life with Hughes, she refused, and the intimate details of her marriage remain a mystery to this day. Any information about her "unusual" marriage that *is* in the public realm came from Hughes's biographers. The most extraordinary fact of all is that there is no record of Jean Peters and Howard Hughes being seen in public together and no photographs.

In 1973, two years after her divorce from Hughes, by which time she was married to her third husband, producer Stan Hough (she also married briefly in the mid-1950s), she decided to go back to acting. Announcing her comeback, Jean said, "There has been no mystery to my life. I've been around all the time, always active. It's just that I wasn't going about my activities publicly."

Jean's oldest friend, Arlen Hurwitz, once said of Jean, who began her career as a trainee teacher in her native Ohio before becoming a Hollywood star and marrying one of the richest men on earth, "Jean's values haven't changed in the slightest. She always knew who she was, so fame had no effect on her personality. Nor has money. She was never owned by her possessions. If Jean was broke, she'd still be rich."

What makes Jean Peters distinctive? The very fact she eschewed the star-studded lifestyle of 1950s Hollywood—turning down roles that were "too sexy," refusing to socialize with other actors, discuss her private life in the press, or lead a glamorous lifestyle away from the cameras—tells everything needed to know about this down-to-earth actress. If she had courted the press a bit more, she would be better known today. In fact, Jean often said that her friend and three-film costar Marilyn Monroe had the drive and the ambition, attributes that she just didn't have.

CHAPTER 1

Farm Girl

It was my experience on the farm plus the inspiring spirit of my mother that gave me so little desire to become the victim of my possessions.

—JEAN PETERS

IN 1924, THE CANTON WET WASH IN STARK, OHIO, WAS AN INNOVATIVE laundry service where family washes were collected, washed, dried, and delivered the same day or the following morning. Twenty-four-year-old Gerald Peters, a truck driver working for the business, met Mary Thomas—a pretty twenty-six-year-old—in one of his daily pickups. Mary was living with her parents and her younger sister, Melba, at 1312 14th Street N.W. in Canton, a five-minute drive from Gerald's house. Every Tuesday afternoon, Mary made sure that the family's dirty laundry bundle was ready for pickup so it could be returned clean twenty-four hours later. At first, Gerald and Mary exchanged only a few words of formal greetings, but slowly, during those weekly deliveries, words became sentences and sentences became conversations. They found a common ground, discovering that both their families were of Welsh descent. Gerald's parents were, in fact, immigrants from Wales. His father, Henry Williams Peters, was a plumber and his mother, Sadie Eliza, a housewife, while Mary's parents were farmers of Welsh and German descent.

Finally, Gerald asked Mary out, and a few months later, the two were officially engaged. On September 12, 1924, after their marriage license request had appeared in a local newspaper, Gerald Morris Peters and Mary Elizabeth Thomas were married at Reverend Pearl Howard Welsheimer's residence. After a quick, simple ceremony, the newlyweds spent their honeymoon in Kentucky. On their return, the couple took residence in a house at 820 Richard Place N.W. in Canton. Although Gerald had been promoted to manager at Canton Wet Wash, his ambition was to find a job as an engineer in one of the local foundries, an aspiration that he fulfilled a few years later.

On October 15, 1926, Mary gave birth to her first child, a beautiful green-gray-eyed baby she named Elizabeth Jean. Little Elizabeth spent most of her early years in the natural landscape that surrounded the Peters's house. Her childhood was happy and carefree, and the house was filled with the arts. Gerald enjoyed playing the piano, and Elizabeth proved herself to be a talented painter. Mary taught her how to sew, and from the age of eight, she started to make dolls' clothes and later sewed clothes for herself, friends, and relatives. She also had a strong work ethic and, from an early age, would help her mother with daily chores around the house.

In 1935, the family welcomed a second baby, Shirley. Sadly, two years later, tragedy struck when Gerald died, aged just thirty-seven, following a long illness. The tragedy shook the family's finances. Practical Mary, who had been raised by farmers, rolled up her sleeves and invested her husband's life insurance into a seven-acre chicken farm—replete with magnolia, elm, cherry, and peach trees—in East Canton by Lincoln Highway.

At first, they lived above a stable until Mary heard of a flood control project that was condemning tract houses. She was able to buy enough material from them to assemble a house with the help of her eldest daughter and an aging uncle. They survived by selling eggs, eating vegetables and fruits from their beautiful orchard, and drinking milk from a cow they owned. Years later, little Elizabeth, who was now Jean, would say, "It was my experience on the farm, plus the inspiring spirit of my mother, that gave me so little desire to become the victim of my possessions."[1]

Shortly after the house's foundation was up and rough framing had been established, the United States entered the Second World War, which made carpenters and builders scarce. If Mary and Elizabeth wanted to get the house finished, they'd have to do it themselves. And they did, as Jean would later recall:

We moved into rooms over the completed garage. And Mother bought a buzz saw and a cement mixer. Then she and I built most of the nine-room house together. Of course we didn't do the heavy work, like putting in the beams. But we laid flooring, built the huge stone fireplace, and I nailed on the basic roof—later, carpenters shingled it. Also, Mother and I cemented all the stonework on the outside of the house.[2]

Once they completed the house, they built a row of cabins, which Mary planned to run as a tourist camp with the help of eleven-year-old Elizabeth Jean.

Jean proved to be a hardworking and determined young girl. Entrepreneurial, too. While in school, she wrote love letters for a classmate who liked a girl but was too shy to make a move. She received twenty-five cents for each letter until, eventually, the girl was won over.

When she came home from school, before she sat down to do her homework, she had to milk a cow named Lulubelle, feed a goat called Josephine plus a lamb named Ali Baba, and attend to three dogs and eighteen cats who lived around the farm. She also had to babysit little Shirley when her mother was not around. Only on Sundays did she rest, along with her mother, without ever missing the service at the local Methodist church. The only shattering of peace on Sundays was the weekly fight Mary and Jean had over the little girl's hatred of hats and her mother's insistence that she wore one to church.

It took four years before the house on the farm was completed and Mary could move in with her two daughters. In the meantime, Jean graduated in the class of 1944 from East Canton High, where she was also part of the high-strutting drum majorette corps. She tried hard to become a majorette leader, but, as she revealed later, she never succeeded. "I had a disappointment and felt very bitter about it," she said. "I tried but failed to become a drum majorette in high school, again at the university. I practiced, could do all the tricks, but other girls were chosen. So I decided I'd better stick to my knitting—my studies."[3]

As a child, Jean had dreamed of becoming a doctor, but once she graduated from high school, she was determined to be an English teacher. She was bookish and, from the age of thirteen, had started building up her own home library, which included some rare first editions. Over the years, through hard work and thriftiness, Mary had been able to save enough money to send her daughter to college, and Jean won a place at the University of Michigan. She chose not to join any sororities because she saw other girls' heartbreak after their failed pledges, so she lived off campus with a professor's family.

For the entire freshman year, she worked as a salesgirl in a department store for four hours every afternoon and all day on Saturday. However, after the first year at college, she was so homesick she transferred as a sophomore to Ohio State University (OSU) College of Education, where she lived with five hundred other girls in the Baker Hall dormitory. Exceptionally studious, on the rare occasions that she went on a date, she preferred the company of medical students, whom she found the most interesting.

Men were intrigued not just by Jean's self-sufficiency, maturity, and slight aloofness but also her sultry looks. They went crazy for her long, dark brown hair, which parted in the middle and hung softly around her face, framing her greenish-gray eyes. Unfortunately, they didn't stand a chance. "I had only three dates the whole year," Jean revealed years later. "At the time, I was quite in love with a boy I'd known in high school. He was in the Army, and I felt it was only right I shouldn't go out much. He was killed during that year. He was the only real romance I've ever had in my life."[4]

Nevertheless, a few months later, Jean almost became engaged to a pre-med student. Their dates were rather unusual, to say the least. "I used to go to autopsies with him," she said. "I was a little squeamish at first, but after a whole semester, I got used to it. That attachment didn't work out, however. I was a bit of a hypochondriac, and he wouldn't pay any attention to my 'symptoms.'"[5]

Among the young men Jean did date at college was Robert Slatzer, who would become one of her closest friends. The two met for the first time in Hayes Hall at the student medical dispensary when they were both suffering from colds. At the time, Slatzer was the campus photographer for *Makio*, the Ohio State yearbook, and *The Lantern*, the college newspaper. He asked Jean to pose for him, but she blushed and said nothing. A few days later, Slatzer visited her at her dorm and asked again, and this time she agreed. She posed for him in the snow near Mirror Lake, where other students were ice skating at the time. "It was freezing, and good sport that she was, Jean came dressed in clothing that did justice to her body but didn't exactly keep her warm," recalled Slatzer.[6] Jean framed the picture and kept it in her room.

In 1945, during her junior year, Jean shared her room with Arlen Hurwitz, a cheerful girl from Cleveland. Arlen would play a key role in shaping Jean's career and become a lifelong friend. Unlike Jean, Arlen dreamed of a future as a screen actress and spent her free time going to the movies and reading film magazines.

Arlen had an outgoing personality but was not a beauty like Jean. She knew her roommate had something special, and when the Homecoming Queen contest was announced on campus, she pushed a reluctant Jean to enter. She made it to the final six but did not win. Arlen was disappointed, but she never stopped pushing her friend toward the road to success.

A few days after the contest and following a long afternoon of Shakespearean studies at the library, Jean returned to her room and noticed the frame of her Mirror Lake photograph taken by Slatzer was empty. Arlen explained that she had sent the photo to the Miss Ohio State beauty contest, which was sponsored by a local newspaper. Arlen had paid the $4 enrollment fee, and it was money she wanted back. At first, Jean was furious and refused to pay her, but Arlen insisted that what she had done would make Jean a movie star. One of the prizes was a trip to Hollywood along with a screen test and $250 cash. Jean paid her the $4.

Jean assumed she would not get anywhere and put it to the back of her mind, but then she was contacted and asked to attend several beauty pageant rehearsals. Unfortunately, illness prevented her from attending. She did appear at a couple of press parties and dinners (beauty contestants would be invited to such events) but told Arlen the evening frivolity was interfering with her goal of becoming a teacher and forcing her to spend money on clothes she could not afford. Nevertheless, something made her continue with the contest, and she appeared in a bathing suit event at a local theater. Meanwhile, model expert John Powers, who had selected the initial 267 contestants from the photographs of more than 1,300 applicants, whittled the number down to forty before reducing it to the final twelve, which included Jean.

On the eve of the final, Jean went around the Baker Hall dormitory asking if she could borrow a dress. A classmate named Ginny Hitchcock loaned her a low-cut black velvet gown, which she wore to the final.

That night, Jean was late because her escort's car had a problem with the engine. She arrived at the RKO Palace Theater in Columbus just in time to be named one of the final six. A few moments later, she heard her name and the words "Miss Ohio State of 1945" with a score of ninety-five. Her closest competitor scored eighty-two. Columbus Mayor James A. Rhodes presented Jean with a trophy, a $250 check, and a voucher for an all-expenses-paid trip to Hollywood sponsored by two Columbus newspapers. The win also entitled her to a screen test at 20th Century Fox and a radio audition with ABC. Later she would say, "I was more surprised than anyone when I won."

As soon as she got home at 2 a.m., she rang her mother from the university lounge phone and shared the good news. She said she had just won a contest and was named "Miss Gooch Face of 1945." There was no chance of her retiring to bed as all the students had learned of her victory, and everyone celebrated until dawn. A couple of days later, Jean returned to East Canton to spend Christmas with her family, and in the first week of January, she boarded a TWA flight to Los Angeles.

Jean said later, "I took the trip, as it was part of winning, but I worried all during the two weeks because I was absent from classes and was afraid

I might not pass in my subjects."[7] Every girl she knew had insisted on lending her clothes and costume jewelry for the trip, so she left for California with a trunk full of borrowed clothes.

That two-week visit to Hollywood was a wonderful experience, and its highlight was the screen test at 20th Century Fox, which Jean took a week before she was due to return home. It was a five-minute love scene between a secretary—Jean—and her male boss, whom she was trying to seduce. Dressed in a see-through black gown, she spent the entire time reclining on a couch, trying to lure a young actor named Michael Dunne into her arms. The last eight seconds of the test showed Dunne breathing heavily as he succumbed. Jean later admitted that she played the whole thing as a gag.

She waited a couple of days, but when she heard nothing from Fox, she boarded the Golden State limited train home. In the meantime, Darryl F. Zanuck, the studio head of Fox, ordered his executives to sign her. He'd been impressed by her light-hearted approach to the scene.

Studio managers hurried to find Jean, but she had already left town. Frantic wires between Hollywood and stops along the train's route east were sent to get her to turn around. Jean got the news in the middle of the night when a wire was delivered to her carriage. She had been offered a seven-year contract with Fox.

Incredibly, Jean did not turn around and instead continued her trip back home to her studies. Her Baker Hall dormmates greeted her warmly, full of questions about Hollywood, and Jean felt overwhelmed. Over the next days and weeks, she withdrew, caught up in the dilemma of whether to complete the current school quarter that ended the following March or return to Hollywood immediately.

Paul Robinson, a photographer from Columbus and Jean's first manager, told the local press, who were fascinated by this student star in the making, that if Jean did return to California immediately, she could finish her schooling there. He explained that Jean was assured six months' employment at $150 a week, and the studio had an option to extend her contract to seven years. The salary would increase annually until it reached $1,000 a week in the seventh year.

After a couple of sleepless nights, Jean decided that her studies came first and Hollywood could wait until the end of the winter quarter. Fox's executives agreed, and her agent informed the press.

On March 15, 1946, after passing all her term exams with honors, Jean left for Hollywood. The night before the departure, she made her last public appearance as Miss Ohio State at a Columbus theater. Her parting statement on leaving the dorm was, "Don't sell my bed—I'll soon be back in it."[8]

Mary Peters was skeptical about a possible film career for her daughter, who was clever and hardworking enough to get a good job elsewhere. Her attitude was, "Have fun for six months and then come back and finish college."[9] In an article she wrote for *Modern Screen* magazine three years later, Mary recalled the frenzy around Jean's departure for Hollywood. She said her hometown friends and neighbors were convinced no good would come from Jean leaving sedate Ohio and moving to "wild" Hollywood:

> All East Canton now suddenly became Hollywood-conscious. Gossip about neighbors and neighborly affairs was suddenly supplanted by the latest Hollywood gossip. According to popular conception, my Jean would have little choice but to get involved shortly after her arrival in the film capital in some sort of love triangle or wild party or some other unfortunate happening that would make sensational headlines. Yet my belief in my daughter and her upbringing remained unshaken.[10]

Even though she trusted her daughter, Mary was relieved to know that Jean would have somebody to look after her in Hollywood. Two years earlier, Mr. and Mrs. Fink, former farmer neighbors and good friends of the family—whose son had gone to school with Jean for several years—had moved to Los Angeles. They offered to have Jean live with them in their modest bungalow with no telephone line until Mary's sister, Melba, could go to California and move in with her niece. While this alleviated a lot of Mary's worries, she still sent Jean regular newspaper clippings about "unhappy people who got their names in lurid headlines—just to remind my daughter what could happen and to caution her never to become like that."[11]

Jean's first day at the Fox studio was hectic. After a talk with Ivan Kahan, head of the talent department, her first job was to pose for her official Hollywood portrait in an elegant white gown that had been lent by Gene Tierney. Later, she was given a studio tour escorted by actors Peter Lawford and Dick Haymes, who took her on the set of *Cluny Brown* (1946), where she met cast member Charles Boyer. This was followed by lunch at the studio commissary.

That same evening, Jean dined with Victor Mature at La Rue, a favorite dining spot for movie stars on Sunset Boulevard, after which they visited Ciro's, Hollywood's trendiest nightclub. The next day she attended the horse races with actor Don Ameche. Every moment was captured by a photographer for a national magazine layout to build up a buzz around her as Hollywood's newest starlet.

In April of that year, Jean, who at nineteen was still a minor, appeared in a Los Angeles court where she received judicial approval of her contract with 20th Century Fox, which provided a starting salary of $150 a week. The judge was visibly surprised to learn of this modest budget from which she had to pay rent and buy food and clothes. Jean, meanwhile, thought it was more than enough to support her and her cow, Lulubelle, who was at home on the family farm and whom she named as her codependent.

Jean's complete lack of acting training prompted the studio to enroll her in the Actor's Lab, one of Hollywood's best drama schools. Classmates included Barbara Lawrence, Frank Latimore, John Russell, and Audie Murphy. For three months, she observed the Stanislavski acting method and attended all the other classes, including singing, diction, and fencing. This was the first time that Jean had come into close contact with professional acting, and she was hooked.

In the summer of 1946, she met actor Norman Lloyd—who starred as Mosca in Ben Jonson's comedy *Volpone*—during a special performance at the Las Palmas Theatre for the young players the studio sent to the Lab for observation and training.

Almost immediately, theater replaced baseball as her passion, as she affirmed years later. "I always loved the theater," she said. "I'm an opening-night, front-row person. I love theaters like the Mark Taper Forum—that little jewel box of a theater; how I would love to play there! But I was never on stage."[12]

When her education at the Actor's Lab was complete, Jean returned to the Fox lot for more training. She reported devotedly to Fox's drama coaches, Helena Sorrell and Craig Noel, who taught her how to speak more slowly. Sorrell had her read aloud for hours every day, and that helped fix her naturally fast speech pattern. The class at the Actor's Lab was made up of a dozen aspiring actors who were all under contract for different film studios and paid anything from $50 to $150 a week.

One day, a screenwriter named Sy Bartlett took Jean and a friend to the local police station to observe its activity, a sort of exercise connected to method acting. Impressed by Jean's intelligence, Bartlett mentioned her name to casting director Ben Lyon, who suggested to producer Walter Morosco that he test her for the role of Rad, a young farmer, in his upcoming film *Scudda Hoo! Scudda Hay!* (1948).

The part seemed tailor-made for farmgirl Jean; however, she was not asked to play in any particular scene but simply to walk around in a bathing suit, sit on a bar stool, and answer a few questions. She wasn't successful, and the role was given to June Haver. "I loved that part," Jean revealed many years later, "because it was a farm girl, there were mules in it . . . instead, I ended up playing a Spanish gypsy."[13]

Scudda Hoo! Scudda Hay! was not a hit, yet it made film history as it featured an unknown Marilyn Monroe in her first screen appearance. Like Jean, Marilyn had just joined Fox as a contract player. The two young actresses had met for the first time in Helena Sorrell's class, where they soon became acquainted. Interviewed by Monroe's biographer Richard Buskin in 1994, Jean talked about her friendship and admiration for Marilyn:

> At the time, I knew her as Norma Jeane. She wanted to come up with a name, and I was arguing with her she should call herself Meredith something. I always liked the name Meredith, but she didn't go for that. Ben Lyon came up with Marilyn Monroe while I was in Mexico for six months shooting *Captain from Castile*, but when we were in class together, she was Norma Jeane. . . . She was a dedicated want-to-be actress/movie star, whereas for a lot of us, it was strictly a lark, and the studio was almost an extension of a college campus. Darryl Zanuck used to call it the Country Club, and it was. It was fun. We were young, we liked each other, and there was a lot of camaraderie. Frankly, I was happier doing the classes than I was making films. I didn't have what Marilyn had, which was this fantastic drive and the ability to really, really work on things.[14]

Within a few years, Jean and Marilyn would appear together in three films: *As Young as You Feel* (1951), *O. Henry's Full House* (1952), and *Niagara* (1953).

In June, Jean left the Finks' residence to move into a two-bedroom house with her Aunt Melba in Westwood, not far from the University of California, Los Angeles (UCLA). Melba "Mel" Thomas Dysle had lost her husband a year earlier. She was Mary's younger sister but only twelve years Jean's senior, and she soon became more of a close friend than an older relative to Jean. The new rented home was filled with over seven hundred books, some of great value, built from the collection Jean had started when she was a teenager. Spending money on books, including rare first editions, was her only extravagance. A portable sewing machine, along with fabric samples, trimmings, and other sewing accessories owned by Jean, was also part of the house furniture.

A few days after Jean and Aunt Mel had settled into the new house, Mary and Shirley drove from East Canton to California. In anticipation of her family's arrival, Jean did some redecorating and repairs around the new house. "I can lay bricks and fix plumbing," she explained later. "In the country, you can't always get help in a hurry, so you learn to do a lot of things for yourself. I love to remake furniture, too—take off the paint or the varnish and clean it right down to the wood and start from there. It rests me to work with my hands."[15]

Jean was thrilled that her mother and sister visited. She had often felt homesick, and their presence cheered her up. She enjoyed showing them all the Hollywood tourist sites and, when possible, sneaking them into the studios.

At the end of July, 20th Century Fox cast Jean in *I Wonder Who's Kissing Her Now* (1947), a musical directed by Lloyd Bacon. She was offered the minor role of an "ugly duckling" that would require heavy makeup with artificial freckles and horn-rimmed glasses. Jean turned down the part. From the very beginning, she had solid opinions about the types of roles she wanted to play, and this was not the one she had in mind for her screen debut. She convinced her publicist that the part was unsuitable and withdrew from the project. It was a bold choice that caused quite a stir among Fox's executives.

That same summer, Jean started dating twenty-two-year-old Audie Murphy from Texas. They had met at the Actor's Lab, and Murphy was also trying to break into the film industry. He was a handsome, boyish war hero and a national celebrity after *Life* magazine proclaimed him America's "most decorated soldier" a year earlier. That magazine cover brought him to the attention of actor James Cagney, who invited him to Hollywood after his military discharge. Murphy accepted an offer from Cagney and his brother and producer Bill for $150 a week as a contract player with their film production company. He enrolled at the Actor's Lab, where he shared a few classes with Jean, whose outgoing personality and striking looks made an immediate impression.

Murphy, who had tried unsuccessfully to conceal his identity and war record at the Lab, found in Jean a kindred spirit and his dream girl. According to one of Murphy's biographers, "The couple fell in love, and their affair caught the attention of the movie press. Gossip columnists dubbed them 'America's most romantic sweethearts.' They swore to each other that they would work long enough in pictures for Audie to buy a spread in Texas or a farm in Ohio, then they would 'retire' from Hollywood."[16]

Alas, the relationship was intense but short. They enjoyed each other's company, but it ended when eccentric billionaire Howard Hughes, at the time, one of the most glamorous and powerful figures in Hollywood, invited the couple to fly on his private plane to Santa Catalina Island for a long weekend.

The weekend started with the Fourth of July party given at Bill Cagney's home near Newport Beach and continued with a cruise on Cagney's boat to Santa Catalina. Most of the invitees wore bathing suits and enjoyed the private beach adjacent to the producer's magnificent villa. The reclusive Hughes was among the guests, and when Jean walked in wearing a dazzling white bathing suit, hand in hand with Murphy, his head was turned. As she walked in his direction, he flashed her a smile, then looked away. "It was like he walked off a farm and into a stranger's backyard,"[17] she said later. Hughes tried to talk to Jean alone, but a jealous Murphy always headed him off.

When the partygoers boarded two yachts for the cruise to Santa Catalina, Hughes took his chance and, while chatting with Murphy about wartime, offered to fly some of the guests—including Jean and her date—to the island. On the flight across the channel, Hughes had his assistant, Johnny Meyer, and Murphy sit in the back seats while Jean sat next to him in the cockpit. Jean was impressed not only with Hughes's ability as a pilot but also his knowledge of the Hollywood establishment, as he was the owner of RKO Pictures.

Despite his wealth, he quickly realized that he would not be able to woo Jean in the usual Hollywood manner, as flashy jewels, trendy nightclubs, and expensive restaurants were not her style. Nor would his power impress her as Jean was too grounded in her midwestern roots. Instead, he charmed her, and Murphy, with his vast general cultural knowledge, came across as more of a father figure to them both.[18] When, a year later, gossip columnist Sheilah Graham asked Jean about that first meeting she had with Hughes, she revealed candidly:

> "We knew right away that we liked each other."
> "What did you talk about?" asked Graham.
> "Propellers!"

Jean explained that she was interested in aviation. "A girl would have to be to go with Hughes," said Graham. However, Jean also explained that in the year since they had met, Hughes "has never let me hold the controls. We both agreed that he never will. Flying is to Hughes what a bag of gold is to a miner. He doesn't let anyone else handle his machine."[19]

Years later, in an article dedicated to Hughes and all his romances, Graham wrote rather caustically: "While Jean was pretty, she was not particularly chic. She made her own clothes, and had no use for a razor or depilatory. Jean was determined to remain as nature had made her. [Some of the studio personnel called her 'Miss Hairy-Legs,' but not to her face.] She was completely honest, and this was her chief attraction for Hughes."[20]

On Sunday morning of July 7, when the party in Catalina was finally breaking up and the yachts sailed home, Hughes invited Jean and Murphy to fly back with him to Hughes Aircraft, his airfield located in Fullerton, California. There he had planned to test an XF-11 spy plane, the fastest, largest private plane ever built.

The couple agreed, and as soon they landed, Hughes got ready to fly. He ignored all the recommendations given by his engineers and flew the plane alone. After a smooth take-off, one of the wings suddenly dipped and the plane plummeted and crashed into a corner of a two-story house in Beverly Hills. When Jean learned the shocking news, she was beside herself. Hughes had been taken to the hospital, but his condition was unknown. It was now obvious that Jean had developed deep feelings for Hughes that she could not hide. She later described him as "the most lost soul in the world."[21]

A few weeks later, she broke up with Murphy. The veteran became so insanely angry that for months he threatened to fight Hughes if he ever saw him again. According to one of Hughes's biographers, an armed Murphy succeeded in bribing all the billionaire's bodyguards but one, so when Hughes made an appearance at the Town House Hotel where he regularly stayed, Murphy planned to shoot him in the parking lot. Fortunately for Hughes, the remaining henchman refused to cooperate.[22]

Murphy was so heartbroken that for a long time, he condemned Jean for her greed and ambition, wrongly thinking that those were her reasons behind the breakup. Yet despite Murphy's hard feelings, the two kept in touch for years discreetly through David "Spec" McClure, a mutual friend. As one of Murphy's biographers recounted, Spec recalled a meeting with Jean on a film set many years later:

When we were out of earshot of the others, Jean would say, "Well, how is the little sonofabitch?" I'd say, "What sonofabitch are you talking about?" She would say, "Audie Murphy." And I would say, "Meaner than ever. Do you want me to tell him something?" She would say, "Tell him I still have a good right hook." Once I told Audie this and he said, "She wasn't kidding. I felt that right hook many times."[23]

An interesting comment. There is no evidence that Jean was violent to her partners, but she did get frustrated and, as will be revealed, would sometimes take an ax to a piece of wood to let off steam.

CHAPTER 2

Catana

I have no delusions about my ability. I think I am a very lucky
girl who got a grand break.
—JEAN PETERS

AT THE BEGINNING OF OCTOBER 1946, JEAN RECEIVED A CALL FROM DARRYL
Zanuck's office requesting an in-person meeting with Mr. Zanuck. Jean had
never met the studio head before and was curious but nervous to know the
reason she had been summoned. The meeting was brief. Initially, the two
engaged in small talk, but then Zanuck told her he had seen and liked the
Scudda Hoo! Scudda Hay! bathing suit screen test. He thought she should test
for the major role of a Spanish peasant girl named Catana in the upcoming
production of *Captain from Castile* starring Tyrone Power.

Jean was speechless. She had, after all, failed the bathing suit screen test,
but Zanuck, sensing her excitement, warned her not to get her high hopes
up because it was a large role and probably too much for an inexperienced
actress. It was just a screen test. While the film's director, Henry King, had
the final decision, Zanuck's final words to her were: "If you don't hear from
me again, you'll know everything is going and it's all alright."[1]

King had struggled to find a convincing replacement after Linda Darnell,
the original choice for Catana, had withdrawn from the picture. She had
been given the opportunity to play the title role in another of Fox's mega
productions, *Forever Amber* (1947). In a letter to producer David O. Selznick
dated September 20, 1946, Zanuck wrote of his regrets that Selznick's wife,
actress Jennifer Jones, was committed to another project and unable to play
Catana. He discussed his personal involvement with screenwriter Lamar
Trotti in what he called a "$4,300,000 subject and probably to be one of
the greatest productions of next year." Zanuck explained that Henry King
was in Mexico and, because of his commitments to Technicolor, shooting
had to start November 25. Zanuck hoped that Jones would be available to

star in *Captain from Castile*. "If there is any change in your plans," he wrote, "please telephone me at once . . . I could probably arrange the schedule to keep away from Catana for one or two weeks."[2]

As the production start date approached, the role remained uncast. Pressure was high until Zanuck called King one day and said:

> I don't know who you have in mind. I haven't anyone to play the part of this peasant girl, but I saw a test of a girl in a bathing suit that, as far as physique is concerned, and as far as having a sort of down-to-earth quality, I believe that she would be my idea of what this girl should look like. Now whether she has any ability or not, that you will have to find out if you are interested.

King watched the test but was not fully convinced, and he asked Jean to meet him at his office. That meeting changed his mind. "She was a very smart, very intelligent girl, but not one of those who knew everything," was his first impression.[3] He added:

> This girl had never spoken a word in her life in theater, stage, screen, pictures—silent, sound, or anything. She hadn't been in anything. She was studying to be a schoolteacher. I decided to make a real test. I had four actors working and I took the most difficult scene in the picture to do. I said, "If she can do this, I'll show her very quickly if she can do anything or not."[4]

King shot the test scene outdoors exactly as it was in the final script. In the sequence, stock player Bert Hicks replaced Tyrone Power as Pedro de Vargas, the film's main character. All the actors involved in the scene wore the costumes that were made for the film. King worked with Jean for two full days. First, they rehearsed the scene, then they shot it. The dialogue showed a gamut of emotions that tested Jean's acting ability, and she did not disappoint with a performance that film editor Bobbie McLean called "wonderful."

Jean and King put together a twelve-minute sequence that Zanuck watched later in a projection room with four people from his entourage. When the lights came on, the producer looked as though he had just witnessed a miracle. A young girl, a complete unknown who had never done anything in show business, had acted in one of the best scenes he had ever seen on a screen test. The producer told King that if he wanted to cast an unknown as Catana, he had his wholehearted consent. King accepted the challenge and agreed with Zanuck that the test had revealed Jean's natural acting talent along with an earthy appeal. Many years later, when discussing *Captain from Castile* in an interview, King recalled Jean's moment of glory, stating, "That girl was a star from that picture on."

Shortly after the screen test, Jean was summoned to an executives' conference. As soon as she walked into the room, someone shouted, "Hello, Catana!" A few moments later, Henry King looked at her and asked, "Think you'll like Mexico?"[5] Before Jean could say a word, an assistant was making plane reservations and instructed her to go to the studio hospital and get typhoid shots. She did as she was told but made a detour to Zanuck's office, where he confirmed that she had been cast as the female lead in *Captain from Castile*. "I could do little but stare blankly," she said later. "I'd never expected any such a thing as this, never in my wildest dreams."[6]

She left his office in a state of shock, not remembering how she made it from that building to the studio hospital. The idea that she would be debuting in a major production opposite Tyrone Power, one of her favorite movie stars, seemed surreal.

That evening, when she returned home and broke the news to her aunt, Jean was still too much in shock to telephone Mary and Shirley. Aunt Mel made the long-distance call to East Canton.

Shortly after, on October 21, 1946, the news that an unknown actress named Jean Peters had been cast in the coveted role of Catana opposite Tyrone Power in *Captain from Castile* appeared nationwide in the print news.

Captain from Castile was based on Samuel Shellabarger's bestselling novel, the rights to which 20th Century Fox had bought for $100,000 in December 1944. A Spanish nobleman, Pedro de Vargas, escapes the clutches of the Inquisition and joins the conquistadors of Cortez in the New World together with Catana, a beautiful young peasant girl. There she becomes Vargas's wife, but their hopes for a better life are threatened when Diego de Silva, the officer who investigates false charges against them, arrives. He is soon killed under mysterious circumstances, and Vargas is held responsible until cleared by a native prince.

In February 1945, writer John Tucker Battle wrote a story outline of the novel, and by late May, he had finished a first draft of a screenplay in collaboration with Samuel Engel. In the meantime, Zanuck consulted director Joseph L. Mankiewicz, who suggested Tyrone Power and Linda Darnell as the leads. Eventually, the script was passed to Lamar Trotti, who wrote all subsequent drafts and ultimately produced the film. The writer had the difficult task of condensing 502 pages of the novel without losing the elements that had made it a success. Trotti also had to tone down the treatment of the Inquisition as the Catholic Church and the Legion of Decency (an organization dedicated to finding and removing objectionable content in movies) told the studio that having a corrupt priest of the Spanish Inquisition as the villain was simply unacceptable.

Captain from Castile was Fox's first costumed film to be shot on location after the war and boasted the biggest crew ever to work outside the US. In early November, before the cast arrived, an army of 205 technicians, craftsmen, and actors landed from a fleet of chartered planes in the picturesque town of Morelia, 190 miles west of Mexico City. Fifty trucks also arrived with more than two thousand tons of equipment, costumes, props, generators, a dry-cleaning plant, and other miscellany. The items had been sent on a special train in eight tightly packed baggage cars and then loaded into trucks for transfer to Morelia.

A laboratory had to be set up in Morelia to develop the film as, according to Mexican laws, no undeveloped film could leave the country. For this reason, three refrigeration units were built to protect the sensitive Technicolor film stock from the tropical heat. An immense commissary was also set up to feed not only the Hollywood company but the huge number of extras as well. When the local hotels were filled to capacity, tents were put up for the less fortunate crew members.

Only players with speaking roles were sent to Mexico, and a record total of 19,500 extras, both Mexican and indigenous, were hired on location. The crew worked on eighty different sets, and these, together with twenty built at the studio for filming interiors, brought the total to one hundred.

Henry King visited Morelia for the first time in 1933 after he spotted it while flying his own plane to the Panama Canal. He stopped there on the way back and was impressed by the beauty of the old town—which was built in 1631—and its well-preserved Spanish-style churches and mansions, not to mention its extravagant gardens surrounded by verdant hills. When *Captain from Castile*'s preproduction started, the director recalled Morelia and decided to fly back with Bob Webb, the appointed second unit director, and air-racing pilot Paul Mantz to see if it would be the right "stand-in" for an old Spanish *pueblo*.

It was, and shooting began in Morelia on November 19, 1946. The company spent six weeks there before moving to another location. Jean arrived in Mexico on November 22, three days after filming started. Fox had agreed to pay all the expenses for Jean to take a companion on the trip, so she invited her former roommate Arlen Hurwitz, who was ecstatic to accept.

A week later, Jean appeared in front of the camera and met Tyrone "Ty" Power, to whom she was in awe, for the first time. "One of the first pictures I remember seeing was *Crash Dive* [1943] starring Tyrone Power," recalled Jean. "When I first met him, he seemed like some kind of god."[7] More than four decades later, in a rare TV interview, she added, "Ty Power was a beautiful man, a beautiful, beautiful person . . . he had glamour and also had eyelashes longer than any girl on the lot!"[8]

For Jean's debut, the director chose the difficult scene in which Catana has to fight off some violent dogs that attack her. King told her that he wanted her to do that particular sequence first so she would not be afraid of anything. Throughout the shoot, King and Power, who had collaborated on seven previous films, showed her constant support, which made her work easier.

In a scene where she had to roast a chicken on a spit, the chicken would fall off every time she turned the handle. Then smoke from the fire got into her eyes and made her cry. It took many retakes to get that scene right, but the director never lost his patience. Another time, Jean and Power had to get up on a horse that was supposed to be trained to carry two people, but apparently, its training had been neglected. The animal became nervous and made a beeline for the camera. When they tried again, Jean got caught in the sword Power was wearing and cut her legs. Only the actor's ability as a horseman avoided more serious consequences.

During an interview on the set, Jean said:

> I tell myself that Catana was a real person, and I am really her. A Spanish girl who lived in the sixteenth century and followed Cortez to Mexico, there to fall in love with one of his captains—in this case Tyrone Power. . . . If I can convince myself that I have acquired Catana's character, it will be reflected in my acting and the audience will be convinced, too. I have prepared myself for this role by doing much research on the period of the story. . . . As a newcomer, I don't know the tricks of acting—yet. So, my only chance to make good in this role is to live it as best I can.[9]

Walking barefoot all day on the farm she grew up on helped Jean with her character, who only wore sandals in one scene and spent the rest of the time walking and even dancing barefoot on all kinds of rough ground. After the film wrapped, Jean had to replace all her shoes because her feet had widened. Costume designer Bill Travilla recalled that off the set, he had Jean wearing shoes that were too small for her to break her of her American walk, and he padded her body to make her short-waisted, as most Mexican women are.[10]

Choreographer Hermes Pan was responsible for teaching Jean and Tyrone Power the *zarabanda*, a sexy Spanish folk dance. Jean admitted that dancing with her costar was one of the most difficult challenges. In preparation, she was given a week of eight-hour-a-day lessons where she learned everything from the waltz to the rumba. "Ty is a marvelous dancer, extremely graceful, but I never learned to dance a bit in Ohio," she said. "Even after rehearsing the dance for a month, I was worried for fear I would make mistakes."[11] Pan found Jean quite clumsy as a dancer and advised the director to shoot the sequence from the waist up so Jean's expressive looks and hand gestures would not be upstaged by her awkward footwork.

One of the biggest thrills Jean had on set was her first screen kiss with Power, at that time one of the greatest male stars in Hollywood. Jean reenacted the memorable moment in an interview printed on the occasion of the film premiere:

> I'll never forget that kiss . . . I didn't know the love scene was next. Without warning, Ty put his arms around me. I was embarrassed, shoved him away. I guess I really didn't know what I was doing. Ty looked surprised: I realized it was a rehearsal and lost no time putting myself in the mood as his arms went around me again. Then Tyrone put both of his hands under my chin . . . and tilted my head back gently. I almost forgot it was a scene.[12]

In a funny anecdote, Jean revealed the less-than-passionate reason the first take of the sequence had to be reshot. As Power breathed gently into Jean's ear and whispered, "I love you, dar . . ." he stopped, incredulous, and pointed to a wad of chewed gum nestling behind Jean's earlobe, attached there by the actress seconds before the scene. A blushing Jean removed the sticky stuff and moved on with the second take that was so passionate that King decided to print it.

Helped by Charles G. Clarke, a skilled director of photography, King used natural weather conditions to enhance the mood of the picture. Instead of turning away from a darkened sky—caused by the unexpected eruption of the local volcano, Parícutin—he had the camera pointed toward the event to add this force of nature to the impact of the story at a climactic moment. Around the foot of the volcano, everything was covered in ash, and the trees had no leaves. To make the whole scene bleaker, it rained every single afternoon and evening. As a result, King had to do most of the shooting in the morning.

Tyrone Power, a Marine Air Corps pilot during the war, flew his own airplane for relaxation in his spare time, while Jean, on her first day off, visited a local public school since she was curious to compare their teaching system with the American one. In her free time, she enjoyed playing the tourist with Arlen, shopping for souvenirs, native clothes, fabrics, and shoes. She bought a sombrero for her sister and had it autographed by all her costars. Overall, Jean loved the Mexican location—except for the food. She was impressed with the local architecture, particularly the old Spanish-style homes with their lovely patios. In Uruapan, where the crew shot for five weeks, she spent her free time reading two books a week and painting landscapes. In Acapulco, the company stayed for almost a month in a twenty-four-hour, army-surveilled area due to ongoing troubles with bandits from the hills. There, Jean spent most of her free time on the beach, tanning and swimming with Arlen.

As the weeks turned into months and continued over the holiday season, King tried to boost low morale by throwing a Thanksgiving dinner and a Christmas Eve party, while Power hosted a New Year's Day breakfast. These were Jean's first holidays spent away from her family, but Arlen's presence and the warmth of her colleagues seemed to alleviate her homesickness. Nevertheless, King's efforts to make the workplace a home away from home weren't always successful. Actor Lee J. Cobb wrote two letters to his wife Beverly in January 1947, which described the heavy atmosphere surrounding the set:

> The morale of the company is pretty low. People are pretty much disgusted. It seems the studio hasn't missed an opportunity to betray its cheapness and smallness, and the people are simply fed up. Some are sick, others drink very heavily, still others are despondent. . . . The work is so uninspired and boring. This is mainly due to the fact that King is not only devoid of a single creative fibre [sic], but he's an unsufferable crank. He's petty and unreasonable, like an aged invalid. Everybody hates and resents him . . . he likes to pick on the little fellow, someone who is holding down some menial job and is afraid of losing it.[13]

Cobb's discontent with King wasn't shared by all, and indeed, Jean had great respect for the filmmaker, who, only a few months later, would direct her in *Deep Waters* (1948).

Once shooting on location ended, Jean planned to go back to Columbus to be part of the yearly Ohio State University Festival, but Fox did not allow her to leave town until all the interiors and retakes were completed at a studio soundstage. She told the press that she still intended to get a teacher's degree because "you never know. I have no delusions about my ability. I think I am a very lucky girl who got a grand break."[14]

Captain from Castile went significantly over budget. Its eighty-day shooting schedule stretched to 112 days as costs swelled to $4.5 million. It took its toll, with King saying, "It's by long odds the toughest picture I've ever made."[15]

The film was scheduled for a November release but had to be delayed because of a shortage of Technicolor prints. It premiered on Christmas Day 1947, with two gala events in New York and Los Angeles, a disappointing choice for Jean, who had hoped that Columbus, Ohio, would be picked for one of the official premieres. When the film opened nationwide in January 1948, critics agreed that it re-created all the grandeur and pomp of sixteenth-century style. They applauded the lavish Technicolor photography and the magnificent score by Alfred Newman but found the script long, disjointed, and often boring.

Jean's work was generally praised. The *Hollywood Reporter* called her "an attractive newcomer [who] shows herself to be an appealing and most convincing actress."[16] *Newsweek* was equally enthusiastic: "Given a chance of a few more roles, Miss Peters is going to be somebody."[17] The harshest critic, however, was Jean's seventy-year-old maternal grandmother. After watching the picture, the strict Methodist commented in a letter to Jean that *Captain from Castile* had only one positive quality for her—and that was to see her walking in bare feet for almost the entire film. Other than that, she was not impressed: "I never would have believed that a skimpily dressed girl cavorting in the arms of a strange man was my favorite grandchild."[18]

Captain from Castile was a box office disappointment. Even though it grossed a large sum of money, it failed to recoup its inflated costs. In a 1949 memo sent to Henry King, Zanuck explained that *Captain from Castile* was not a failure as a picture; the failure was that Fox had spent more for it than the market could afford. The film cost more than it could take in, in spite of being a hit with cinemagoers throughout the world.[19]

In February 1949, Jean reprised the role of Catana for a *Lux Radio Theater* broadcast of *Captain from Castile* with Cornel Wilde in Tyrone Power's role. She also appeared in her first printed advertisement as a sponsor of the popular soda Royal Crown Cola. Things were fizzing for Jean.

CHAPTER 3

Sense and Sensibility

I don't know whether Ohio lost a good teacher—but certainly,
Hollywood found a lovely actress.
—JESSIE ROYCE LANDIS

TWO WEEKS BEFORE THE WORLD PREMIERE OF *CAPTAIN FROM CASTILE*,
William R. Wilkerson, owner and publisher of the *Hollywood Reporter*, raved
about Jean's screen debut in his influential front-page column "Tradeviews."
Wilkerson, one of the most powerful men in Hollywood, called Eliza-
beth Jean Peters "the hottest thing that's hit our screens in many a day."
He enthused about her next starring role in *Deep Waters* opposite Dana
Andrews and forecast a very bright future for Jean:

> We have never seen a girl (or a boy) zoom to such a sensational begin-
> ning as has Jean Peters. Zanuck probably has the greatest potential
> ticket-seller in the entire picture world in his hold on this Peters girl,
> and unless she is given a lot of baloney for picture stories or some
> bad direction in her next few starts, she's a cinch to become the
> screen's greatest star. . . . She'll have the ticket customers frothing at
> the mouth after her first scene in *Castile* and those same customers
> will be begging for a new Peters picture and will probably go back to
> see the old one, many, many times, because of her sensational screen
> beauty, poise and, believe it or not, her acting.[1]

Once *Captain from Castile* was completed, Jean devoted her free time to
the sewing machine, adding to her wardrobe for her trip home to see her
mother and sister, who was about to graduate from junior high school. Mary
was waiting to see how her daughter's career turned out, but her ultimate
plan was to sell the farm and move with Shirley to Hollywood.

On her return from Ohio, Jean was involved in a series of public appearances, which included the opening of the Lou Costello Jr. Youth Center in East Los Angeles and working as a special tour guide at the 20th Century Fox studios. Even though Jean's face had not appeared on the big screen yet, her name had achieved two claims of fame in the public eye: the much-awaited debut role opposite Tyrone Power and her personal association with Howard Hughes.

After Hughes's terrible plane crash, Jean regularly visited the convalescent billionaire, first at the hospital and later at his mansion in Beverly Hills. She recounted that as Hughes lay in bed during his recuperation from the accident, he would "talk for hours about his feelings, his dreams and his sorrows." Often, she would sit next to his bed, knitting or making her own clothes. Gradually, she became not just a friend and confidante but also a lover. When she flaunted a big Cartier square-cut stone ring, a gift Hughes had bought for her birthday a few months earlier, the media went crazy.

She wore it publicly for the first time in Superior Judge Frank Swain's court when she obtained approval for her contract scaling from $300 to $1,000 a week over six years at 20th Century Fox studios. "Mr. Hughes gave it to me," she told the press brightly, "and the romance is serious." Asked if she contemplated marriage, she said, "No, we haven't discussed matrimony yet."[2] She was more specific with columnist Sheilah Graham a few days later:

I'm very much in love with Howard. But neither of us wants to get married just yet. Howard told me that he always wanted to marry, but something always happened. Either he decided it was wrong, or she did. He wants to be very sure that when he does marry, it's for keeps. So do I. We both feel that if we wait a year, we'll know more about whether we want to get married. But please do not say we are engaged now, because Howard gets annoyed . . . he's a businessman and doesn't like that sort of publicity.[3]

Hughes's courtship of Jean continued when she left to film *Captain from Castile*, and he flew to Mexico twice to see her. They had met at the Hotel Reforma in Mexico City, and while they were there, he told Jean something that drew her to him strongly. He said that when he died, his fortune was to go to a medical institute; this was something he had envisioned when he made out his first will at age eighteen. He was concerned that this meant she would not be protected. Jean, with her characteristic good humor and pragmatism, told him, "Don't worry about me, I can always work."[4]

Jean was different from all the women Hughes had met before. She was sensible, unspoiled, and independent. She refused to bestow him special treatment just because of his fame and money, which stimulated his interest even more. When they went out together, she did not care for the trendy Hollywood night spots, preferring simple restaurants away from the cameras. She often wore handmade clothes and preferred to eat at a diner and watch a movie than dance in a popular nightclub. She even started sharing his interest in planes and took a few flying lessons.

Despite being seriously smitten by Jean, Hughes did not stop seeing other women—mostly famous young actresses or models. It was a behavior Jean disapproved of but never commented about in public. In December, a few days before *Castile*'s premiere, while trying on a pair of gloves at a store, she took Hughes's ring off, laid it on a counter and forgot it. When she came back, it was gone, and she never saw it again. She was devastated.

In 1947, Jean's name was attached to the 20th Century Fox productions *Julie* (1947), *By the Night Star* (1947), *White Fang* (1947), *Apartment for Peggy* (1948), *The Street with No Name* (1948), and *Call Me Mister* (1951), films that, for one reason or another, she never made. Her second starring role was in *Deep Waters*, based on Ruth Moore's bestselling novel *Spoonhandle*, the rights for which were purchased by Fox in December 1946.

Initially, Louis de Rochemont was assigned to produce the project, but Zanuck gave it to Samuel Engel. Henry King was chosen to direct. King was critical of Richard Murphy's verbose screenplay and cut many superfluous scenes that obstructed the flow of the story. He also eliminated the strong Yankee-accented dialogue of the characters, which was present in the original novel. Although Zanuck was surprised to see the script cut to the bare bones, he did not interfere with the director's decisions. However, he made it clear that after the enormous cost of *Captain from Castile*, the production would have a limited budget.

Deep Waters told the story of a lobster fisherman, Hod Stillwell, and his efforts to rescue a young orphan named Danny Mitchell from the state reformatory. Stillwell tried to adopt Danny and win back the love of his ex-girlfriend Ann Freeman, a welfare worker in charge of the boy's well-being. Actor Mark Stevens was the first to be considered for the leading role but lost the part to Dana Andrews, Fox's hottest new male face. Jean was King's first choice for the female lead after their Mexican collaboration. She was equally keen to work with him again, as she told Louella Parsons: "It's really a break for me because he knows where he's going and what he wants, and I naturally have a great confidence in him."[5] The director returned the compliment calling the actress "a natural talent.

... Jean has something that is very rare in a young woman, the ability to listen. I believe in her."[6]

Deep Waters' exteriors were all shot in Vinalhaven, Maine, a colorful New England fishing village located on a tiny island ten miles off the Rockland coast. It was a location King had scouted while flying his plane around the area. At the end of September 1947, when preproduction was complete, the director flew to Maine with his assistant Joe Behm and cameraman Joseph LaShelle, followed by a crew of twenty-five people, including an oceanographer to advise on the course of ocean tides for the fishing scenes.

The complete cast with Jean, Dana Andrews, Anne Revere, and Cesar Romero flew east a few days later. Dean Stockwell, the eleven-year-old child star, had to report on location two weeks earlier than the rest of the cast to learn how to row a boat and handle a shotgun. During the entire course of instruction, the young actor never revealed how much fun he was having. But the moment Jean and Dana Andrews arrived on the set, he challenged them to a shooting match.

Costume designer Charles LeMaire chose clothes that were appropriate for Jean's character of a young state welfare board worker, as she explained to Louella Parsons: "I play a girl who earns about $100 a month . . . so Mr. LeMaire saw to it that I wear clothes that are logically within those means. He didn't go out and select gowns that looked simple but actually cost a fortune. He bought honest-to-goodness cheap clothes, the same as he did for *Captain from Castile.* In that one . . . I wear peasant clothes." The residents of Vinalhaven welcomed a Hollywood film unit taking over the island. The one resort hotel in Vinalhaven, which was usually closed off-season, remained open to accommodate the actors and crew. Locals clamored for a chance to play bit roles and extras, with King seizing the opportunity and using them and their fishing boats. One of the extras, a lobster fisherman, asked Jean to marry him. Although she turned him down, the man kept besieging her on set with letters and small gifts. Finally, she told him that she had an aunt, a grandmother, a mother, and a young sister all dependent on her and that her prospective husband would have to assume that responsibility. She never heard from him again.

Shooting started under the constant check of weather reports since a hurricane was forecast to be approaching the Atlantic coast. The storm did not hit Vinalhaven, but the heavy rain altered the production's schedule, which amounted to twenty-two shooting days in the outdoors. On October 15, 1947, just before shooting was complete, Jean celebrated her twenty-first birthday with a party organized by the production on the set. The friendly locals swamped her with twenty birthday cakes that made her feel a little less homesick since this was the first birthday she had spent away from her family.

After leaving Vinalhaven, the company returned to the studio to film all the interiors, and on her way back to Hollywood, Jean made a stop in East Canton to visit her ailing grandmother. She had more time with her than she'd previously thought, as shooting at the Fox studios was postponed for two weeks due to a violent gasoline tank explosion. It had happened on a lot just as Ralph Hammeras, a special photographic effects cameraman, was about to start processing the Maine shots for *Deep Waters* at the edge of the tank. Seven technicians for different productions were hospitalized, but no film material was damaged. Shooting resumed at the end of October.

"When *Deep Waters* was completed," King explained in an interview, "it was a little gem. It was a small subject, and the amazing thing was, it got good reviews; audiences liked it, it got all the business it demanded, and it made a little money. Zanuck said if we spent another dollar on the picture, it would have been a flop."[7]

The fine acting of young Dean Stockwell and the warm sepia photography that enhanced the Maine landscape were the talk of the critics. A six-minute storm scene earned the film an Academy Award nomination for special effects. Unfortunately, Jean's performance did not excite the reviewers, who wrote kind but unenthusiastic words including "lovely to look at," "natural," and "pleasant but unspectacular in the role of Ann."

In the spring of 1948, Jean took a stand that shocked Fox executives. She rejected major roles in two films: *Yellow Sky* (1948), opposite Gregory Peck, and *Sand* (1949), opposite Mark Stevens. It was considered outrageous for a contract player to act this way. Turning down a script was a privilege only granted to established stars. Jean stood her ground. "I frankly thought that *Sand* was a very poor script," she said bravely in an interview, "and I didn't want to do *Yellow Sky* for another reason. The girl in it was too sexy. I'd already played a low-necked role in *Captain from Castile*, and I didn't want to establish myself as that type. I just said I wouldn't act in it."[8]

Fox put Jean on immediate suspension and took her off the payroll. She took that moment of "disgrace" calmly, with the knowledge that she had plenty of free time to enjoy. She took a course in American History at UCLA, read, sewed, cooked, and went to the beach with her friend Arlen, who was now living with her and Aunt Mel. Hughes offered his help, but Jean's great sense of independence and stubbornness forbade him to intervene.

For a moment, she even considered going back to Ohio and finishing the two semesters she needed to complete her college degree to become a teacher. She told a reporter that her suspension had come at an opportune time. First, it was the beginning of the baseball season—her favorite sport—and second, she was entertaining a troop of visiting relatives from Ohio. Nevertheless, only a month after she was ostracized by the studio, Fox announced Jean as the female lead in *Mr. Belvedere Goes to College* (1949), a sequel to the box office hit comedy *Sitting Pretty* (1948) starring Clifton Webb.

When the production was delayed, Jean was invited to star in *It Happens Every Spring* (1949), a role originally offered to Jeanne Crain. Jean loved the script and was attracted to the idea of playing a strong-willed woman in a romantic comedy set in the baseball world. "I like the lighter themes," she said, "because in them, I can be myself. Then, too, you can have so much fun in comedy."[9]

She played Debbie Greenleaf, the daughter of the president of a Californian college, who was in love with a wacky chemistry professor played by Ray Milland. Milland had replaced Gary Cooper, who was Fox's first choice. The teacher discovers, by accident, a chemical compound that, when applied to a baseball, makes it repulsive to wood. He becomes an overnight pitching sensation and a big-league star. However, his secret is exposed when his roommate, played by Paul Douglas, mistakes the compound for hair tonic with funny results.

Milland (on loan from Paramount), Douglas, and Jean had great chemistry on and off the set, as she confirmed: "In *It Happens Every Spring*, we had a grand time playing baseball between shots, particularly pepper ball games. You'd have died laughing at Mr. Milland when he first started to pitch. I don't believe he'd even seen a game before. But he is a fine actor and picked up the principles of the game very quickly."[10] To look the part of a skilled baseball player, the British actor had to practice with a professional coach. The makeup department had to dye his gray temples black as, according to the producers, the gray made Milland look too dignified. It was rumored that Joe DiMaggio was to play a cameo after he read and liked the script, but a health problem prevented him from appearing. Negotiations were underway with Steve O'Neill, manager of the Detroit Tigers, and several other big-league names to play extras, but the expense involved in hiring them was not justified by the comparatively minor roles they would have played.

In November, a month before filming was due to begin, Fox faced major difficulties with representatives of professional baseball. Despite the studio's numerous pleas, commissioner Albert "Happy" Chandler would not allow the use of actual team names in the film, as it was a story of a cheater set during the World Championship Series. Fox offered to include a disclaimer that explained the fictionality of the story, but Chandler wouldn't budge.

Despite his refusal to get on board, most of the sports scenes were filmed at Wrigley Field, home of the minor league baseball team of the Los Angeles Angels and a local spring training camp. All the other exteriors were shot at the University of Southern California (USC), just a few blocks from Jean's home.

It Happens Every Spring went before the cameras in the middle of December 1948, with William Perlberg at the production helm and ex-ballplayer and avid fan Lloyd Bacon directing.

Jean arrived very excited to be in a baseball comedy. She had been a fan of the sport in Ohio, where she supported the East Canton High School team and the Cleveland Indians. In California, she had become a fan of the Hollywood Stars and bought a box at Gilmore Stadium, where she never missed a game. Jean's passion for baseball resulted in her sponsoring a team on the lot made up of carpenters, grips, actors, clerks, and other Fox employees. They got together twice a week for practice or games with other teams on the lot, and Jean was in the heart of it, pitching and catching. When the "Peters Team" lost a studio tournament against the "Rex Harrison Team," she was heartbroken.

During the six-week shooting of *It Happens Every Spring*, Jean took several trips to an osteopath. She explained that her back was out of place after she had bought an ax and chopped some wood, something she had been doing on the Ohio family farm since her teens. Whenever she got mad, Jean would take the ax and whack it through a pepper tree and the eucalyptus limbs in her backyard. This worked the anger out of her system, and the wood ended up in her fireplace. Once, she held up traffic on Sunset Boulevard for twenty minutes while wrestling a roadside log into her car to take home. Her stress reliever had, however, also left her with chronic back pain.

On set, Jean became friends with Jessie Royce Landis, who was cast in a minor role. In her autobiography, the veteran actress talked about the happy times they shared together. "Jean is a very beautiful, charming, intelligent girl," she wrote. "I don't know whether Ohio lost a good teacher—but certainly Hollywood found a lovely actress."[11] Landis tempted Jean with the possibility of working with her in *Magnolia Alley*, a comedy she was about to rehearse on Broadway as soon as the film was complete. Jean loved the idea of acting on stage—an experience that would have enriched her persona and increased her value as an actress. Unfortunately, her strict contract with Fox would not allow her to leave Hollywood for a few months of theater work in New York.

On May 12, 1949, a special screening of *It Happens Every Spring* was organized at the University of Michigan in Ann Arbor, where Governor G. Mennen Williams of Michigan, city officials, and other notables honored the university's Vice President Emeritus Shirley W. Smith, author of the original short story. She shared honors with screenwriter Valentine Davis to turn the story into a picture.

The film's official premiere was held in St. Louis, Missouri, on May 26, with Paul Douglas and Jean making personal appearances along with Fox superstar Linda Darnell. The trio arrived in St. Louis two days earlier to fulfill a packed schedule of broadcasts and appearances, including one at a Cardinals' baseball game, before flying to Pittsburgh for another press junket. Reviews were mixed. The humor was perceived by the critics as rather thin, and Jean's presence was generally described as being more decorative than performative. Nevertheless, *It Happens Every Spring* grossed $1 million, and Shirley W. Smith and Valentine Davies received an Academy Award nomination for Best Writing for a Motion Picture Story.

CHAPTER 4

Dallas Pruitt

It was my first bad girl part, but I hope it isn't my last.
I wondered how long I could be sweet on the screen.
—JEAN PETERS

AFTER TWO YEARS IN HOLLYWOOD AND ONLY THREE FILMS, JEAN WAS
able to invest her first savings in real estate. She and her mother bought
two duplexes in Laguna Beach, and the rent helped meet the payments.
Meanwhile, Shirley, now fourteen, enrolled in Emerson High School in
Westwood and moved in with Jean. Mary, who still owned and ran the sea-
sonal tourist camp on her property in East Canton, traveled to Hollywood
every chance she got.

While her mother was in Ohio, Jean had to take care of Shirley, who had
to be fed and sent off to school early each morning. One day, the teenager
asked Jean to go to an open house at her school to meet her teachers and
represent the Peters family in their mother's absence. Jean agreed, but once
she arrived at Emerson High School, her fresh-faced looks meant she was
mistaken by teachers and students as one of the seniors.

Jean's professionalism and acting ability in *It Happens Every Spring*
had impressed Lloyd Bacon favorably. In the spring of 1949, the director
intended to borrow Jean to star in *Cabin in the Sky* (1949), an independent
production he planned to direct. Unfortunately, Fox refused to loan her
on the grounds that she had been assigned to appear in two upcoming
productions: *Wildcat* (1949), opposite Richard Widmark, and *The Australian
Story*—later titled *Kangaroo* (1952). Bacon was disappointed and aborted
his project shortly after Fox's refusal. Even though Jean did not appear in
those two films, she was cast in a picture with the working title of *Turned
Up Toes*, a remake of *Tall, Dark and Handsome*, a successful comedy produced by Fox in 1941.

Shooting began on June 15, 1949, and Jean was reunited with two familiar faces—*Captain from Castile*'s Cesar Romero and *It Happens Every Spring*'s Paul Douglas. Romero had played the lead role in the original film *Tall, Dark and Handsome*, whereas in this remake, he was cast as the villain. Keenan Wynn was borrowed from MGM for the role of a gangster named Bugs, while comedienne Joan Davis took time off from a popular radio program she hosted to appear in the funny role of Mamie Sage.

The original story, a comedy satire set in 1928 Chicago during the Prohibition era, was adapted slightly. It depicted a turbulent romance between the leader of a racketeer gang and a naïve young woman hired by the gangster to work as a governess in his home. In postproduction, Fox changed the title to *Love That Brute* (1950) after *Life* magazine published an article on Paul Douglas with that same title. The film was shot mostly on a Fox lot except for a few school scenes filmed at St. John's Military Academy in Los Angeles.

For the filming of a long park sequence involving Jean, Paul Douglas, and a number of ducks, the director Alexander Hall had to find "quackless" ducks to avoid spoiling the dialogue. The mute ducks were duly found and hired by the production with an animal trainer, but the benefit of their silence was outweighed by their inability to float. Their feathers lacked the amount of natural oil that squawking ducks have, and they would not stay in the water for a long time. They would waddle out of the studio pond to dry out, interrupting the scene constantly and making Jean and Douglas laugh hysterically. The trainer and a crew of technicians had to prod the winged animals with poles to scoot them back in the water for several takes.

Another moment of uncontrollable laughter happened a few days later when ten-year-old actor Peter Prince lost one of his front teeth during a scene with Jean and Douglas. The director ordered the boy to rush to the studio dentist for a false tooth, but he disliked the idea, believing the process might be uncomfortable. In a bid to reassure him, his studio schoolteacher pulled out a bridge connecting three false teeth of her own to show him. Prince was so fascinated with the idea of being able to show off a removable tooth that he agreed to visit the dentist. Meanwhile, Hall had to make a fast schedule switch so that Jean and Douglas could work while Prince had his tooth-fitting in the morning and returned to work that same afternoon.

In *Love That Brute*, Jean had a nightclub scene in which she had to dance elegantly and sing while wearing a $1,500 silver-beaded evening gown. As she couldn't sing, Jeri Sullavan ghosted vocals of "You Took Advantage of Me," the song Jean lip-syncs in the scene while walking gracefully up and down stairs in high heels, aided by four handsome tuxedoed men. To prepare for the scene, Jean took a few lessons with Angela Blue, Betty Grable's dance instructor. She wasn't a natural, and the sequence, along with all the others set in the nightclub, took seven days to complete.

Throughout the week, Jean was unable to sit down for fear of tearing the expensive tight-fitting gown; she was only allowed to relax against a studio leaning board. As soon as the scene was completed, Jean ran into her dressing room and changed into a plain blouse, skirt, and low-heeled shoes. She complained that she was not used to wearing high heels, not even for walking, and that she needed to go home to soak her aching feet.

She was out of her comfort zone with the singing and dancing, and Hall's words of encouragement about her performance and her seductive appearance failed to convince her that the number was perfect. "Don't kid me," she laughed, "clothes do nothing for me. The less clothes for me, the better. I can't even stand stockings. Me—I'm strictly a no-girdle gal."[1]

Nor was she a heavy makeup gal, as the cosmetics she had to wear for the film caused an eye allergy. Between scenes, she went to see a specialist in Beverly Hills, and when she got out of her car, she found herself in the center of a whistling group of parking lot attendants. She realized then that her period picture skirt barely reached her knees. The stares and the whistling continued up the street, in the elevator of the medical building, and after she received a histamine injection for her reddened eyes. "Wow," she exclaimed to Paul Douglas when she returned to the set. "I'll never leave the lot in these clothes again. I felt like a circus sideshow freak, and some of the people gave that 'haven't you heard of the new look or are you crazy?' look."[2] When filming was over, Jean sent a gracious note to the dancers saying that when it came to the nightclub scene, it was their talent that made her look good.

Love That Brute premiered in New York in May 1950, almost a year after it had been completed. The picture had very little weight as a box office attraction, but it received a warm critical reception. *Variety* called it "a farce with plenty of sparkle and speed,"[3] while the *New York Times* described it as "bright and breezy entertainment."[4]

During the summer of 1949, while working on the set of *Love That Brute*, Jean took an evening course in sociology at the University of Southern California. "I like to keep up with things," she commented to a local newspaper.[5] A film career wasn't the be-all and end-all for Jean. Her thirst for knowledge and eagerness to learn encouraged her to succeed in different fields. When the course was complete, she drove with Shirley to East

Canton to help Mary finalize her permanent move to Hollywood. Aunt Mel had left Jean's house a few months earlier to get married to realtor Nelson Doss. Mary thought that it was the right time for her to leave Ohio and move in with her daughters.

In October, Jean and Paul Douglas reprised their roles in a radio adaptation of *Love That Brute* broadcast on the *Lux Radio Theater*.

Even though Jean did not appear in front of a camera for fifteen months, she had become a regular in the social column of several newspapers, which kept speculating about her mysterious relationship with Howard Hughes and their possible marriage. In an article written for *Modern Screen*, Mary tried to dampen the rumors of a serious romance and possible betrothal between her daughter and the reclusive billionaire:

> There are no romantic implications in Jean's life. Even the much-publicized "romance" with Howard Hughes . . . must have sprung from the fertile imagination of columnists or publicity men. Certainly, Jean has gone out with Howard Hughes. But she has gone out with other famous men as well. Probably the cause for all the comments has been the fact, while she appears so very seldom at nightclubs and almost never at big Hollywood parties, she has been seen dining with Mr. Hughes a few times. But there's absolutely no foundation to these marriage rumors. For that matter, Jean feels she's too young to get married . . . she still wants to concentrate on her career for the next years. And when Jean makes up her mind about something, she sticks to it. She's a Peters.[6]

It was true that Jean felt too young for marriage, as she often told the press, but a major deterrent to her walking up the aisle with Hughes was his unfaithfulness. He simply could not stop dating and flirting with other beautiful women. This insensitive behavior hurt Jean's feelings and left her feeling humiliated. In retaliation, she started to keep Hughes at arm's length and refused his invitations more frequently. Incredibly, Hughes tried to reassure her that their relationship was special and that seeing other women was just part of his work.

In February 1950, Jean was faced with a challenging opportunity when the production of a film titled *Take Care of My Little Girl* (1951) was announced in the press. From the beginning, the project became the center of a strong debate.

According to studio publicity, Peggy Goodin originally wrote *Take Care of My Little Girl*—which exposed the snobbishness of the college fraternity and sorority system—as her master's thesis at McGill University and then turned it into a novel. Fox producer Julian Blaustein encouraged Zanuck to purchase the film rights, which he did, assigning Blaustein the task of an immediate production.

Anatole Litvak was announced as the director, with Frank McCarthy serving as the associate producer, and the project was then shelved for almost a year. In the meantime, Litvak got involved with a different film and Jean Negulesco was asked to replace him. However, threats from the Greek societies it sought to mock were exerted on Fox to cancel the project. The studios stood resolute and ignored the pressure. L. G. Balfour, chairman of the Interfraternity Research and Advisory Council, wrote to Spyros Skouras, president of Fox, saying the story was "Communistic propaganda and would give comfort to the enemies of the country." In Skouras's reply, he mentioned the American right to free expression and the wisdom of withholding judgment until the picture's release. He also reminded Balfour that his studio had made *The Iron Curtain* (1948), the first purely anti-Communist film, the patriotic features *The Fighting Lady* (1944), *The House on 92nd Street* (1945), and *Twelve O'Clock High* (1949), as well as other pictures that dealt with defects in the American system. Skouras wrote:

> *Take Care of My Little Girl* does not condemn the fraternities and sororities, but it does expose the evils and practices such as segregation and intolerance. . . . It is un-American, we think, to bar a girl from a sorority because she belongs to a certain religious faith or happens not to dress as well as her sisters or comes from the wrong side of the railroad tracks. Some of the things that do occur are heartbreaking and wrong.

Balfour threatened to bring the matter to the attention of the five million fraternity members, warning, "I can assure you that you will not be favorably received."[7] As usual in these situations, the controversy got so much media coverage that it generated more publicity for the picture and resulted in a very strong showing at the box office, outgrossing every other Fox premiere in 1950.

To assure authenticity, Blaustein employed Goodin as the technical advisor on the film, which was scripted by twin brothers Julius J. and Philip G. Epstein. Goodin worked closely with the screenwriters before and during the shoot. She also advised on costumes with fashion designer Bill Travilla and set design with Lyle Wheeler and Joseph Wright.

Jean had read Goodin's book and thought that the role of ruthless Dallas Pruitt, the snobbish campus fashion victim of the Tri-U sorority, was perfect for her. "They were thinking of me only as the loving wife [but] I wanted to look sophisticated,"[8] she said. She also wanted the role because the story represented exactly the type of sorority that made an independent of her during her days at the University of Michigan and Ohio State.

She was afraid to talk to the studio about the part—she never had the nerve to walk into a producer's office to plead for a role—so she decided to try her luck in a different way. After it was confirmed that the part was still uncast, she wore an elegant plaid vest and cap that she had handsewn matched with a pair of black velvet slacks and entered the studio commissary when the director was having a meal. "I planned it deliberately," she admitted later. She cast a smile at Negulesco as she passed his table. "That," Negulesco exclaimed to his table companion, "is Dallas."[9] That same afternoon the director called Jean and asked her if she could possibly consider the part, although he was afraid that she would not be interested in playing a second lead. Jean agreed to do a screen test. She spent that same night sewing a sophisticated dress for the occasion. She had used some of her free time hanging around Charles LeMaire, the head of Fox's wardrobe department, who, as she often joked, could even give her a job as a designer. The dress she made that night was sensational and helped make her screen test successful.

Susan Hayward was originally set to play Liz Erickson, a naïve freshman who gets wise to the sorority's manipulative scheming, but Jeanne Crain's increasing popularity landed her the lead. Dale Robertson played a levelheaded medical student, while Jeffrey Hunter was a drunken, womanizing fraternity boy.

Take Care of My Little Girl went into production on October 14, 1950. The narrative centered on the experiences of Liz Erickson, whose fondest dream is to belong to Tri-U, the same sorority as her mother. Yet Dallas Pruitt, the egotistical Tri-U president who chooses her friends by appearance and background, makes it harder for Liz and other freshmen to be part of it. Meanwhile, Joe Blake (Dale Robertson), a soft-spoken senior, war veteran, and an outcast from the rest of the students, opens Liz's eyes to her drunken, womanizing boyfriend Chad Carnes (Jeffrey Hunter). Eventually, Joe makes Liz realize that the serious side of life is more important than a sorority badge.

The production hired twelve hundred college-aged Hollywood extras, and continuity was a nightmare as it was not easy for Negulesco to place his chattering cast in front of the Technicolor camera in the exact same way for each take. He wanted them to be relaxed in front of the camera, as naturalness, he said, was the key to making the film work:

> As relaxed, as cute, as nice, and sweet and caring and bantering, as catty and cutting and as cruel as only young persons can be. That way, we will have a picture great for its naturalness, for the intolerance of youth, which is a very cruel thing, even if it is unconscious. And what we have to tell in this picture is exactly that: the unconscious cruelty of youth. But it must be told without offending the nostalgic memory of millions of American women who once were young and thoughtlessly cruel, too. So, we do it lightly. We let it tell itself by peeking indiscreetly through the keyhole of a composite sorority house.[10]

When Romanian-born Negulesco was asked why he, a foreigner, happened to be directing a subject specific to American life, he replied, "A 'foreigner' has as much a sense of dramatic situations as anyone and may be a little more objective about an American subject. Besides, I have so much experience with Americans. My wife is part Cherokee Indian—and what can be more American than that!"[11]

Drama coach Helena Sorrell and dialogue director Herschel Daugherty helped Jean and Jeffrey Hunter during rehearsals. Jean was excited to play her first bad girl, as she recalled later:

> Ah! The villainess! I was that in *Take Care of My Little Girl*, a sophisticated, snobbish college girl. And to help me in my wickedness, I wore some glamorous clothes, something exceptional for me. I played that part as though I believed the girl believed she was right. . . . Jean Negulesco was the director. He seemed to think my approach got results, and I count it as one of my favorite parts.[12]

Jean summed up her experience in a short article titled "The Role I Like the Best," which she wrote for the *Saturday Evening Post*:

> There were tons of girls on the set, a lively, friendly group. We formed our own chorus to sing between scenes, took ballet lessons from Mitzi Gaynor, and trooped off the lunch each day as a unit. . . . With all this happy background, I should have been playing a lovable, life-of-the-party girl. Actually, my part, Dallas, was a fashion-conscious

snob with a completely mistaken sense of values. . . . Most people who saw Dallas loathed her. But I liked playing the part because it was my first really interesting character role on the screen. . . . Although the picture was very critical of some phases of sorority life, I have remained neutral on the subject. However, I don't think the idea behind a picture is an actress's responsibility. That's up to the producer. My job simply was to play Dallas as well as I could, and I enjoyed it thoroughly.[13]

Jeanne Crain arrived on the set six weeks after the birth of her third son and requested a trailer equipped with a nursery where she breastfed her baby between takes and played with her two other children. "I have to take care of my little boys!" became her usual cry every time she left the set. She and Jean became instant friends.

A few days into shooting, Negulesco had to rearrange the schedule after Dale Robertson was involved in an accident at a golf tournament. The director had to wait until the actor's infected foot healed so that he could walk without a limp.

When they had time on their hands, Jean taught Jeanne Crain how to sew. The results were a black crepe dress Jean sewed for herself and another one Crain made with pink felt and Halloween faces decorating the hem. Both showed off their creations proudly at a party given by Negulesco to celebrate the end of the shooting, which was brought in seven days under schedule.

Take Care of My Little Girl received lukewarm reviews. Some writers thought the picture was one-sided, and *Newsweek* pointed out that "no hint of the novel's objection to religious or racial prejudice sneaks into the movie." However, as Dallas Pruitt, Jean was welcomed with general critical acclaim: "Jean Peters, a gorgeous beauty, plays the top snob of the bunch to near perfection"[14] and "Miss Jean Peters looks and acts the parts."[15]

The picture was profitable domestically, but it had a very limited release overseas because Fox believed the subject would not arouse much interest outside North America.

CHAPTER 5

Lady Pirate

If you sit back and let life pass you by, you have only yourself
to blame if you are overlooked.
—JEAN PETERS

AS *TAKE CARE OF MY LITTLE GIRL* WAS ABOUT TO GO INTO PRODUCTION,
filmmaker Elia Kazan suggested to Zanuck that he promote longtime Fox
film editor Harmon Jones to director status. Zanuck agreed and assigned
Harmon—who had been at Fox for more than ten years and had edited
many of the studio's top pictures—to the comedy *Will You Love Me in
December?* with Lamar Trotti as screenwriter and producer. *Will You Love Me
in December?* was based on an unpublished short story by Paddy Chayefsky
titled "A Few Kind Words from Newark." According to Chayefsky, the part
was written for William Powell, but Trotti preferred to use sixty-two-year-
old Monty Woolley after his popular and critical success in *The Man Who
Came to Dinner* (1942). Thelma Ritter was signed in a small role, but with
her popularity on the rise, the script was changed and her part expanded.

The numerous changes didn't please the original author: "The story was
made by another writer, and the director was an editor—his first job as a
director," complained Chayefsky. "By the time that picture showed up on
screen, it was completely deformed."[1]

The first treatment of the story submitted by Trotti was called *The Great
American Hoax*. The script was later revised and changed into *Will You Love
Me in December?* but prior to the film's release, it was retitled *As Young as
You Feel* (1951). The comedy was about a printer forced into retirement at
sixty-five despite still being in love with his work. The man dyes his hair
and beard and poses as the president of the business to change the rules
and recover his job.

At Zanuck's invitation, David Wayne and Constance Bennett played secondary roles. Jean received fourth billing as Alice Hodges, a role in which she was cast as a last-minute replacement for Mitzi Gaynor. The picture was filmed entirely at Fox's Western Avenue studio, starting on December 15, 1950, just a few days after Jean had reshot a couple of scenes in *Take Care of My Little Girl*.

Monty Woolley's flamboyant personality kept the cast and crew on their toes and entertained. Jean described the veteran actor as "an elderly man with great reserve, but really a dreamboat when you get to know him. He's nervous and gets everybody into a big lather, but it's an act. He's just a white-bearded clown with a divine sense of humor."[2] She added: "He was so funny when he'd go up on a line. Instead of just stopping, the weirdest thing would come out of his mouth, and he'd just keep going. I mean, really weird things, but he was fun."[3]

Some of the press attention focused on Fox's rising star Marilyn Monroe, who was cast in a marginal role of a sexy secretary. Monroe had signed a new contract with Fox five days before principal photography began. The cast soon realized that Marilyn worked to her own schedule and was treated differently from everyone else, as David Wayne recalled:

All extras and all of us so-called stars waited and waited the whole morning, and I asked, "Who are we waiting for?" The assistant director said, "It doesn't matter. Just sit tight." Anyway, after we'd all broken for lunch and come back, in she finally came, this very pretty young girl. She didn't have one line, but they told her where to sit, and I said, "You mean to tell me that we have waited all this time for an extra?" So, we went ahead and shot the scene, and then I realized that something was going on which I didn't know about; this girl had a little power going for her.[4]

It was on the set of *As Young as You Feel* that Marilyn met her future third husband, Arthur Miller. The playwright was brought along by Elia Kazan, an old friend of Harmon's, who was often visiting the soundstage. Jean remembered being introduced to Miller: "I was nervous," she said. "[I] had an idea he'd be an academic snob, but he was so easy to talk to. He went to Ohio State also, worked his way in one of the student hangouts, and we had great fun talking together."[5]

As Young as You Feel was completed in six weeks. Marilyn was the only cast member who created a commotion as she was going through some personal problems, and Jones was worried about the impact her misery was having on his picture. "Every time I need her, she's crying," he told Elia Kazan. "It puffs up her eyes!"[6] The movie was released in the summer of 1951. Critics' reviews were varied, and the box office return was modest.

Even though neither *Take Care of My Little Girl* nor *As Young as You Feel* had been released yet, on January 30, 1951, Fox informed the press that Jean's old contract had been torn up and a brand new one had been handed to her, along with a hefty salary hike. Jean's first job under the new setup was to act in her first starring role as a lady pirate in *Anne of the Indies* (1951).

Anne of the Indies was a fictionalized version of the historical figure Anne Bonny, an Irish female pirate operating in the Caribbean. The film was an action-packed swashbuckling yarn about Captain Anne "Bonny" Providence, who terrorized the seas in the seventeenth century. The script was based on a *Saturday Evening Post* story written by Herbert R. Sass, whose film rights were acquired in 1948 by Walter Wanger as a vehicle for Susan Hayward, whom Wanger had under contract. The producer hired Jan Fortune to write a script to be made into a Technicolor picture for the British-American film company Eagle-Lion. However, the estimated budget of $1.5 million was considered too high and risky for Wanger, who shelved the project.

Hayward, who loved the part, proposed the picture to Fox, for whom she owned a film, but the studio bought the rights from Wanger only in May 1950. Arthur Caesar was asked to write a script, and George Jessel was to produce. Susan Hayward was still attached to star, but when the production was ready to begin, she became unavailable. Linda Darnell was linked to the title role, and Patricia Neal was tested, but at a press conference in December, Zanuck indicated that Valentina Cortese was being considered for the part of Anne. The Italian actress had starred in a few films in Hollywood, and Fox was trying to make her a star.

The announcement caused ripples of discontent, and she wasn't attached for long as Jessel was convinced that the character of a lady pirate had to be flat-chested, and voluptuous Cortese did not fit the bill. When Jean learned that the role was still uncast, she campaigned for it. In a disagreement with Jessel, who obviously thought a strong female pirate should look more like a man than a woman, she argued, "All she has to be is tough enough to make men believe she's the boss. She doesn't masquerade as a man. The part needs somebody who can climb a yardarm, whatever it is. I'm strong enough to make it believable."[7] Those words were enough to get her a screen test.

Being slightly superstitious, on the day of the test, Jean put a lucky penny in her shoe, but the coin fell out while she was walking across the lot on the way to the studio. She looked back and saw a man pick it up. She chased him halfway across the lot, got the penny back, nailed the test, and got the part, despite not having all the dramatic skills required, as she recalled later:

> In *Anne of the Indies*, I had to be hard, bossy, and able to fence like a veteran. I must admit, once I was very keen to do it—so much that I lied to my big boss, Darryl Zanuck. I wrote a note telling him I could fence, which meant he would not have to use any doubles. I went around singing, "Yo! Ho! Ho! And a bottle of rum" each time I saw George Jessel, the producer. Well, the part was really mine, and then the truth was out: I had to be taught to fence. What a master I had! Fred Cavens, who has taught the finest swashbucklers in the business from Douglas Fairbanks to Ty Power, Stewart Granger, Errol Flynn, and now a would-be teacher from Ohio.[8]

Dissatisfied with Arthur Caesar's script, Zanuck assigned Philip Dunne to write a new screenplay that could incorporate unused footage from the 1942 Fox pirate film *The Black Swan*, starring Tyrone Power. French filmmaker Jacques Tourneur was hired as director in January 1951. In his memoir, Philip Dunne hinted at disquiet between Tourneur and producer George Jessel. "On the first day of shooting, Georgie marched briskly onto the set, saluted Jacques Tourneur and the rest of the crew, said, 'Okay, fellas, see you at the preview,' and marched briskly out again,"[9] he wrote.

Jean was excited about the makeover she had to go through to become a convincing pirate. A hairstylist dyed her hair pitch black and made it curly, and she spent several hours with costume designer Edward Stevenson in order to fit in all her period clothes. She loved her wardrobe, as she enthused to Hedda Hopper:

> The costumes are delirious. Any girl would look good in them; they have tightfitting trousers and open-throat skirt down to here, and free top boots—I'm in rags, really, but so picturesque and flattering. And the character is terrific. She's a complete primitive, a girl raised by Blackbeard, the pirate, who knows no other life than the law of might. Just an animal. I can't wait to begin it.[10]

Tourneur was keen for accuracy, and before cameras started rolling, he dismissed a large group of young men hired as extras because they had one or more tattoos on their bodies. The director explained that although the principle of tattooing had been known for many centuries, the art had been refined in the last one hundred years or so, and the modern tattoo looked nothing like those seen on anybody in the seventeenth century. Normally, those marks could have been covered by greasepaint, but the actors were scheduled to spend most of their time in the water and Tourneur did not want to be bothered by possible visible anachronisms.[11]

Shooting commenced on February 26, 1951, when Tourneur introduced Jean to Louis Jourdan, whom, together with Debra Paget, was the first to be cast. The handsome French actor played the part of a suave prisoner who steals Anne's heart. Years later, Jourdan complained that, just as in *Bird of Paradise* (1951), the second film he shot for Fox that year, his character in *Anne of the Indies* was half-naked the entire time. "It was the so-called period 'French sexy,'" he said. "Those films were idiotic but sexy."[12] His lack of clothing might have been why he struggled with flu symptoms in the middle of filming and had to stay at home for a few days. Tourneur had to change the schedule and shoot scenes that did not require the French star's presence.

In several action sequences, firemen stood around the soundstage with extinguishers ready to intervene in case of an emergency. Once, while special effects men set fire to the sails of Anne's ship, and smoke was poured over the top structure—which was mounted on a hydraulic lift to simulate the ocean's roll—fiery, flaming pieces of canvas fell all around Jean, who was jumping and running around the vessel. At the end of the scene, crew members congratulated Jean on her iron nerves. She had insisted that, whenever possible, she would do her own stunts.

Besides the physical challenge, capturing the character of Anne Bonny felt like a huge responsibility for Jean:

> It took a lot of fortitude to go after a big part. If I am a flop, I thought—and a woman pirate is a difficult role to play because women in the audience won't be able to create any identity with her—then I have brought about my own downfall. However, if you sit back and let life pass you by, you have only yourself to blame if you are overlooked.[13]

Anne of the Indies was completed in April 1951, but after watching a rough cut, Zanuck was not fully convinced. He asked for a new ending that, according to many, saved the climax of the final scene but not the film as a whole. The Technicolor adventure premiered in New York on October 24, 1951, and ranked number 75 in the top-grossing charts of 1951, earning $1.5 million at the domestic box office.[14] Reviewers were more impressed by Jean's energetic performance and less by the script that, according to some, put "too great a strain on adult credulity."[15]

• • •

Being directed by Negulesco in *Take Care of My Little Girl* created a long-lasting friendship and collaboration between Jean and the Romanian director. The two often bumped into each other at Fox's studios and met again on several social occasions afterward.

When, in the spring of 1951, Negulesco was confirmed as the director of *Lydia Bailey* (1952), he started thinking about casting. He thought Errol Flynn would be the perfect hero for the story, so he made an appointment with the star to discuss the part. He was just about to get in his car to drive to Flynn's house when he saw Jean in a studio parking lot. Seeing her gave him the idea to ask her to play the role of Lydia opposite Flynn.

When he mentioned it, she was ecstatic because working with Errol Flynn had been her childhood dream. Flynn, who was having trouble with his heavy drinking, seemed interested in the part. But then Howard Hughes, who was seeing Peters on and off at the time, learned of the possibility of her working with the womanizing Flynn and made sure it was not going to happen. When Negulesco went back to his office, he found a short note from Zanuck that read: "Cast set for *Lydia Bailey*. Do not approach Errol Flynn or Jean Peters."[16]

He had been warned.

CHAPTER 6

Kazan and Brando

I was determined to have her.

—MARLON BRANDO

A FILM ABOUT THE LIFE STORY OF EMILIANO ZAPATA, THE MEXICAN REVO-
lutionary who commanded the Mexican Southern Army from 1910 to 1919,
was a project director Elia Kazan had in mind for a long time. In 1940,
MGM purchased *Viva Zapata*, a story by Edgcomb Pinchon, author of the
book *Viva Villa!* When the writer published *Zapata the Unconquerable*, the
studio also acquired the film rights but shelved the project for seven years.

Eventually, in 1947, MGM announced that a Zapata film based on Pinchon's book was about to be produced by Jack Cummings. The producer
arranged for a specialist camera crew to go into the jungle of Mexico's
Yucatan Peninsula to shoot background and scenic vistas for use in the
film. In November 1948, the *Hollywood Reporter* wrote that Robert Taylor
had been cast in the starring role of Zapata.[1]

Unexpectedly, two months later, MGM sold the rights to Fox, but after
almost two years of work and eighteen completed scripts, the studio tossed
it into the "impossible" file. In 1949, in a phone call between Kazan and the
novelist John Steinbeck to discuss a possible collaboration on a film about
Christopher Columbus, the conversation shifted to the Mexican Revolution
and a biography on Zapata that had just been published.

The character of the Revolution intrigued both men, and in a few
months, they came up with a draft script that they pitched to Zanuck. His
interest was piqued, and he hired Steinbeck to revisit the script.

In February 1950, Kazan flew to Hollywood and told Zanuck that he
wanted to direct the project. As for the role of Zapata, at first, he thought
of Jack Palance, who was Marlon Brando's understudy in the Broadway
version of *A Streetcar Named Desire*, but then he thought Brando would be

the better choice. However, Zanuck agreed to produce *Viva Zapata!* (1952) only on the condition that Tyrone Power would play the title role.

Kazan, however, had already settled on Brando and insisted that he was Zapata. Finally, Zanuck caved in and agreed to screen-test Brando, whom he felt mumbled incomprehensibly. He also thought that Brando and Julie Harris, whom Kazan had tested for the role of his wife, Josefa Zapata, looked ridiculous as Mexicans. Zanuck had Debra Paget and Geraldine Brooks screen-test, but Kazan was not impressed with them.

In May, Jean was asked by the Fox home office talent department to fly to New York to see the director and test for the role of Josefa. She was scheduled to rehearse one afternoon and shoot the next day, but when she arrived, Kazan, who was a big baseball fan, called off the rehearsal because the Red Sox were playing the Yankees. They all took off for the ball game, discussed the test between innings, and shot it the following day. Jean looked more convincing than Harris, Paget, and Brooks, but Kazan still wasn't sure. Finally, a trade-off was agreed between Kazan and Zanuck: Brando would play Zapata, but Jean would play his bride.

Years later, in discussing *Viva Zapata!*, Kazan said:

> I liked the cast and the whole experience very much, although I wasn't satisfied with casting Jean Peters as Zapata's wife. I tried to get some-one else, and I couldn't, so finally. I gave up. . . . I tested Julie Harris, but she wasn't right for it. I don't think I looked hard enough. Part of the difficulty was that if I cast a true Latin as Josefa, Brando would have looked like the Indiana [Brando was from Nebraska] boy he was.[2]

Jean knew she wasn't Kazan's choice, as she explained in an interview: "Darryl Zanuck wanted me to appear in *Zapata*. I am not sure that our director, Elia Kazan, wished to have me in the first place, but you can imagine how much working with him meant to me, and he was wonderful to me during the picture."[3]

Zanuck reluctantly agreed to pay Brando, who was then a big star, $100,000 to be Zapata, but paid Jean, who was a Fox contract player, only $6,000 a week. Besides Brando, Kazan cast Anthony Quinn as Zapata's passionate brother Eufemio, Joe Wiseman as the agitator Fernando, and Mexican-born actress Margo as a camp follower.

Jean described her character Josefa as a "sweet, self-centered, rather stupid heroine. . . . A part of many sides: the young, spoiled, petted sev-enteen-year-old daughter of a doting family who married a man who left her completely embittered, a dead soul, her life smashed."[4]

Kazan wanted to make the film in Mexico and submitted the script to
Gabriel Figueroa, who was head of the Mexican syndicate of film technicians. However, Figueroa and the Mexican national censors demanded
several radical changes in order to have the film shot locally, including
casting Mexicans, not Americans, in the lead roles.

Kazan refused and decided to shoot in Texas on the Mexican border.
He scouted an old Mexican-style town, Roma (in Texas), and presented
himself to the local authorities, who were delighted to host the production as it would bring significant economic opportunities to their small
town. Five hundred citizens put on makeup and costumes to go before
the cameras as extras.

On May 28, 1951, Jean flew to Del Rio, Texas. Howard Hughes asked
Jeff Chouinard, a private investigator he used to surveil his women, to
have his wife Betty Lou accompany Jean. She was ordered to stay with
Jean at all times and call Hughes immediately if there was any trouble.
The billionaire's greatest fear was Marlon Brando and his reputation as
a consummate ladies' man. Mrs. Chouinard didn't disappoint. She was a
strict chaperone and the reason behind Brando's failed attempts to seduce
Jean, as the actor revealed in his autobiography:

> Jean was seeing Howard Hughes at the time, and he had sent a
> woman with her to Mexico [sic] to accompany her twenty-four hours
> a day as a kind of security guard, chaperone, and lady-in-waiting.
> Since nothing ever energized my libido more than a well-guarded
> target, I was determined to have her. We did a little casual flirting,
> but her chaperone was always in watchful attendance, so I didn't
> get anywhere. Deciding to bring the matter to a head, one night,
> about two a.m., I climbed up on the roof of the house she was living
> in, intending to implement my plan of seduction. But just as I was
> about to lower myself on a rope to Jean's window, the chaperone
> woke up and saw me, so I had to make a quick exit. Undaunted, I
> tried other ways to effect my plan, but was never able to get past
> Howard Hughes's security.[5]

Jean recalled more details about that night. Brando had climbed up
to her window and serenaded her by playing his recorder, but she slept
through it. The following morning, the actor asked if she had heard him,
but she told him she had not. Brando was deflated and confessed that with
that daring romantic gesture, he had almost broken his neck. Jean told a
Brando's biographer that she enjoyed his playfulness and sense of humor.

Sometimes during breaks, he would write a line of verse, and she would write another until they had composed a complete poem.[6]

Jean's natural beauty and down-to-earth persona had caught Brando's attention. He was impressed by the fact that she did not act like a star and wore jeans and no makeup. He also appreciated Jean's culinary skills as she made him what he called "the world's best Caesar salad."[7] She enjoyed his attention but was never interested romantically, telling Hedda Hopper, "I think Marlon's very sexy. But not for me."[8] She enjoyed his friendship, and anyway, Brando was already involved with Maria Luisa "Movita" Castaneda, a stunning Mexican actress who had a bit part in the film. They would later marry.

Jean often gave Brando a ride in her new car, a convertible with red leather seats that replaced her 1940 sedan from her Ohio college days. When he accepted the lifts, he was often in the company of his pet raccoon, Russell, who had been given to him by his mother. He had the pet on a chain and would play with him as though he were a dog. Once, when she was driving them from a ranch to Fox Studios, Russell escaped from Brando's grip and bit Jean in the ribcage. Scared and surprised, she subsequently swerved the car. Brando explained that the raccoon signaled that he was hungry and asked Jean to stop at a drive-in café. He ordered Russell a milkshake that the raccoon tried to hold with his little paws, but he spilled it all over Jean's new car.

On another occasion, the raccoon stuck his paws in Jean's straw bag and pulled everything out. The final "straw" was when Russell left a sizable puddle on the rear seat. Jean was furious, but Brando calmed her down by pointing out that the raccoon was only a baby. She relented and their friendship continued, but Russell never stepped a paw inside her car again.

Kazan insisted that Brando look like Zapata, complete with a heavy drooping mustache, cartwheel sombrero, dirty cotton pajama suit, bandana around his neck, and split curly hair. Brando also suggested that the makeup artists flare out his nostrils with plastic rings and glue up his eyeballs to enhance his resemblance to the Mexican leader.

Jean's makeup was simpler and less sophisticated. Her hair was dyed black, and long extensions were sewn in so it hung down her back. Kazan insisted that the makeup artists used real dirt on the faces, feet, and fingernails of the cast and the extras—something Zanuck disapproved of. According to Brando, the head of Fox was a bigot from old Hollywood, where studios often cast whites as Black or Asian. Zanuck kept warning Kazan that Jean looked too dark in the rushes, and no one would buy a ticket to see a film whose female star did not look white. He made her change her makeup and kept ordering the director to reshoot scenes with different lighting so that she would not appear "so dark."[9]

Jean hated her stay in Roma—one of the five Texan locations chosen around the Rio Grande—where the average daily temperature was 105 degrees. Every morning, she and other members of the cast had to be driven out in old station wagons a couple of hours away from their non-air-conditioned hotels along dusty roads while sweltering in their heavy costumes. For a few days, Jean felt unwell—it may have been the heat or a stomach ulcer—but it did not prevent her from continuing with her work. During breaks, she enjoyed playing baseball with other crew members, but Kazan ordered her to stop for fear she would hurt herself.

A funny thing happened while Kazan was directing a scene between Jean and Brando on the Texas side of the Rio Grande. A group of women from the Mexican riverbank swam naked toward the cameras every time the lights were turned on. They appeared in the daily rushes and the director was forced to repeat the scene, but only after production had appealed to Mexican authorities to stop those nude ladies from swimming into view of the cameras.

Years later, Jean revealed that many of the lines in the script irritated her, in particular, a scene in which Zapata proposed to her:

> It was very stylized. The words were hard to say and hard to feel you were doing naturally. . . . Marlon kind of set me back on my heels because he was so believable. He had the fire and the excitement. Marlon would give a scene full-blast even if he was off-camera and I was in closeup. He'd never let down, as many actors do sometimes out of exhaustion or fatigue. And he also amused me, help[ed] to relax me. Once, he spilled something, and I said, "Don't be such a slob!" with a laugh, of course. He replied, "I am not a slob." He spoke in the elegant accent of a duke or a prince, and he was so precise and prissy! He added, "I can be the most perfect gentleman you've ever seen." And he did the perfect imitation of how a perfect gentleman would sip his coffee. It was magnificent.[10]

On June 25, after four weeks of location work, the cast flew back to Hollywood in a chartered plane. Shooting resumed on a Fox lot, but a painfully bruised knee caused Brando to drop out for a few days, making it necessary for Kazan to shoot around him. Between scenes, Jean relaxed by knitting an outfit for Anne Baxter and John Hodiak's baby, who was about to be born.

After *Viva Zapata!* was completed, Jean said of her costar, "Marlon is one of the greatest people I've ever worked with—everyone loved him, the cast and the crew."[11]

Viva Zapata! was a problematic film to release after the American Legion put it on a short list of possibly Communist-influenced movies. It only received a seal of approval after Spyros Skouras's intervention, when he asked some of the participants in the film to write letters explaining their past political activities.

It worked, and the film's world premiere took place in New York on February 7, 1952, with Kazan and Brando in attendance. An exhibition of Nancy Ranson's Mexican paintings was held at the Rivoli Theatre in conjunction with the event. Five weeks later, a Latin-style Hollywood gala premiere was organized at Grauman's Chinese Theatre. The forecourt was transformed into a Mexican-style fiesta plaza with an orchestra providing Latin music. More than two hundred members of the local Mexican community attended wearing folk costumes, along with several authorities of the Latin American consular corps. Jean and Anthony Quinn were among the many celebrities who showed up for the event, but Brando did not attend.

Viva Zapata! received some acclaim, mostly international, yet most critics did not think it was a four-star picture. The *Hollywood Reporter* felt that the film had "many of the qualities of the documentary without being oppressive."[12] The *Saturday Review* saw it as a "misfire, too slow at times" and "obscure."[13] Jean's performance was, however, widely praised, with one critic writing, "Jean Peters is the 'fuel to Brando's fire.' As Zapata's wife who has a foreboding of his martyrdom and doom, she evokes anguished poignancy."[14]

The film established itself as a solid box office hit abroad, but the domestic box office stagnated after the initial buzz. Ultimately, the picture was a financial flop with a domestic gross profit of only $250,000, which barely recuperated its cost. Zanuck said, "It was a disappointment. I made a mistake in subject matter. It was alien to American audiences."[15] Despite this, *Viva Zapata!* obtained five Academy Award nominations, including one for Marlon Brando as Best Actor, yet only Anthony Quinn won the Oscar as Best Supporting Actor.

In November 1952, Jean returned to play Josefa opposite Charlton Heston, who took Brando's title role, in a *Lux Radio Theater* broadcasting of the film.

A few weeks before *Viva Zapata!* opened nationwide, Fox's contractual option on Jean was renewed for another year and *Wait Till the Sun Shines, Nellie* (1952) became her first film under the new agreement. Originally, Zanuck had acquired the rights to Ferdinand Reyher's novel, *I Hear Them*

Sing, as a starring vehicle for Anne Baxter, due to her standout performance in *All About Eve* (1950). The story follows a temperamental bride brought by her barber husband to live in a small Illinois town. The picture was planned to be filmed in April 1951 under the title *See Nellie Home*, with George Jessel producing and Maxwell Shane directing. Later, Henry King replaced Shane, who instead cowrote the final script and changed the title to *Wait Till the Sun Shines, Nellie*. When Anne Baxter became unavailable, Marilyn Monroe was the studio's first choice for the title role. Monroe took a screen test opposite David Wayne under King's supervision, but it didn't work out, and he decided on Jean instead.

Years later, Jean learned why King preferred her over the blonde actress who was a hugely popular sex symbol. "The movie wasn't that successful, but if Marilyn had been in it, then it might have been a different story," Jean mused. "I told Henry that. He said, 'Well, it wasn't that I didn't want her. It was just that I told Darryl [Zanuck], if you make me use her, you'll really have to give me another ten days of shooting time to get her to stop talking that way!'"[16] After considering the budget cost of ten extra days, Zanuck cast Jean.

In preparation for her performance, which was a dual role, Jean began extensive makeup and wardrobe tests. On August 14, 1951, two planes carrying the principal cast took off for Hutchinson, Kansas, for two weeks on location. King had previously scouted two main Kansas locations, flying his plane over Hutchinson and the nearby hamlet of Castleton. Later, he visited them for a closer look to confirm that they had the authentic small-town backgrounds necessary for the story.

Once they arrived and cameras were ready to film, King had to delay the shooting for twenty-four hours due to heavy thunderstorms.

Interviewed on the set, Jean recalled her excitement at playing two parts in the film:

> This is the type of assignment every actress would turn handsprings to get—a chance to play a dual role. I first appear as David Wayne's wife, then show up later in the picture as my own granddaughter. Talk about a chance for plenty of histrionics! In the first characterization, I am a woman dissatisfied with her lot, making life a nightmare for Wayne, but when I show up later as my granddaughter, I am a totally different person—the sort that everyone wants to have around. The roles call for a completely different approach—just the type of challenge an actress likes to meet. There's only one problem involved. During the shooting of the picture, the sequences presenting the

two characters are interwoven. One day, I'll be one person, the next, the other, and then back again. Director Henry King has helped me straighten out the two roles by always referring to me as "Miss Peters," very formally, when I'm Wayne's wife, and dropping into a friendly "Jean" in the second characterization. It's easy for me to stiffen up into a difficult customer when people become over-proper, which is what is needed for the opening role, and then to be a pretty friendly character when folks get around to calling me "Jean." There is only one type of vehicle I'll be aiming for after this—a picture with a one-woman cast.[17]

After two weeks in Kansas, the troupe returned to Fox Studios to shoot the interiors. However, Jean had left a few days earlier after falling ill. She was diagnosed with a lingering bronchial condition and was ordered by her physician, Dr. Verne Mason, to take a rest before resuming her film work. However, "Punctual Pete," as Jean was referred to by her coworkers (she was never late on set or for an appointment), wanted to complete her scenes first. On the first week of October, she finally checked into the Good Samaritan Hospital for ten days of further examination. Due to her health condition, she was forced to cancel her next film, *Way of a Gaucho* (1952), which was scheduled to be filmed entirely in Argentina. Gene Tierney replaced her.

Zanuck was so pleased with the first screening of *Wait Till the Sun Shines, Nellie* that he ordered only very small cuts from the original footage. King was proud of his work but added, "I wouldn't want to go through it again. I would rather film two *David and Bathsheba*s [the 1951 epic he directed] than one *Wait Till the Sun Shines, Nellie*. The trouble with *Nellie* is that you must get inside the characters and live with them. It's a job of interpreting human nature, and that's the hardest job in the world. The spectacle stuff is easy compared to this."[18] A petition carrying the names of thirty-five thousand residents of Hutchinson was presented to Fox executives in Hollywood by Mayor William Shaw, asking that the world premiere of *Wait Till the Sun Shines, Nellie* be held in their town. Jean was photographed together with Zanuck, King, and Shaw at the official presentation of the request, which was agreed to. May 14, 1952, was the date fixed for the event.

Jean, her costars Hugh Marlow, Helene Stanley, and producer George Jessel returned to Hutchinson to take part in an unprecedented three-day series of events, including a costume ball and street parade. Almost a hundred thousand people showed up for the occasion, and according to the local Chamber of Commerce, close to $1 million was spent on the celebration. The town stepped back in time to the early 1900s, with every shop in Hutchinson displaying merchandise in their windows at 1902 prices, and residents wore clothes and hats from that period.

When it came to the release of the film, Fox adopted an unusual strategy. It was first shown in towns of every size in all the Midwest states, where it was assumed that local people particularly would enjoy the film's nostalgic Americana. New York and Los Angeles had to wait more than a month before the film opened in their cities.

Unfortunately, the film was often mistaken for a musical because its title was based on the popular 1905 song of the same name, and this kept away all the spectators who were not aficionados of that genre. Reviewers appreciated the beautiful Technicolor photography that depicted the turn-of-the-century, small-town life and its amusing characters, but it was not enough to draw more theatergoers.

Disappointing commercially, *Wait Till the Sun Shines, Nellie* grossed $1.25 million domestically and disappeared from theaters after a few weeks. More than a year later, in May 1953, David Wayne and Jean starred in a radio rendering of the film for the *Lux Radio Theater*.

CHAPTER 7

Negulesco's Muse

You couldn't not be in love with Jean Peters.
—JEAN NEGULESCO

JEAN MADE A SPEEDY RECOVERY FROM HER RESPIRATORY PROBLEM JUST in time to travel to the Okefenokee Swamp Park near Waycross, Georgia, where she was expected to play the female lead in *Swamp Water*. At the same time, Debra Paget was alerted to be ready as a replacement in case the doctors would not allow Jean to travel.

Swamp Water, quickly retitled *Lure of the Wilderness* (1952), was a Technicolor remake of Jean Renoir's *Swamp Water* (1941) based on Vereen Bell's debut novel, which was originally serialized in the *Saturday Evening Post*. It tells the story of Ben Tyler, a young man who stumbles upon Jim Harper, a fugitive from justice hiding in the Okefenokee Swamp in Georgia, and his attempts to help clear him of the charges. Meanwhile, the young man falls in love with Laurie Harper, the fugitive's beautiful and wild daughter, played by Jean.

Lure of the Wilderness was directed by Jean Negulesco and produced by Robert Jacks, the husband of Darryl Zanuck's daughter Darrylin. Jacks, who was just twenty-six, had started in the Fox publicity department before switching to the story department and gradually moving up to the job of administrative assistant. Working with Negulesco was Jacks's first experience in a long, fruitful career as a producer of mostly Western and adventure films for Fox in the 1950s and subsequently for television.

When she arrived on location on October 26, Jean was greeted by a gala welcome, which included a one-hundred-car motorcade from the airport in Waycross, Georgia, to town. As she stepped from the plane, she was overwhelmed by the crowd of hundreds who turned out to greet her. Wearing a conservative gray suit, she joked with the local press by tweaking the lyrics of a song to say, "If I had known you would be here, I'd have dressed for the party." The mayor of Waycross presented her with the key to the city and escorted her to the Ware Hotel, where hundreds of autograph seekers swarmed around her car and pursued her into the hotel lobby. It was Jean's first visit to the South, and she fell in love immediately. "Now I know what they're talking about when they mention southern hospitality," she told the local press. "I'll be talking with a southern drawl before I leave here."[1]

Lure of the Wilderness was not an easy shoot as it was filmed in harsh weather conditions. Throughout the entire schedule, from dawn till dusk, all members of the production, cast and crew, were either wet with sweat or swamp water. The hazards of shooting the picture in the four-hundred-thousand-acre Okefenokee Swamp were extensive and constant. The troupe worked in the heart of the swamp where no tourists and few guides had ever been, most of the time in water up to their waists. Their "alligator patrol" was a constant reminder of the ever-present danger they were in. "I don't believe that I'll even look at an alligator purse without being a little afraid of it," Jean told Hollywood columnist Sidney Skolsky, who visited the set.[2]

The wardrobe crew carried three extra pairs of khaki pants for Negulesco since he would fall into the swamp water more often than anyone else. Wardrobe director Charles LeMaire dressed Jean in leather pants and a jacket throughout most of the picture, but the same outfit had to be made in several duplicates to be replaced every time she got soaked in sweat or swamp waters. "Yet Jeanie remains feminine and desirable at all times," LeMaire stated in an interview, "because her long hair made up for the fact she wasn't wearing chic gowns."[3] Jean also joked about her makeup being de-glamourized. "I get into makeup in the morning. With other actresses, it's pin curls and stuff," she said. "With me, it's 'dirty up her hair, throw oil on her face, and let's go.'"[4]

Jean and the cast made Waycross their headquarters for the film, traveling to the swamp each day. Her costar, Jeffrey Hunter, had to keep a tape recorder running to catch the local accent so he could copy it for his character. "We grunt and groan instead of talking," Jean explained. She and Walter Brennan played daughter and father who had been hiding in the swamplands for years.[5]

In discussing the film, Jean recalled the practical skills she picked up on the set: "In *Lure of the Wilderness*, I had to be taught the art of handling a bow and an arrow and to pole a boat. Both proved to be fun. Jeffrey Hunter and I had to practice poling on the lake on 20th's back lot. The water was so cold, I made up my mind not to fall in, but we had a couple of narrow squeaks."[6]

Of the rather unusual location, she said, "The real star of the picture is the Okefenokee Swamp, and any poor human who thinks otherwise is just kidding himself. With its 180 species of birds, twenty of frogs and toads, thirty of fish, twenty-eight of snakes, and forty-five of mammals, it's a world apart. Some of those captured on film include panthers, black bears, deer, alligators and others. No, I don't want to go back there."[7] The animal stars were unpredictable. Gloria Cesar, a professional snake handler, was bitten on both hands by one of her "pets" and had to be rushed to the hospital.

Negulesco had developed a great fondness for Jean, with whom he had worked a lot, but this film crystallized his feelings. In an interview, he said, "Peters was superb, gorgeous physically with animal-like movements, like someone who had always lived in the jungle. I admired her and loved her a lot. You couldn't not be in love with Jean Peters. She neither wanted to play in any film nor to be a star, but the agents and the producers would fall in love with her and keep casting her in their pictures."

After three weeks in the rugged location, the troupe returned to Hollywood looking like a lost war battalion. Jean flew back home, suffering from poison oak, which caused an itchy rash all over her body. Walter Brennan had also contracted poison oak so severely on set that the makeup artists had to mix their body paints with a soothing medical lotion to give him some relief while he was in front of the camera.

After a week off, shooting resumed on a huge Fox back lot, where a fifteen-acre area included a large pool masquerading as the Okefenokee Swamp. Working on the lot proved to be just as challenging as being in the actual swamp. Negulesco was supposed to shoot mid-summer scenes on the main street of a hot, dusty southern town on the edge of the swamp, but that winter in Hollywood, the average temperature was thirty-five degrees and was often accompanied by a chill northern wind. "I know now what the cry of the swamp is. . . . We better be careful. This is in Technicolor, and before the day is over, it's going to show me turning blue,"[8] Jean joked with the press. For most of the film, her character wore a short-sleeved, thin cotton dress. When she finished a scene, Jean would race for the sidelines where a wardrobe woman waited with a sweater and a heavy coat.

Filming in such conditions exhausted Jean. "I feel I could sleep six months," she told the press. "Every night I go home, bathe, drench myself in black narcissus, [and] put on a lace nightie. Otherwise, I wouldn't know I was a woman."[9]

Despite the challenges, the stars were encouraged to invite their families to the set. Jeffrey Hunter was visited by his wife, actress Barbara Rush, and his parents, and Jean welcomed Mary and Shirley. A few studio executives showed an interest in her younger sister, and for a moment, Jean thought Shirley was interested in a film career. Yet the young girl revealed that she had no acting ambitions, and her only plan was to become a teacher of either English or speech.

In December, a few days before Negulesco wrapped shooting, Jean paid for an ad in a trade paper to thank Zanuck and each crew and cast member for the amazing job they had achieved and to wish them happy holidays. In February, the director summoned her back to the Fox lot to shoot two new scenes with Hunter and Brennan.

Lure of the Wilderness' world premiere was held on July 16, 1952, in Waycross, and was followed the next day by a gala event in Atlanta, where a four-block section of the city was transformed into swampland to provide the atmosphere for a colorful parade led by Walter Brennan, Jeffrey Hunter, and Fox's new starlet, Anne Francis. Unable to leave the set of her latest film, *Niagara* (1953), Jean could not take part in the event.

The critical reception for *Lure of the Wilderness* and for Jean's performance was varied. *Photoplay* noted that "Jean Peters is sullenly handsome as the girl who distrusts all humans,"[10] while *Variety* commented, "Jean Peters is okay as the sulky jungle girl and looks good in the swamp-type costumes the role calls for."[11] The *Hollywood Reporter* seemed more taken by Jean's performance than by her looks: "Miss Peters handled the part . . . with sensitivity and appeal."[12] The film grossed $2 million.

With four films released in 1952 and vastly increased visibility, Jean's fanbase skyrocketed. Nevertheless, as she insisted on keeping her private life private, she was still seen as an enigma. "Mystery girl," many movie fan magazines called her, because she avoided glitzy social events, including film premieres and studio gatherings. She never attended trendy restaurants or star-studded nightclubs, much to the bafflement of the press. Jean would happily sit down with them and discuss her career, her new films and her dressmaking ability, but her personal life remained off-limits, especially the on-and-off relationship with Howard Hughes.

Jean spent her free time indulging her passions, which included sewing, reading, oil painting, playing tennis or golf, and keeping a record of her observations on the people and places of Hollywood with the intention of writing a book. This project would never materialize after she decided to destroy her journal a few years later. Jean also found time to design the costumes for the musical *On the Town*, performed at the Gallery Stage, a small theater in Hollywood. The show starred Jean's old university mate Arlen Hurwitz—now Arlen Allen—who had pursued a career in the theater.

Jean attended the gala premiere, and her input as a costume designer certainly helped the musical gain more column inches in the press.

On February 13, 1952, the *Hollywood Reporter* announced that director Jean Negulesco had given February 20 as the starting date for filming *The Last Leaf*—the fourth sequence in Fox's *The Full House*, based on a quintet of short stories by William Sydney Porter, who used the pseudonym O. Henry. Fox had decided to produce *Bagdad on the Subway* (as the film was originally titled), a star-studded film in five episodes featuring the contribution of five different filmmakers: Negulesco, Henry Koster, Henry Hathaway, Henry King, and Howard Hawks.

Negulesco's *The Last Leaf* was based on a short story originally published in O. Henry's 1907 collection, *The Trimmed Lamp*. A couple of weeks before shooting was due to start, Fox changed the title to *O. Henry's Full House* (1952). Of the film, produced by André Hakim, who at the time was Darryl Zanuck's son-in-law, Negulesco recalled:

> The story I had to adapt told the fight against death of a woman sick with tuberculosis [played by Anne Baxter]. She knows that she is going to die when the last leaf, which she sees from a window in her bedroom, [falls] from the tree. Her sister [played by Jean] asks an old painter [played by Gregory Ratoff] to draw on the wall the soaring leaf. The sick woman starts to recover, thanks to that tiny particle. I wanted Gregory Ratoff so much that I refused to make the picture if he wouldn't be cast in the part. The studio wanted Edmund Gwenn, but I did not find him too close to the character I had imagined. We shot each episode in six days.[13]

Jean was excited to work opposite Anne Baxter, who was a friend and colleague she respected highly. It is lightly suggested in the original story that the two women are lovers, but the Hollywood moral code changed them into sisters.

According to Negulesco, Jean gave "a touching performance. She never wanted to be an actress," the filmmaker explained. "She would much rather have been a teacher; in fact, I think she had a slight inferiority complex about it."[14] Many years later, Jean told Marilyn Monroe's biographer that *The Last Leaf*, at just twenty-three minutes, was the favorite of her films.[15]

The premiere of *O. Henry's Full House* took place on August 7, 1952, at the Carolina Theater in Sydney Porter's birthplace, Greensboro, North Carolina. *The Last Leaf* was found by many to be too melodramatic and not the best episode of the film, the reception of which was scarcely enthusiastic.[16]

• • •

In the spring of 1952, Mary and Shirley Peters returned permanently to the Ohio farm while Jean moved to a rented, unfurnished home in Beverly Hills with her grandaunt, Cis Francomb. The relocation was completed a few weeks before Jean was set to star in Henry Hathaway's *Niagara*. That May, the *Los Angeles Evening News* reported that Jean stood a good chance of starring in Otto Preminger's *The River of No Return* (1954) opposite Dale Robertson, but Marilyn Monroe and Robert Mitchum were the final casting choices when the film went into production in the summer of 1953.

After giving Monroe her first leading role in *Don't Bother to Knock* (1952), Fox knew that they were onto something big with the blonde actress, but the studio was unsure how to exploit her sexual magnetism to best effect. Producer Charles Brackett cowrote a suitable script titled *Niagara* that seemed the perfect vehicle for Monroe—a murder mystery set in the world's most famous waterfalls. Brackett had been born very close to Niagara Falls and lived around that area all his life. He had the idea of a story using Niagara's natural spectacle as an important part of the plot. He brainstormed with screenwriter Walter Reisch, who came up with the idea of a thriller involving honeymooning couples at the resort. Although Brackett was not totally convinced, he discussed the concept with Zanuck, who loved it.

Shortly after, Brackett, Reisch, and screenwriter Richard Breen traveled to Niagara Falls and lived for a while on both the Canadian and American sides of the falls, where they blocked out the script. Meanwhile, Zanuck appointed Henry Hathaway as director and James Mason as the male lead. Titled *Niagara*, the script tells the story of Rose Loomis, an adulterous wife who brings her husband George, a war-shocked Korean veteran, to Niagara Falls. Rose then plots with her lover to have her spouse pushed into the falls. At the same time, another couple of honeymooners, Polly and Ray Cutler, become involved with Rose and George in a series of circumstances that lead to two murders.

Maureen Stapleton and Anne Baxter were both being considered for the role of Rose, while Jeanne Crain and Anne Francis were discussed for Polly. In September 1951, Zanuck suggested Louis Jourdan as George Loomis, Constance Smith as Rose Loomis, and Jeffrey Hunter as Ray Cutler.

Eventually, in April 1952, Hathaway, cameraman Joe MacDonald, unit production manager Abe Steinberg, and special effects photographer Ray Kellogg flew to Niagara Falls, Ontario, where they scouted locations for twenty days. Finally, Fox announced Joseph Cotten and Anne Baxter as leads, and he had another surprise, as Walter Reisch recalled: "Zanuck wired or phoned us that he wanted to put Marilyn Monroe into the picture.

We thought that was a nice idea until there came a second phone call that he wanted her to be the villainess, not the girl in the honeymoon sequences. . . . He insisted it was a great idea, so we finally did it."[17]

A month later, Monroe signed the contract, followed by Jean, who was cast as Baxter's replacement. Some accounts wrongly reported that Marilyn's role was originally written for Jean, but the truth was that Jean stepped in to replace Anne Baxter, who pulled out of the project when the Polly Cutler part was downscaled so as not to upstage Marilyn's character. The *Hollywood Reporter*'s columnist Mike Connolly wrote, "Know how Jean Peters go [sic] that part in *Niagara*? She walked up to Henry Hathaway and ASKED for it."[18] (This was a rumor, but there is no proof that it happened, and as Hathaway was a bad-tempered and feared director, it seems unlikely.)

Years later, Jean admitted that during filming, even though Marilyn's part was more interesting than hers, she felt that they were equals, and she never thought she was in a Monroe vehicle. However, this all changed when the film came out and she received third billing after Monroe and Cotten.

Jean and a crew of seventeen flew out to Niagara Falls on May 31, 1952. The production encountered some difficulties in finding enough single beds for the cast, and the crew and Jean and the other main cast members stayed at the fancy General Brock Hotel. To comply with the story, a realistic "Rainbow Motel" was built from scratch in Queen Victoria Park, facing the Horseshoe Falls, which cost $48,000. In addition, a construction shack was set up on a hill overlooking the falls near Burning Springs.

Henry Hathaway had a reputation for being a difficult director and was known to fire an entire technical crew if one person did not follow his commands exactly. "To be a good director," he once said, "you've got to be a bastard. I'm a bastard, and I know it."[19] Even though his relationship with Jean was very good during the entire shooting, she said that he could be very unpleasant, and he bullied cast and crew members.

Hathaway was meticulous in his craft and knew the exact length each sequence required before it was shot. He gave precise instructions to his actors on the duration and pace of the scenes they had to play. Although Monroe's recurrent tardiness on set tested his patience, he was able to contain himself. Other cast and crew members could not and became upset and angry about her disrespectful behavior that repeatedly held up production.

While on location, Jean enjoyed a visit from her mother and sister. She also reunited with Robert Slatzer, her old OSU friend, who had come to visit Marilyn for a few days. Jean and Robert enjoyed a couple of meals together, and they also watched Hathaway shooting Monroe make the longest walk in motion picture history—a 116-foot walk in a tight skirt.

According to Slatzer, when he mentioned that he was having dinner with Jean, Marilyn said, "Jean's really great . . . I like working with her."[20]

There was no chance of Slatzer and Jean rekindling their college romance. Casey Adams, who played Jean's husband, recalled that, once again, Howard Hughes sent a female friend to prevent any males from getting too friendly: "Jean Peters I absolutely adored right from the time we met. Of course, Howard Hughes had sent a girl to watch over her. Jean and I would skip away and have dinner together, then we'd come back, and this girl would beat me with an umbrella and say, 'You stay *away* from her!'"[21] This plan may have worked on set, but a few months later, Jean and Adams had a brief affair after a series of dates organized behind Hughes's back.

Following twenty-two days of location filming at Niagara Falls, Canada, Hathaway resumed shooting at a Fox lot for twenty-four more days, ending in the middle of July. *Niagara* was widely considered to be a gripping thriller/melodrama that blended clear film-noir elements with high-contrast Technicolor cinematography. As many reviewers pointed out, Jean's and Cotten's superb performances also contributed to the movie's success. The *Hollywood Reporter* wrote, "Jean Peters turns in a warm, sensitive performance as the honeymooner drawn into the murder intrigue."[22] *Variety* stated, "Miss Peters portrays the honeymooning wife with a wholesome quality and generally makes a favorable impression."[23] *Niagara* became one of Fox's greatest hits of 1953. It cost $1.25 million to produce and enjoyed a return of $6 million.

CHAPTER 8

Femme Noir

Jean was a good sport, easy to work with, fun to be around.
—SAMUEL FULLER

SEVERAL ACTRESSES APPROACHED DIRECTOR SAMUEL "SAMMY" FULLER about playing the role of Candy in his upcoming production, *Blaze of Glory*, based on a story by Dwight Taylor. Ava Gardner was one of the first who asked to read for the part, but the director dismissed her as too glamorous to be believable as Candy, an ordinary-looking, unsophisticated woman. Shelley Winters campaigned for it desperately and Fox eventually gave it to her, against Fuller's wishes as he thought she was not right. A few days after the press reported that she'd been cast, Winters discovered she was pregnant and pulled out.

Blaze of Glory was a tough melodrama set in the New York underworld. Petty criminal Skip McCoy accidentally picks the purse of a girl named Candy that contains microfilm belonging to the Communists. Suddenly, the pickpocket becomes involved in a plot between the "Reds" and the FBI. In the story, Candy is frequently the object of excessive brutality by men, and in one dramatic scene, takes a severe beating. Those violent scenes were to be shot according to Fuller's realistic style, with the use of close-ups and no doubles, which was why pregnant Winters felt compelled to turn the part down.

As soon as the news broke about Winters, Betty Grable asked Zanuck for the role but insisted that a dance number had to be included in the picture. Fuller was outraged at the request and felt that Grable, who was, at the time, one of the highest-paid actresses in Hollywood, was not right for Candy. Zanuck thought otherwise and cast her, but the actress refused the role because her wish for a musical number was dismissed. Grable explained that she was not suited for a straight dramatic role and would not be received well by her fans. Fox placed her on immediate suspension.

The role remained uncast as preproduction began. Some columnists speculated that Anne Baxter, Linda Darnell, and Jean were being considered for the part. Meanwhile, Fuller had Marilyn Monroe read for it. Although the filmmaker was impressed by Monroe's seductive look, her soft way of speaking—almost purring—seemed inappropriate for Candy's strong character. Monroe was disappointed, but Fuller's dismissal did not stop her from visiting the set during the shoot.

At this point, with time running out, Bill Gordon, one of Fuller's collaborators, proposed Jean for the female lead. Fuller rejected the idea because he remembered disliking her in *Captain from Castile*, the only one of Jean's films he had ever watched. Then one day, Fuller had lunch at the studio commissary with Henry King, Henry Hathaway, Ray Kellogg, Leon Shamroy, and Jeanne Crain. Just before the meeting, Crain saw Jean in the hall and asked her to join the party. She agreed and was duly introduced to Fuller, the only person in the group she did not know. She made an immediate impression, as Fuller wrote in his autobiography: "She had a lilting voice. As she walked away from us, I looked at Peters's pert figure and her legs and thought to myself that she had Candy's bowed legs, the kind of gams you get from streetwalking. Peters came to read for me on a Friday afternoon. The sets were all built. We were going to shoot a week from that coming Monday."[1]

Like others before him, Fuller became smitten by Jean's cerebral qualities and her knowledge of a wide range of subjects, from literature to politics. After she read just one scene, he knew he had found his Candy. Jean was aware that she had been at the bottom of the list of Fuller's casting choices, but the director told her the only reason he had not screen-tested her earlier was his dislike for "those fake representations of gypsies" in *Captain from Castile*. Jean defended herself by saying that it was her first film and Henry King had to be blamed for the clumsy portrayals.

Once Fuller confirmed Jean got the leading role, she asked for some rehearsal time—first alone and then with costars Richard Widmark and Thelma Ritter. With only a week before principal photography began, Fuller and Jean rehearsed together every day from 6 a.m. to 10 p.m. She would show up on time at Fuller's office bungalow in a chauffeured car and the driver would wait outside, in dark sunglasses, the entire day. Eventually, Fuller realized that the mysterious man had to be Jean's boyfriend and asked her if she wanted him to wait inside. With a smile on her face and without offering any information about his identity, she declined.

By the end of the week, Richard Widmark joined the rehearsals and ran through all the love scenes he had with Jean. Standing outside, leaning on his car, the driver would stare into the window and watch every passionate clinch. Finally, one of Fuller's secretaries recognized Jean's mysterious escort as Howard Hughes. Fuller was shocked—this was one of the most powerful, wealthiest, not to mention reclusive men in the world, and here he was, sitting in a car outside his office all day.

Jean and Hughes were acting in a low-key manner in an attempt to avoid publicity, as Hughes had only just emerged from the eye of a press storm after settling a two-year legal battle with Jean Simmons. The British actress had a contract with Hughes's studio, RKO, but the billionaire would not let her work because he was infatuated with her, despite her marriage to actor Stewart Granger.

The shooting of *Blaze of Glory* started on September 18 on a Fox lot where man-sized utility tunnels were used for several underground sequences. The subway backgrounds for the picture were shot in New York, while office buildings in downtown LA stood in for some Manhattan buildings.

Jean turned down suggestions to bleach her hair. Fuller agreed to let her keep her natural dark hair since he wanted her to avoid comparison to Shelley Winters or Betty Grable. Jean told Hedda Hopper that her character was "a sexy moron who falls in love with a pickpocket."[2] For the character, she developed a "sexy" walk. "Ordinarily, I have a stride that could cover two country miles in half an hour," she told columnist Bob Thomas. "But I've worked out a sexy shuffle in the picture." Marilyn Monroe, whose bottom-wiggling walk was part of her sex symbol persona, joked with Jean on one of her regular visits to the set: "If you steal anything from me, I'll sue," she said. "Don't worry," laughed Jean. "This is all mine."[3]

On their first day filming together, Jean and Richard Widmark had to have a nurse on standby as they performed a violent courtship scene. Jean suffered a sprained ankle, a loosened tooth, bruised lips, neck scratches, and a torn dress from the scene, while Widmark got a lump on the head, a scratch over the right eye, bruised shins, and sprained ribs. This playacting had serious consequences.

One day, on a break between scenes, Jean asked Fuller what had changed his mind about her that led him to give her the part. "Your legs, kid," he said candidly. "They're very sexy. They're a little arched. I'm not saying a tank could drive through them. But maybe a small Jeep." Jean laughed.

"She was a good sport, easy to work with, fun to be around," recalled Fuller. "To shoot those legs the way I wanted, I placed a camera below the rickety bridge to Skip's shack. Jean walked across it with a little sashay, her hips swinging, the bridge swinging, the whole set swinging."[4]

Jean and Widmark had great chemistry that translated to the screen. "[Richard] can do anything—things Brando couldn't do,"[5] she said, flattering her costar. He returned the compliment by saying that of all the leading ladies he had worked with, Jean was his favorite.

The same couldn't be said for Widmark and Fuller. "He was not a favorite of mine, but we got along okay," Widmark said of Fuller years later. "Jean Peters and I rehearsed by ourselves—at length. We wanted to get it right. Neither of us was crazy about doing the movie or working with Sam. For what it was, I think it came out a pretty good little movie."[6] Fuller found Widmark "cantankerous and insular, sometimes thoroughly uncooperative. As a star at Fox, he had an attitude," he said. "I didn't give a damn about his status."[7]

In the middle of production, the title was changed to *Pickup on South Street* (1953). Jean also celebrated her twenty-sixth birthday midshoot. She received a script binder from the crew, flowers from Fuller, and a gag cake that wouldn't cut from Widmark. *Pickup on South Street* was finished on schedule in only twenty days, but a month later, Fuller asked Jean to return to the set for retakes. A scene where she and Richard Kiley frisked each other for loot was too explicit for Joseph Breen's production code office and had to be toned down.

The film's critical response was mixed, but Jean's performance was generally applauded. "[Fuller] draws superb performances, particularly from Jean Peters, who is brilliant in a change-of-pace role as a sexy, rather slowwitted ex-B girl," wrote the *Hollywood Reporter*.[8] From the *Washington Post*: "Jean Peters couldn't be more striking as the 'cannon' and the babe,"[9] while the *New York Times*' Bosley Crowther praised her for "doing very well."[10] In September, the picture won the Bronze Lion at the 14th Venice International Film Festival, but Fuller did not attend as he was busy on the set of his next film. The award was presented to him four months later in Los Angeles by the Italian consul at a Fox luncheon.

Seven months after its release, *Pickup on South Street* passed the $4 million box office mark, making it Fox's top black-and-white grosser for 1953. In France, the picture was released as *Porte de la Drogue* (*Port of Drugs*) and re-edited so that the French version, which was dubbed, told a story about drug smugglers and did not offend the French Communist Party. Despite the film's success, only Thelma Ritter received an Academy Award nomination for Supporting Actress.

Although it did well, it is not a film that has been revered over the decades, although in recent years, *Pickup on South Street* has been reevaluated by critics who now consider it a cult movie and a classic of the film noir genre.

In May 1952, Jean agreed to be part of a group of entertainers who volunteered to perform during the Christmas and New Year season for GIs stationed and hospitalized overseas. The Hollywood Coordinating Committee assigned Jean, Paul Douglas, Jan Sterling, Walter Pidgeon, Debbie Reynolds, Rory Calhoun, and several other stars to one of the three units scheduled to tour bases and hospitals in Korea.

In December, Jean was invited to be the "lady editor of the week" on Bob Hope's daytime NBC radio show, where she discussed her film career along with her forthcoming trip to Korea. She spoke enthusiastically about the efforts she was making to prepare her outfits for the tour. Many of the items she had sewn herself for what she described as "a full wardrobe of fur-lined evening gowns."[11]

Two days before Christmas and shortly before she was due to leave, Fox asked Jean to screen test opposite Scott Brady for the female lead in *A Blueprint for Murder* (1953). She got the role, but the studio took her off the Korean tour since the dates clashed with the production schedule. Jean was heartbroken and offered to go off salary during her absence. Fox refused and demanded she report immediately for work but promised her that she would be permitted to join the next scheduled tour.

In January 1953, after six years at the studio, Jean's contract with 20th Century Fox was renewed for two more years. The new exclusive agreement provided a substantial salary increase but also indicated that she would have no choice in picking any of her films; the studio had total control.

So, with no choice in the matter and with limited time for preparation, Jean joined the cast of *A Blueprint for Murder*, a mystery melodrama featuring Joseph Cotten, Gary Merrill, and Catherine McLeod. Gloria Grahame, who owed Fox a picture, was originally set to play the lead opposite William Lundigan, but for unknown reasons, both artists were replaced by Jean and Cotten. Initially, the picture was planned as a high-budget production, but the idea was abandoned for a more appropriate cost revision. To save money, sets from other productions were borrowed, including the use of the lavish ship set created for the film *Titanic* (1953).

A Blueprint for Murder was completed in only twenty days, with the first scene filmed on February 12, 1953. The picture tells the story of a man who, on the basis of substantial evidence, suspects that his young sister-in-law is responsible for the deaths of her husband and one of her stepchildren.

Andrew Stone, the picture's director and screenwriter, revealed that in writing the script, he and his wife conducted two years of research, breaking down reports of 1,055 cases of death by poison. Most of the shooting was done at Fox studios except for a scene filmed at a new wing of Cedars of Lebanon Hospital, where Jean was the first occupant before the space was open to the public. Later, Stone remarked on Jean's professionalism, strength of character, and willingness to succeed: "[Jean] was a charming girl. I don't think she had the greatest screen personality, but she was a very competent actress. I'll never forget a Friday afternoon when she read for a part and wasn't good. I was concerned. She said, 'Don't worry, Monday I'll be in and I'll be a different girl.' Monday came and you wouldn't know it was the same actress."[12]

Joseph Cotten and Jean had become acquainted on the set of *Niagara*, but their friendship was cemented when they were reunited in *A Blueprint for Murder*. "What a conversationalist!" Jean said about her costar.[13] When she discovered that Cotten had just finished building his own home, she expressed a wish to visit it and Cotten invited her over. He welcomed her wearing an old baseball cap and rough corduroy. While he showed her around, the actor explained that he had also built a fireplace from floor to ceiling. "I built the walls and the terrace," he told Jean, "But something went wrong when I mixed the cement. You see, that line dried a different color halfway across, and it looks terrible. Someday I'll have to do something about it."[14]

She was fascinated with Cotten's interest in construction and shared her own experiences of building work, having grown up on a farm. She told him why she thought there was not much he could do to fix the problem and how to prevent it from happening again.

Cotten was impressed not only with Jean's technical knowledge but also with her interest in the practicalities of everyday life and the fact that it meant more to her than being a movie star. Her down-to-earth qualities made the reserved actor open up. He told her that whenever he felt tense, he would buy tons of picture stone and build himself a wall, the only activity that genuinely relaxed him.

A Blueprint for Murder premiered in the summer of 1953 but received divided reviews, and along with its modest success at the box office, it did very little to help Jean's career. That same year, her name was attached to several productions, including two major studio projects: Fox's second film in CinemaScope, *How to Marry a Millionaire* (1953), and the historical epic *The Egyptian* (1954). But by the time the final casting choices were made, her name was no longer there.

The next picture Jean made that year was *Vicki* (1953), the third and final film noir of her career, in which she played the title role of a ruthless and ambitious model. Producer Leonard Goldstein, together with director Harry Horner, had announced the project at the end of 1952, and Goldstein told Hedda Hopper that Jean was one of the greatest sirens of the screen he had ever seen. So he bought the story of *Vicki* by Steve Fisher especially for her.[15] The picture was a remake of 1941's *I Wake Up Screaming*, a film noir starring Betty Grable, Victor Mature, and Carole Landis.

The film was particularly exciting for Jean as she would be starring opposite her close friend Jeanne Crain, who played her sister. The picture marked their reunion on the screen three years after they played "sorority sisters" in *Take Care of My Little Girl*. In interviews, Jean would often talk about her special friendship with Crain and how she wished that one day she'd have a happy marriage like hers. Jean, who had been seeing Hughes on and off for years, was impressed by how Crain had a good marriage with a fine, intelligent man (actor Paul Brinkman) and continued to be serious about her work. "Her career did not dominate her," Jean said. "Fame isn't an influence that is wrecking her devotion to her husband. She's made it just that extra self-expression almost every woman needs besides the family circle."[16]

One week before the cameras rolled, Fox dropped the original decision to shoot *Vicki* in 3D. Production started on March 2 on a Fox soundstage and later moved on location at the studio ranch in Calabasas, California.

From the first day on set, Jeanne and Jean agreed that they would have fun in their roles playing bad girls, especially since they had to wear glamorous clothes, work in luxurious settings, and monopolize the camera for a large percentage of the running time. Although Jean's character dies before the picture begins, she appears throughout the entire film in a series of flashbacks. Interviewed on the set, Jean said of the glitzy role:

> I've never regarded myself as a clothes horse, but since my assignment in *Vicki*, I can see where a girl can become one. I play a waitress who overnight is turned into a fashion model and cover girl, and the studio has turned out the fanciest assortment of apparel I've ever worn—on or off screen. Most are evening dresses, the sort of things in which a girl can really look her best. I'm great for loafing around the house in blue jeans and a sport blouse, but I'll have to admit they just don't provide the lift you can get from a well-turned-out party gown. I never thought I'd like to own a fur coat, but even that is changing since they put me in sables for one of the love scenes

with Elliott Reid, who plays a publicity man. I'm afraid that *Vicki* is going to bring about a change in my budget. I've always managed to spend more money each year on books than on clothes, but now I believe I'll reverse the order![17]

While making *Vicki*, Jean and Crain took part in the 25th Academy Awards ceremony. They dressed up for the occasion, ready to accept the golden statue—Jean on behalf of Marlon Brando, who was nominated for *Viva Zapata!* and Crain on behalf of Susan Hayward, nominated for *With a Song in My Heart* (1952). It was the first Oscar ceremony to be televised and the first ceremony to be held in Hollywood and New York simultaneously. However, Jean complained that "not a single TV camera caught us during the entire evening."[18]

Everybody wanted to know the identity of her mysterious male escort. Later, she revealed that it was Paul Marino, an old school friend, who had been spotted several times already on the set of *Vicki*.

Jean surprised and impressed director Harry Horner when she agreed to sing two songs without being dubbed. Her bravura performances of "I Know Why" and "How Many Times Do I Have to Tell You?" proved she had what it took to pass as a sultry blues singer. It was a far cry from her poor vocal performance in *Love That Brute* when her singing had to be ghosted.

Horner completed the shooting in twenty days, four days earlier than scheduled, at a $560,000 cost. American critics found *Vicki* insipid and contrived, but they praised the acting of the leading players as first-rate. The *Hollywood Reporter* wrote, "Misses Crain and Peters are both decorative and competent."[19] Box office revenue barely covered production costs, and the picture quickly disappeared from screens.

In October 1953, after *Vicki* had been released nationwide, Fox was sued by playwright Siegfried M. Herzig, who claimed that the studio had appropriated the title of his play *Vickie* in an attempt to capitalize on its distinctive name and title. Herzig's play ran for forty-seven days on Broadway in 1942. Fox stated that their picture was based on entirely different material written by Steven Fisher. Two years later, a federal court in Hollywood ruled in favor of the studio and dismissed Herzig's $250,000 lawsuit.

· · ·

On March 31, Jean attended the opening of the Pacific Coast Baseball League season and was photographed kissing Stan Hack, manager of the Los Angeles Angels. A few months later, she was invited to throw the first ball at Gilmore Field to open the season. The event was televised and marked her first TV appearance. After years on the big screen, she was coming to the attention of the small.

CHAPTER 9

No Time for Love

What a perfect wife Jean would make!
—ROSSANO BRAZZI

IN 1953, DIRECTOR JEAN NEGULESCO, WHO WAS HAVING MARITAL PROBLEMS, asked Darryl Zanuck to assign him a project in Europe so that he could be close to his wife, Dusty. Tired of her husband's recurrent infidelities, she had left him and moved to Paris. The filmmaker chose Italy after Sol C. Siegel, producer of the film *We Believe in Love*—later called *Three Coins in the Fountain* (1954)—accepted him as director.

The two men left Hollywood for Italy to scout locations, making a stopover in New York where they watched *Roman Holiday* (1953) starring Gregory Peck and Audrey Hepburn. Negulesco liked the picture and wrote a memo to Zanuck telling him that *Roman Holiday* was made on location but in black and white, while *Three Coins in the Fountain* was going to be shot in color and CinemaScope. Zanuck resented Negulesco's memo since his plan was that once the locations had been scouted, he would send a second unit to Rome to film backgrounds and long shots with doubles. All the scenes, including close-ups and interiors, had to be shot on the Fox lot. He also pointed out that if Negulesco did not agree with his idea, he would gladly take him off the picture.

Siegel and Negulesco were upset by Zanuck's reaction and by his refusal to shoot the entire film in Italy. The two men asked Sid Rogell, head of studio production, if filming on location would be cheaper than creating studio replicas of some of the locations. The obvious answer was that shooting in Italy would have cost a third less than in Hollywood. When the cost study report was presented to Zanuck, he could not oppose the idea any longer but, according to Negulesco, resented him thereafter. *Three Coins in the Fountain* became the first CinemaScope picture made on location.

The original cast of *Three Coins* included Marilyn Monroe and Frank Sinatra as leads, but Monroe got engaged to Joe DiMaggio and did not want to leave the States. Sinatra turned down the part but later agreed to sing the theme over the title credits. The romantic song became the hit love ballad of the year.

The press had announced that Barbara Stanwyck, Clifton Webb, Gene Tierney, Vittorio Gassman, Jeanne Crain, and Louis Jourdan were all set to star. Yet only Webb and Jourdan appeared in the final cast, which included Dorothy McGuire, Maggie McNamara, Rossano Brazzi, and Jean.

Before leaving for Italy, Jean spent four days at the Hotel Flamingo in Las Vegas as a guest of Howard Hughes. As usual, he wanted her to be accompanied to Europe by a female chaperone, but after a fight, Jean won and flew to Italy alone. She joined the set in the first week of August when principal photography was scheduled to begin. During his first weeks in Italy, Negulesco filmed breathtaking panoramas of Rome and Venice along with the most famous monuments and landmarks.

Italian star Vittorio Gassman, who was then married to Shelley Winters, was chosen to play the role of Giorgio, a simple romantic Italian who falls in love with Anita Higgins, the character played by Jean. However, Gassman, a veteran of several Hollywood productions, turned down the role after reading the script. It was a decision he later regretted since his replacement, Rossano Brazzi, received a huge career boost from the movie.

Three Coins in the Fountain was a romantic comedy based on a novel by John Secondari, an American writer living in Italy. It told the story of three American girls working in Rome who throw their coins into the Trevi Fountain and hope for romance. Secretary Dorothy McGuire gradually wins the love of her employer, played by Clifton Webb. Jean, who also played a secretary to an American official in Rome, is romanced by a local Italian, Rossano Brazzi. Maggie McNamara lands herself a prince, Louis Jourdan.

Negulesco discovered that the best time to work quietly in Rome was between one and four in the afternoon, when the shops were closed and the streets deserted, because the Romans rested through the heat of the day.

Shooting a key scene at Rome's famous Fontana di Trevi cost Fox ten barrels of water. At the time, some of the Romans living near the world's most beautiful fountain got all their drinking and washing water there. Before Negulesco was granted permission to film, he had to provide two barrels of water for each of the five streets that converged on the fountain. Romans needing water while the film was being made could get it from the barrels without interrupting the shoot.

Having locals nearby also helped with the authenticity of the film. In a sequence shot near the landmark, the three women had to throw coins into the fountain to bring them luck. After a few takes, an onlooker told the director that people traditionally threw the coins over their shoulders, so the scene had to be reshot.

Talking with the American press, Negulesco said that CinemaScope added greatly to the realism of pictures and to their acceptance abroad. But CinemaScope on location, with its vivid colors, presented new types of problems. While Jean, McGuire, and McNamara's dresses looked superb when shot indoors under artificial lights, outside in the Roman streets next to the Italian extras, they looked as though they were made for a masquerade ball. Negulesco told Jean to buy new clothes at local stores that were more in line with the current Italian fashion.

Another issue arose due to the fact that no studio-type incandescent lamp could be found in Rome,[1] which meant some of the interior shots were later shot on a Fox stage.

During filming, Jean became conscious of the public way in which actors would have their makeup applied. In Hollywood, this was usually done in a partially private setting, or depending on the temperament of the star, in complete privacy. But in Italy, when Jean was being made up, people would gather from all over the set to watch the operation and make comments. This made her uncomfortable, but she let it pass because the observers were all so cheerful and interested.

Jean shared most of her scenes with Rossano Brazzi, the handsome Italian leading man considered by many to be the perfect embodiment of the Latin lover. The two hit it off perfectly. "What a perfect wife Jean would make!" was Brazzi's comment on his costar.[2] "He's a typical Italian," responded Jean. "I like Italians; they are happy people."[3]

Jean had a wonderful time in Italy, and not speaking the language didn't seem to restrict her social life at all. She received many invitations, all of which she accepted. The Italians liked her, and she returned their affection. She was impressed particularly by the charm of the Italian men, whose attention she found pleasantly flattering. "Italians are so very detailed in their expressions of appreciation," she said. "An American may say to a girl she has pretty eyes or hair, but the Italians can discourse a chapter or two on the beauty of one's feet. I regretted I didn't speak Italian so that I could understand all they said, but it was lots of fun anyhow."

By the end of her stay, she had come to understand that gallantry toward women was almost a reflex with Italians, and their compliments were like a game. "But," she exclaimed, "what an amusing game!"⁴ She reported to the press that Italian men "take longer to tell you how wonderful you are, but what a wonderful way to get bored!"⁵

While she was bemused by the flirtations of the local Casanovas, she was less enamored by a cast member who did not behave very gallantly. One evening, as a group of actors was lounging in a hotel room having cocktails after the day's work and Jean was curled up on a bed, an actor reached over and ran his hand along her leg. She picked up a portable radio on a nightstand and threw it at him. She missed, but the radio bounced through the open door and clattered down the steps, creating some commotion among some other hotel guests.⁶ The episode was reported to Howard Hughes, who called her almost every night to make sure everything was well with her.

In Rome, Jean was introduced to American Ambassador Clare Boothe Luce, who was also an author and a friend of Clifton Webb's. Luce threw a party in the embassy garden in honor of the cast. At that time, *Pickup on South Street* had just been shown at the Cannes Film Festival and was causing a stir for its political implications regarding communism. Mrs. Luce, who participated in the debate, was not in favor of the film in which Jean starred. Yet despite their differences, Jean was impressed by the charismatic diplomat. "She's a handsome, dignified woman," Jean told the press, "but there is this jazzy side of her that comes out now and then, as if to remind you that she wrote *The Women* and *Kiss the Boys Goodbye*."⁷

While making *Three Coins*, Jean's sister Shirley visited Rome, a trip she was bestowed as a graduation present. The young woman had just completed high school and had been admitted to USC. She planned to move in with Jean and her great-aunt Cis at the Beverly Hills house when she returned from Europe.

Shirley joined her sister when production moved to the Italian Alps for a few days. In the Northern Italian town of Merano, Jean bought a complete Tyrolean outfit, including a brightly colored skirt, embroidered bolero, and feathered hat. Having a couple of hours free one afternoon, she put on her new costume and rode the cable car up to Avelengo peak. As she took her place in the car, she could not help overhearing a couple of American soldiers in the back seat. "Boy, these Alpine cuties are really something," said one after a low whistle. "You can say that again," his friend agreed. "That one is pretty enough to be an American movie star!"

According to Jean, that month in Italy was one of the best times in her life, although she was disappointed she could not visit more places:

I can't say I've seen Europe. We went straight to Rome, and on the return trip, stopped off in Paris fifteen minutes. It was maddening. The studio was crazy to get us to Italy because scenes at the Fountain had to be shot on Sundays. We were scheduled to work within two days after we got home. So, I didn't get to Venice. Our production manager had a harum-scarum trip planned for my sister and me to go to Venice. We would have been jumping off buses to catch trains, then transferring to planes, but we were a day late in our shooting schedule, so we couldn't do it. But I saw everything in Rome.[8]

In the Eternal City, Jean had a friendly dinner date with Frederick Worden, editor of *Screenland* magazine. The journalist mentioned the evening in a long article he wrote on Jean, in which he described her beauty and down-to-earth qualities and mused about why she found it impossible to find Mr. Right:

As we walked through Rome's crowded streets, I kept glancing at the girl considered one of the most important young stars in Hollywood. . . . Hardly a soul that we passed in this ancient and worldly city realized that the girl beside me was a famous Hollywood personality. With her long turquoise and silver earrings, dark brown hair cut in [a] cowl effect, and her marvelous black eyelashes, she could easily have been mistaken for any of the large number of attractive Roman girls that gracefully walked by. Jean seemed to read my thoughts. "Don't you think I blend perfectly with the Italian background?" she asked. I told her that I have been thinking exactly the same thing: "I'm very often mistaken for Italian," she added. "I'm really of Welsh extraction, but there's a great similarity in type with the Latin races."[9]

Filming on location in Italy was completed in the middle of September and then resumed in December at Fox's studios. *Three Coins* cost $1.7 million, and Fox hoped it would repeat the commercial success of *How to Marry a Millionaire*. However, according to a Zanuck biographer, when a rough cut was shown to the studio head, he got up and left the screening room without any comment. Negulesco was so upset that he went out and threw up in the street. The film had to be reedited and some new dialogue added. Zanuck decided to personally take care of the re-editing in the hope of making it a commercial success.

In his memoir, Negulesco told a different story. In that retelling, the rough cut was shown for three nights in a row to friends in the industry, the crew, and studio people, and their reactions were unanimously positive. After it was shown to Zanuck and Spyros Skouras, both left the projection room without a word. The following day, Negulesco and Siegel were summoned by Zanuck, who, with the help of a cutter, went through all the scenes that they had edited, cut, or changed. Finally, the newly edited version was ready.

Negulesco and Siegel watched it and were shocked by the butchery done to their picture. They both signed a memo to Zanuck expressing their disappointment and added that if he decided to release this new version, their names should not appear in the credits. Zanuck asked them to rewatch the new cut with him, but after the viewing, he told the cutter to return it to its original state and ship it to all the American exhibitors, who subsequently raved about the picture.

Three Coins in the Fountain received generally positive reviews, particularly for its color and CinemaScope widescreen cinematography of the Italian locations. *Variety* wrote: "Once before, in 20th [Century] Fox's *How to Marry a Millionaire*, director Jean Negulesco CinemaScoped a trio of feminine beauties into a lucrative attraction. In *Three Coins in the Fountain,* he repeats this feat but obviously has gained some experience. The film has warmth, humor, a rich dose of romance, and almost incredible pictorial appeal." The magazine also commented on Jean: "Miss Peters has voluptuous appeal. She's also quite charming in the sequence involving her introduction to Brazzi's farmer parents."[10]

Strangely, Jean was not invited to the film premiere held in New York in May 1954. She complained in an interview, "I didn't see it. I don't understand why actors aren't invited to see their pictures, but they're not."

In later years, the film became one of her favorites: "I loved it; it gave me a chance to smile," she said. "I'm usually being beaten to death [in pictures]. This one was full of life and living—and love."[11] According to a rumor years later, once Jean was married to Howard Hughes, *Three Coins in the Fountain* became the film she liked to watch most with her husband in the privacy of their screening room.

The picture grossed $5 million domestically and got three Academy Award nominations including Best Film. Negulesco received an award nomination for Outstanding Directorial Achievement in Motion Pictures from the Directors Guild and a nomination for the Golden Lion at the Venice Film Festival, where the picture was presented in 1954.

In conjunction with *Three Coins in the Fountain*'s release, movie fan magazines printed a few articles discussing the reasons behind Jean's difficulty in finding a partner. Some blamed an overactive ambition that she had developed to compensate for fear of losing her heart. Others blamed Fox's demanding contract, which kept her hopping from one picture to another and not leaving her enough time to date men.

The truth was somewhere in the middle. Certainly, Jean did not have much time and room in her life for romance simply because it did not fit into her busy schedule. However, as per her own admission, she constantly fought emotional entanglements and erred on the side of self-protection. The moment she felt she was about to fall for a guy, she would take strong hold of herself and run away. Jean was a perfectionist in everything—including men. She feared that once she got to know a man too well, she would discover that he was not what she wanted him to be, and then she would become disillusioned.

Instead, she kept busy, pushing aside anything and everything that could possibly interfere with her success. She did not need a man around. She had never had men around her and had not grown up with a strong male influence. Everything she had accomplished she had done by herself. After her father's death, she and her sister were raised by her mother. The three women got along perfectly with no men around to tell them what to do. In an interview, Jean said:

> Since then, I had a well-developed sense of responsibility. Each of us had specific duties to perform, and part of mine was to look after Shirley. All my life, I had to work hard for the things that mattered to me. . . . Even now, in my Hollywood house, we are all females . . . I'm full of insecurities, and they make me painfully introspective. I spend a lot of time alone just thinking things out. I carefully and meticulously analyze every situation that confronts me—and that includes men, love, romance, and marriage. I'm always weighting and evaluating. I never seem to be able to accept things for what they really are. And until I can, I'm afraid I'll keep putting barriers around my emotions.[12]

And then everything changed.

On the day Jean headed back home from Italy, there was a mix-up in her luggage at the customs counter of Rome's Ciampino Airport. Her suitcases had been routed to the Paris address of a handsome businessman, while his were sent to Jean's in Los Angeles. As a result of the confusion, they both had to wait for twenty minutes, during which they made conversation—the typical chat between strangers in a public space. The tall, blond, blue-eyed gentleman recognized Jean only when she said that she had been in Rome to work with a motion picture company as an actress. Suddenly, he remembered her as Catana from *Captain from Castile*. He explained that her approachability, far from the typical movie star's behavior, had prevented him from recognizing her in the first place.

Stuart Cramer III was the name of the well-mannered man, a native of Charlotte, North Carolina, in the oil-drilling business in Wichita Falls, Texas (although not an oil millionaire, as some tabloids would report). He was the grandson of the legendary industrialist Stuart Warren Cramer (1868–1940), a textile industrialist, founder of eleven textile mills and close friend and former West Point classmate of Dwight D. Eisenhower.

Stuart Cramer III was traveling to Texas via Paris, and once the misdirected luggage had been sorted out, the two sat next to each other on the plane to Paris. They chatted for the entire flight, said their goodbyes, and went their separate ways. Jean took her connecting flight to New York while Stuart stayed in Paris.

Landing in Los Angeles, she was disappointed to not be welcomed formally by Howard Hughes, but she got over it when, a few weeks later, Cramer called her from Texas, announcing an upcoming trip to Hollywood. Jean took him to the studios and gave him a grand tour. After that, Cramer's visits became more frequent and they started to date, visiting trendy nightlife spots such as Ciro's and Mocambo. According to Jean, they never worried about being seen together or what anyone would think. Strangely, no one seemed to notice them.

Jean did not introduce Stuart to the studio publicity department or to any member of the press since it was her custom never to talk about private matters, not even to her closest friends. Her friends would meet him often at her Beverly Hills house, but they never heard details about the nature of their friendship.

Jean and Stuart had a long courtship because Howard Hughes was still in her life, and in the middle of it all, Jean made *Bronco Apache* opposite Burt Lancaster.

For the first time in her career, Jean was loaned from Fox to Norma Productions, an independent production company formed by Burt Lancaster and his agent Harold Hecht, later renamed Hecht-Lancaster. The company agreed with United Artists to produce two pictures. The first was *Bronco Apache*, adapted from a 1936 novel by Paul I. Wellman, whose rights Lancaster and Hecht had purchased in May 1952. The book was based on a historical retelling of Massai, an Apache who refused to surrender to the oppressive authorities and, by doing so, became a legend to his people.

James R. Webb, a master in the Western genre, was hired to write the adaptation, and Robert Aldrich was on board to direct. Hecht knew thirty-six-year-old Aldrich had a reputation for making films on time and within budget and believed he was the right person to keep *Bronco Apache* under $1 million. "Hecht-Lancaster let me do a Western, *Apache*," Aldrich explained, "because I was young, ambitious, eager, and inexpensive."[13]

Jean was excited to be cast in her first Western. Her character was Nalinle, Massai's devoted wife, a gentle woman who brings her fierce fighting Apache man back to the path of peace. Her performance was true and tender. Aldrich admired Jean's tenacity and determination to do a good job:

> [Jean was] a delight to work with—very responsive and courageous. ... The film involved an awful lot of physical work. When someone's done something that's *almost* good enough, you don't want to make them go through all that again just to improve it that one little bit, because who will know, except you and maybe the actress later? And she would never cop out on that kind of thing. "I didn't do it quite right, did I?" she'd say. "I'd like to do it again." It's not easy to bring yourself to ask someone to do that kind of thing repeatedly because it was terribly strenuous, and she was marvelous.[14]

Actor Charles Bronson, still known as Charles Buchinsky at this time, had fourth billing in the small but crucial role of Hondo, the Indian scout, part of the federal troops, who eventually kills Massai.

Principal photography began on October 19, 1953, but a week later, shooting had to be halted after Lancaster was hospitalized with leg and hip injuries sustained after a horse he was riding stumbled and fell sixty feet down a mountain on location fifty miles north of Sonora, California. The actor was discharged from a local hospital but had to return to Los Angeles for further examination. When shooting resumed a month later in Sedona, Arizona, Lancaster had a physiotherapist on the set and used a double for all dangerous stunts.

Since the film was now behind schedule, Aldrich was forced to shoot under any type of weather conditions. After a tremendous mountain snowstorm hit the location and held up production again, Lancaster hired a local medicine man to pray for good weather. It didn't work, as a few days later, high desert winds afflicted the set. Once the sand hit Jean's face and head so hard that after a couple of takes, she approached Aldrich and said, "There's just one thing. When my wig flies past, just be sure the camera pans with it."[15] The director understood and stopped shooting until the wind had calmed down.

In December, the production resumed at a Columbia studio ranch before moving in mid-January 1954 to Key West Studios in Hollywood. Jean would have the makeup and wardrobe crew visit her home early in the morning to have herself put into costume before going to the studio. She would go to work in a long black limousine, driving alone through Bel Air, wondering what people must have thought seeing her dressed in rags in such a car.

Once she arrived at the lot, she would walk from the set to the commissary, past all the tourists and star-spotters, and no one would recognize her. They thought she was just another Indian extra. Back at home, her aunt Cis would not let her take the costume off in the house, forcing her to undress on the back porch.

Jean talked about her experience in the film that was retitled *Apache* (1954) in an interview released just before its opening. "I liked working with Lancaster, he's an active guy who never stops," she said. "I had a wonderful part . . . but nobody will ever know me; it took ages to get the makeup on and the two full hours at night to become white again. I had a disreputable scroungy old wig, and my clothes were assorted rags."[16]

Jean's admiration for Lancaster contradicted Aldrich's perception of the two stars. Not only was he quoted as finding Lancaster "not an easy man to get along with, but quite responsive," he also said, "Jean had a personal animosity toward Burt Lancaster, and she hated the corporate contract she had with Fox. . . . [Despite all,] she was marvelous to work with."[17]

It is a sign of her professionalism that Jean completed the film despite battling fatigue throughout the shoot. The doctor advised rest, but she was determined to keep working. She took several blood tests to find out the cause of her exhaustion, but everything seemed fine. The problems seemed more psychological than physiological. According to Robert Aldrich, Jean was going through a difficult time. "She was deeply embroiled with Howard Hughes at the time," he said. "That broke off temporarily in the middle of the picture, obviously causing her great concern."[18] Nevertheless, she never let the emotional turmoil impact her work.

Apache was made in only thirty-four days, and Aldrich wasn't overjoyed with the result. "It was a moderately expensive epic that I should have done better," he said later.

The original story was somehow believable, yet an alternative happy ending, which compromised the film's credibility, was imposed by United Artists, the film's distributor. Lancaster's character was required not to die in order to appease the movie fans. The actor-producer and the director strongly opposed the altered ending, but the "box office pressure" was so strong that Lancaster and Aldrich were overruled by United Artists.

Although *Apache* was an example of a pro-Indian Western that questioned the white man's superiority, reviewers criticized the film's upbeat ending along with the unrealistic casting of Lancaster and Jean as Native Americans. As Britain's *Film Monthly Bulletin* commented: "We remain conscious that these are two actors doing a very decent best in an impossible task. The strangeness is missing; Indians are not just White Americans with a different colored skin and a simple vocabulary." That review also summed up Jean's acting in the film: "Jean Peters plays soberly and well."[19]

In late June 1954, *Apache* premiered at the Roosevelt Theater in Chicago. To mark the event, the production sponsored an Old West parade. Although Jean did not make a personal appearance on the promotional film tour, she was invited to the premiere. "I was amazed when Burt Lancaster's office called and invited me to *Apache*," she said. "I could not believe my ears."[20] As a part of the film promotion, her face appeared in several women's magazines advertising Lux Soap.

Apache was only moderately well received by the critics, but audiences loved it. The Technicolor picture was a box office success, earning $3 million domestically, which doubled after its international release.

While Jean's public persona was increasing in popularity, she was having a tough time privately. She was dating and slowly falling for Stuart Cramer (who had visited her on the set of *Apache*), but she still had feelings for Hughes.

However, the wealthy Lothario kept behaving as if he had no interest in an official commitment, even though he demanded Jean's exclusive and constant loyalty. There were long periods when he could not see her, and he always chose business over romance. When Hughes learned of her "secret courtship" with Cramer, he did not give it much importance as he was busy on other romantic fronts and entangled by problems with his airline, TWA. But Hughes underestimated Jean, and a few months later, she caught him and the entire world by surprise by accepting Cramer's marriage proposal.

CHAPTER 10

Surprising Girl in Surprise Wedding

One of the most breathtaking women I've ever seen was Jean Peters.
—ROBERT WAGNER

IN JANUARY 1954, JEAN ACCEPTED A STARRING ROLE IN THE *LUX RADIO Theater* broadcast of *The Day the Earth Stood Still*, based on the 1951 sci-fi film. She played opposite Michael Rennie in a role performed onscreen by Patricia Neal. At the end of that month, she and Stuart attended a glamorous dinner party in Miami, followed the next day by a luncheon at the exclusive Bath Club. In Florida, Jean officially met Stuart's parents. Later, the couple flew to Nassau for some relaxation on the beach.

In February, several publications announced that Jean had been cast opposite Robert Wagner in the Fox Western *Broken Lance* (1954), a Cinema-Scope-Technicolor picture in which Spencer Tracy, Richard Widmark, and Dolores Del Rio also starred. Producer Sol C. Siegel and director Edward Dmytryk—who had just completed *The Caine Mutiny* (1954)—planned to start production near Nogales, Arizona, on March 1. A week earlier, Dmytryk, cameraman Joe MacDonald, and dozens of Fox technicians arrived there for preproduction before the 115-strong company of cast and crew joined them to begin shooting.

Just a few days before cameras started to roll, Mexican actress Dolores Del Rio had a problem getting a work visa and was unable to travel to the States. She was replaced with another Mexican actress, Katy Jurado— whose previous American films included *High Noon* (1952)—for the role of Señora Devereaux, Spencer Tracy's second wife and Robert Wagner's mother. Since Jurado and Wagner were not far apart in years, heavy makeup was used to age Jurado's face, with dark and deep pencil lines around her eyes. Her acting ability and the skillful application of cosmetics aged her so convincingly that eventually, she received critical recognition and an Academy Award nomination for Best Supporting Actress.

Spencer Tracy played Matthew Devereaux, a ruthless cattle baron and stern father, who is forced to divide his ranch among his four sons, including half-brothers Joe (Robert Wagner) and Ben (Richard Widmark), who are both fighting over their birthright. Jean starred as Barbara, the daughter of the governor, who defies convention in her love for the mixed-race Joe.

Cast and crew were impressed by Jean's unstarlike attitude. She would appear on the set, always on time with her lines learned, ready to do anything she could to make everything harmonious. No one heard her complain about the blistering sun or the sandstorms that afflicted the production on location. She would laughingly spit out grains of sand and carry on with her acting.

Off the set, Jean spent a few evenings with Wagner's parents, who visited their son on location. Jean and Robert "Bob" Wagner had met a year earlier when they took a screen test together for *Beneath the 12-Mile Reef* (1953). They both got the part, but Jean was later assigned to *Vicki*, whose production dates overlapped, and she was replaced by Terry Moore.

In his autobiography, Wagner confessed his attraction to Jean:

Nothing happened because I was with Barbara [Stanwyck]. Later, when Barbara and I broke up, I developed what I can only call a crush on Jean. We never had an affair because she was already interested in Howard Hughes. Actually, Hughes was passionately interested in her, and Jean . . . well, Jean acquiesced to his passion . . . but [that] wasn't the reason Jean and I didn't get together. That was strictly because of Jean Peters, who was not one of those ladies who hopped from bed to bed. She was a loyal woman. That meant that we were friends and had fun together, but it never went beyond that. Unfortunately.[1]

Jean was equally as admiring of Wagner, but not in a romantic way, as she explained in an interview:

I'm happy to have Bob as a friend because he's very easy to be with, even to the point of a refreshing shyness. . . . I enjoy Bob's sense of humor and his ability to laugh right along with others. I like to rib Bob about his one extravagance—a comparatively insatiable affection for sports clothes. Checks, plaids, or stripes—it doesn't matter, and he's always on the prowl for them.[2]

According to the British film magazine *Picturegoer*, when Jean and Wagner rehearsed their first love scene, the whole cast clustered around—not to advise, but to tease him. A giggling Spencer Tracy warned him, "Don't forget, son, this stuff separates the men from the boys."

When Richard Widmark chimed in with: "Why not just knock her out the way I did in *Pickup on South Street*? Use the old positive approach," Jean snapped back, "Your positive approach was to revive me by pouring beer over my face. You're just a tough guy. Take no notice, Bob, and do the best you can." Wagner took all the teasing well, and after completing the love scene, the company applauded.[3]

Spencer Tracy, who usually ate dinner at a motel in Nogales, invited Jean to dine with him a few times, but she always refused, explaining that she preferred to eat in her room to be near the phone in case Hughes called. Both Wagner and Dmytryk confirmed with Tracy that when Jean was not working, she had to stick close to her dressing room or hotel room just in case Hughes telephoned—something he rarely did. Tracy, who was not a fan of Hughes, asked Jean bluntly, "What the hell is it about this guy? . . . What makes him so damned special? Is it his money?"

"Money!" Jean laughed. "He owes *me* a bundle!" She named a sizable figure. "Whenever we go out, he just doesn't have the change in his pocket, and I have to foot the bill."[4]

Tracy was deflated and never asked Jean to dine with him again.

Fascinated by the rural location that reminded her of her childhood in Ohio, Jean accepted a dinner invitation from Peter Lewis, the owner of a seventy-seven-thousand-acre oak bar ranch, which was used as background in some scenes. Lewis asked Richard Widmark and Jean to visit the property, stay for dinner, and watch a recent film in his private screening room.

Like some other cast members, Jean was given a car to drive around when her presence was not requested on the set. Once, she parked the vehicle in Nogales, and upon her return, found a policeman writing out a ticket. She had failed to put a coin in the parking meter. "Parking meter!" she gasped. "I glanced at it as I left but thought it was a hitching post!"[5]

That wasn't the only hitch. During the fifteen days spent in Arizona, Jean burned her hand picking up a branding iron without a glove, and Tracy suffered bruises and scratches after falling from his horse. Luckily, the accidents did not delay the shooting that resumed on a Fox lot in the last week of April.

Back in Hollywood, Wagner asked Jean to escort him to the world premiere of his last film, *Prince Valiant* (1954). Fox's executives encouraged the date with the hope that a presumed romance between Jean and Wagner would attract a great deal of publicity. Jean accepted the invitation, but only as a token of friendship—she usually avoided Hollywood social events that didn't involve her own films. That evening, she surprised everyone when she appeared at the after-screening party at Romanoff's, where she was photographed dining and dancing with Wagner.

In May, after fifty-five days of work at a cost of $2 million, *Broken Lance* wrapped. The picture was edited quickly and rushed out for a summer release. It was well received by the public and the press. The *Hollywood Reporter* found Jean to be "excellent as the strong-willed girl."[6] The picture won a few awards, including the Silver Spurs for Best Western of 1954. As well as Jurado's Academy Award nomination, Richard Murphy's script, which was based on Philip Yordan's screenplay for the 1949 Fox film noir *House of Stranger*, won an Oscar for Best Screenplay. Although not a single line of Yordan's had been used in the quite different Western version, the award went to him and not to Murphy. Though Yordan protested, nothing could be done about it, and he had to accept the Oscar.

That year, Jean was rumored to be appearing in three other Westerns: *The Garden of Evil* (1954), *Siege at Red River* (1954), and *Lewis and Clark* (1954), but it was Jean Negulesco who gave her a major role, once again, in the star-studded cast of *Woman's World* (1954)—a production that would have marked Jean's fifth collaboration with the filmmaker. The picture was scheduled to start two weeks after *Broken Lance* was completed.

Before reporting on set, Jean and Shirley traveled to East Canton for a short visit to their mother and to check on a local theater whose financial interest she had acquired during the summer. With some childhood friends, she had become a stockholder in the Chagrin Valley Little Theatre. She hoped to squeeze in a guest appearance if her film commitments permitted, but unfortunately, the opportunity never arose.

Back in California, Jean fell ill with a bad case of flu. Her sudden sickness almost blocked the production of *Woman's World*, which could not be postponed due to the tight schedules of the film's other stars, and Arlene Dahl was quickly cast as Jean's replacement. *Woman's World* turned out not to match the commercial success of *Three Coins in the Fountain*.

Jean recovered from her flu, but after the missed opportunity to work with Negulesco again, Fox had no immediate plans for her. So, when Cramer proposed, she accepted. Both agreed to keep the news of their engagement quiet. Stuart's father was ill in the hospital, and they wanted no publicity. The wedding date was set for just a few days later when Cramer senior was able to participate in the ceremony. Stuart was smitten by his new bride, as he confessed in a rare interview:

I found Jean had a beautiful, compelling, unhappy quality. Not only did I think this, but I talked to two or three other men who had gone with Jean, and it seemed everyone was interested in doing things for her. Anything just to make her happy. She had a mystery about her even though people said she was sweet and simple. Her great charm was making a man want to reach out and care for her. We courted several months before we married. She was an attractive, interesting girl and highly intelligent.[7]

At 3 p.m. on May 29, 1954, in the sanctuary of the New York Avenue Presbyterian Church in Washington, DC, only two blocks from the White House, twenty-seven-year-old Elizabeth Jean Peters said, "I do" to twenty-seven-year-old Stuart W. Cramer III. She wore a pink chiffon taffeta one-piece dress trimmed with Chantilly lace and a little pink pillbox hat with a veil. She carried a bouquet of sweetheart roses and walked down the same golden carpet on which Queen Elizabeth II had stood at her coronation a year earlier. It was a historical piece of carpet that Rev. Dr. George M. Dockerty, pastor of the church and wedding celebrant, had obtained from London's Westminster Abbey.

The private and informal ceremony was a secret to everyone but the three other guests: Jean's mother and the bridegroom's parents, Mr. and Mrs. Stuart W. Cramer Jr. Before the ceremony, Jean called 20th Century Fox to announce her wedding plans: "I just wanted to tell you that I will be a married woman in about ten minutes," she told a studio executive calmly.[8] Fox disclosed the news to the press only a few hours after the happy event. Louella Parsons expressed her amazement at the surprise marriage in her column:

> Just a few days before Jean Peters was married, somebody told me that she was getting married and I didn't believe it because I knew she had carried the torch for some other man for such a long time. So I was as surprised as everyone else when a call came from the East that she had just married Stuart Cramer. I never heard the name, never heard of her going out with him, and it was a real surprise to her studio and her friends, although I suspect she herself knew it for some time.[9]

Parsons's rival, Hedda Hopper, declared triumphantly that the love story had not been a secret to *her*. Jean had told her about it three weeks prior to the ceremony but swore her to silence.

Jean explained that the wedding had to be a secret because Stuart had as many friends in North Carolina as she had on the West Coast, and if they had known, they would have been forced to have a grand event, which was something neither wanted. That was one story. Yet on another occasion, she insisted that the marriage had not been that secret at all as she had ordered eight hundred wedding announcements at a department store before the event, and her closest friends helped her get ready for the special day.

Whatever the truth, the word never got out, as no one had spilled the news.

After the ceremony and before departing for the honeymoon, the newlyweds changed to pose for photographs. The few journalists alerted by the studios reported that Jean demurred when asked to kiss Cramer. "He's not an actor yet," she said.

Stuart, who was one of the owners of Mineral Wells, a Texan petroleum company, told the reporters that he should not be described as a Texas oil billionaire. "Please don't call me that, because I'm not one," he exclaimed. "I'm just beginning in the business."[10]

The couple flew to Bermuda on the first lap of their honeymoon and basked in the sun for a week. They then toured by car through the Smoky Mountains and stopped for two days at Cloudcroft, the Cramers' summer house in Linville, North Carolina, before driving to Charlotte, where his family lived. In their beautiful townhouse, Stuart's parents gave a tea dance for the newlyweds before the couple returned to Washington, where they had rented a house. Jean had, in fact, given up her Beverly Hills home and shipped all her belongings to her mother in East Canton.

Jean asked for an eight-week leave of absence from Fox to stay in Washington with her husband. Hollywood gossip speculated that she was considering giving up her film career for home life, a notion fueled by rumors that she and Stuart had been heard arguing the point during their honeymoon.

The first weeks of Jean's marriage were harmonious. "I always wanted to marry happily. I never wanted to just marry, period. And I haven't," she told columnist Gladys Hall. "I married a wonderful man who has all the qualities I've always wanted my husband to have. He's kind and gentle and thoughtful and—if need be—forceful, and most important, I feel we have a solid foundation for marriage."[11]

Yet by the time the interview was printed, only three months after the wedding, the marriage was overshadowed by problems. In the beginning, living in Washington as Mrs. Cramer was enjoyable for Jean as she could go anywhere unnoticed. "It's a very sophisticated city," she said. "A motion picture actress doesn't make a very big dent when you consider the much bigger celebrities there."[12]

Of the gossip surrounding her career, she said: "I'm not retiring from pictures. I like being an actress. I just don't want to do one picture after another. By cutting down, I don't feel I'm giving up anything because I never tried being a movie star." Still, Jean was not used to long periods of inactivity, and being away from a set was harder than she thought. When, in the summer of 1954, Fox offered her the female lead in *A Man Called Peter* (1955), Jean was conflicted. While she had clearly stated her intention to continue working, leaving Stuart for two months felt as though she was deserting him. She wanted his approval, as she explained:

> [Work] is an important part of my life *and* because my husband has no objection to my doing so; [he] is interested, in fact, in my career. The career will depend, however, on his wishes and reactions. If, for instance, a picture should come up for me that my husband, for some very good reason, objected to my doing, I would not do it. . . . What a man's wife does is very important to a man and should be.[13]

Eventually, Jean's desire to return to acting and Fox's pressures to have her back on a set prevailed. After that year's successful releases, *Three Coins in the Fountain*, *Apache*, and *Broken Lance*, Zanuck considered Jean a "hot" star and was not ready to lose her. Nevertheless, her reluctance to accept the lead in *A Man Called Peter* had Fox considering back-up actresses, including Eva Marie Saint, Elizabeth Taylor, Jean Simmons, Dorothy McGuire, and Donna Reed.

Finally, only six days before principal photography was scheduled to begin in Georgia, Jean agreed to play the part of Catherine Marshall. She justified her comeback to the press as a contract obligation she had with Fox—one last picture she owed that year. However, on the day Charles LeMaire's office expected her for wardrobe fittings, she did not show up. Her role as Catherine Marshall required many costume changes, and most of the clothes had been fitted to a dummy duplicate of her figure, yet she was needed for final fittings.

Jean's out-of-character absence created a lot of concern as she was known for her punctuality and professionalism. When Zanuck was asked of her whereabouts, he said, "Nobody's seen hide nor hair of her. The last I heard from her [was] when she agreed to do the picture. We're supposed to start shooting on location next Monday, and if she doesn't make an appearance, I don't know what we'll do."[14] Jean did appear on the set on the first day of shooting, but she wouldn't disclose the reason for her erratic behavior. In fact, her marriage with Cramer was on the rocks, and Howard Hughes was back in her life.

Based on Catherine Marshall's bestselling biography, *A Man Called Peter* was the story of her husband, Reverend Peter Marshall, a humble, young Scotsman with a vocation to serve God. Marshall emigrated to the United States where, in 1931, he was ordinated as a Presbyterian minister serving as a pastor in Covington, Georgia. He later rose to renown as a minister of the historic New York Avenue Presbyterian Church in Washington (the same church in which Jean had recently married Stuart Cramer) and as chaplain of the US Senate.

Jean's role was Catherine Marshall née Wood, daughter of Reverend John Ambrose Wood and a student attending Agnes Scott College in Decatur, Georgia. She and Peter Marshall fell in love and married in 1936. Catherine assumed an active part in her husband's work, helping him write many of his sermons and speeches that brought him fame.

Despite the book's success, only a few studios bid on its film rights, as it was thought it would be too difficult to adapt into a box office hit. Yet Darryl Zanuck saw enormous potential in the subject and bought the rights for $30,000. He handed the project to screenwriter Sylvia Richards, who quit after six months, finding enormous difficulty incorporating Marshall's words in a simple story. Oscar-winning screenwriter Eleanore Griffin took over and delivered such a captivating script that Zanuck assigned the production a budget of $2.5 million.

Irish-born, British-bred Richard Todd, a stage-trained actor whose other noteworthy films included Vincent Sherman's *The Hasty Heart* (1949) and Alfred Hitchcock's *Stage Fright* (1950), was cast in the title role. Todd got the part after first-choice Richard Burton and second-choice James Stewart were unavailable. While the picture was in preproduction, Todd, who was then in England, sent some recordings of him doing one of Peter Marshall's sermons. He did it in a perfect Scottish accent and so intensely that it convinced the producers to give him the part over the other contender, Dennis Morgan.

For the first time in her career, Jean played the role of a living person. She never met Catherine Marshall in real life, but they corresponded frequently during the production. Jean bore a distinct physical resemblance to Mrs. Marshall in her proportions and facial features, and she captured the essence of her personality without doing a simple impersonation.

Jean flew with a female companion to Georgia on a large Constellation TWA aircraft provided by Howard Hughes. They were the only two passengers. Once at the hotel in Atlanta, she received a dinner invitation from Richard Todd, who wanted to meet her before filming started. Jean's companion responded, saying that Jean was tired and would not be leaving her suite that evening.

The following morning the two costars were introduced on the set in Covington, where Peter Marshall had met his future wife for the first time. Todd wanted to get to know Jean but found her aloof and unavailable, as he wrote in his autobiography:

> I found Jean to be a very lovely young woman, ravishingly pretty, intelligent, and great fun to be with, though we rarely chatted except when we were actually rehearsing or shooting. She and her rather taciturn female companion took themselves off to their trailer and never sat with the rest of us. Everything went well with our first day's exterior, and the weather was lovely. That evening, I again phoned to ask if Jean would care to dine with me but got the same response as the previous day. By then, the message was clear: Miss Peters wanted to be alone. And this message was to be the pattern throughout our filming. Jean never left her trailer-caravan, even for meals, except when actually working on the set.[15]

Three days later, the crew flew to Washington, DC. When Todd arrived on the set, he was surprised to find not Jean but a lookalike, wearing her costume and ready to start filming with him. He was told that Jean would not join the Washington set at all but that her double would take her place since Jean had no dialogue in those scenes. The two costars resumed their work together a few weeks later at Fox's studios.

Todd learned through the Hollywood grapevine that Jean's marriage was in crisis, and she was again seeing Hughes, who was a persistent and possessive suitor. That explained Jean's secretive behavior during the shooting and the constant presence of a chaperone.

Filming was not without incident. One day, on the set, Jean escaped injury when a ten-thousand-watt lamp exploded above her head. Her scalp was protected because she was wearing a heavy felt hat. She got so scared by the near-miss that shooting was paused for a few hours.

Richard Todd described the whole film experience as pleasant, yet columnist Erskine Johnson claimed that on set, Jean's eyes were so swollen and her nose so inflamed she could not do close-ups and had to be shot around. Her crying was blamed on "smog," but others considered her marital problems with Cramer to be the real culprit.[16]

The film's director, Henry Koster, was so impressed with Jean's work that he said, "Someday, Jean will do something spectacular on screen, and there will be a great rush of awards and cheers—a shouting recognition at her talent."[17] The filmmaker also praised Richard Todd's performance and would go on to collaborate with him in two more films.

On the last day of filming, Koster gave an end-of-the-picture dinner party at his house for cast and crew. Everybody was surprised when Jean turned up. But at 10 p.m. sharp, while everyone else was enjoying the night, she left in a large black limousine that had waited for her outside the entire time.

A Man Called Peter was rushed out at amazing speed to catch the Easter holiday season. The picture marked the first international world premiere of any 20th Century Fox CinemaScope production with simultaneous openings in Glasgow (Peter Marshall's hometown), New York, and London on March 31, 1955. The three-country event was designed to rank among the most glamorous film events, with government leaders, stars of the entertainment world and prominent religious, social, civic, and business figures in attendance. However, Jean displeased producer Samuel G. Engel by not participating in any film publicity, and she did not attend the New York premiere with Richard Todd and Catherine Marshall.

The picture was a triumph, with unanimous praise from reviewers and audiences. It made every top-ten film list of 1955 and became one of the highest box office hits of the year. Strangely, it obtained only one Academy Award nomination for Best Color Cinematography.

Jean received some of the best reviews of her career. The *Hollywood Reporter* called her work "superlative,"[18] while *Films in Review* wrote, "Jean Peters, as Mrs. Marshall, continues to exhibit an acting ability she did not possess a few years ago, and in at least two sequences, contributes to the film's success (her speech on the truck to college kids, her wooing of the young clergyman in the scenes that followed)."[19]

Sadly, even though Jean considered *A Man Called Peter* to be the best theatrical release of her career, it would also be her last.

CHAPTER 11

Bye-Bye Hollywood

Ever since I know Jean Peters, she's been madly in love with
that man [Hughes]—including all her days at Twentieth.
—JEANNE CRAIN

DURING THE TWO-MONTH SHOOTING OF *A MAN CALLED PETER,* THE CRAMERS
lived apart. Stuart traveled for business around the East Coast, while Jean
rented an apartment in Beverly Hills. Henry Koster's wrap party was the
last social event in which Jean participated before she disappeared from the
public eye and from Stuart, who could not reach her by telephone. When
Jean did not return his calls, Cramer would call his mother-in-law in Ohio.
Mary did not know Jean's whereabouts either but shared her suspicions
that Howard Hughes was interfering in her daughter's marriage.

Two different accounts of how the situation evolved have been reported
by Hughes's biographers. The first was told by Noah Dietrich, chief executive officer of the Howard Hughes business empire. He affirmed that when
Jean married Cramer, she did not tell him about her on-and-off relationship with Hughes. This was confirmed by Cramer in an interview when
he admitted that "it had never been mentioned."[1] Stuart explained that he
had learned about the tie between his wife and Hughes directly from the
tycoon, who invited him to Los Angeles to discuss the situation.

He flew out from Miami and met Hughes at the Beverly Hills Hotel,
where the billionaire bluntly told him that he had been in love with Jean
for years and that his feelings were reciprocated. Hughes asked Cramer
if he was willing to give her an uncontested divorce if she confirmed the
fact with him.

Shocked by the news, Cramer later confronted Jean, who admitted her
relationship with Hughes but denied her intention to ask for a divorce.
According to Dietrich, Jean was distraught and racked with grief. She was
upset with Hughes and refused to take his calls. Hughes called Cramer and

exploited Jean's distress, saying that if he cared for her, he would let her go. But Stuart insisted that he loved Jean and was ready to fight to save his marriage. He tried to contact Jean, but she refused to see him.

Hughes decided to use the situation to his advantage and offered to talk to Jean about a reconciliation. In the meantime, he had surreptitiously gathered a detailed file on Cramer in an attempt to dig up dirt from his past and discredit him. He spied on Cramer but discovered nothing compromising aside from the fact that he was genuinely in love with Jean.

Hughes's obsession with Jean intensified. His desire to have her now that she was married became stronger than ever. As Jeanne Crain explained: "When Hughes wanted something, he could be overpowering." According to Dietrich, when Jean and Stuart finally met to discuss their marriage, she was depressed, in high distress, alcohol dependent, and with suicidal thoughts. Jean felt guilty for abandoning him, but she was also questioning Hughes's intentions to marry her if she agreed to divorce Cramer. New, exhausting arguments between husband and wife made reconciliation doubtful.[2]

Jean went off to Florida and hid in a little house on an island in Biscayne Bay near Miami. There, she finally realized it was a huge mistake to have gotten married. Some speculated that the elopement with Stuart was simply to prove to herself her independence from Hughes. In announcing her marriage to her close friend Jeanne Crain, Jean allegedly said, "Forever is just too long to wait for Howard." Years later, Crain was quoted as saying: "Ever since I've known Jean Peters, she's been madly in love with that man [Hughes]—including all her days at Twentieth. She tried to get away when she married Cramer because she thought it wouldn't work out with Howard. But she just couldn't forget him."[3]

A different account of the events alleged that when the marital relationship became extremely tense, Stuart asked for Hughes's intervention to get Jean back. Stuart knew how much Jean and Howard were fond of each other and hoped Hughes would help them reconcile. However, he had foolishly underestimated the extent of the tycoon's scheming to win back Jean's love.

Hughes organized a private meeting between Jean and Stuart on a chartered fishing boat. But without the couple's knowledge, he also arranged for a fake deckhand to spy on them discreetly and report what was said. Yet the encounter resolved nothing. Jean and Stuart argued about lots of petty matters for several hours before they separated again.

In the subsequent days, Cramer, thinking Hughes was on his side, pestered him to try and find out Jean's whereabouts. Hughes told him to be patient and wait a week until another meeting was set up—this time at

Jean's place. Hughes asked his personal private investigator, Chouinard, to spy through the window and report everything, but the clumsy sleuth had a silly accident in the garden that prevented him from snooping on the couple.

Remarkably, this meeting seemed to work, and Jean and Stuart started seeing each other every day and appeared to be on the path to reconciliation. Angered by this, Hughes ordered Chouinard to follow them everywhere they went. Then Jean surprised both her suitors and flew to Los Angeles with no warning. The reconciliation had failed. Stuart followed his wife but failed to woo her back.

In California, Cramer's friendship with Hughes became stronger. Not only did the business magnate give Cramer a job as a junior executive at Lockheed Aircraft Corporation, but he also organized social events so he could meet new and interesting companions and forget Jean. As a final grotesque touch, Cramer would date and eventually marry Hughes's former girlfriend, actress Terry Moore.

Despite which of the two accounts is more faithful to reality, both ended in Hughes's victory.

In September 1955, Jean publicly announced her intention to divorce Cramer, stating that they had been separated for almost a year. Three months later, she filed a divorce suit in Los Angeles Superior Court, giving "mental cruelty" as the reason she could no longer remain with him. She estimated the length of her cohabitation with him to be thirty-three days. She asked for the return of her maiden name but did not make any financial demands on him.

According to the law at that time in California, she had to wait one year before the divorce became final. Three months after it was granted, Elizabeth Jean Peters, who had all but disappeared from public view, married Howard Robard Hughes in secret.

Remarkably, Cramer was not resentful of Jean or Hughes. "I don't think she knew what the hell she wanted to do," he said years later. "I'll say this: if your wife is going to get a divorce, you might as well let her marry someone who can afford to support her. It's the cheapest way out."[4]

· · ·

After the successful release of Jean's last film, *A Man Called Peter*, many in Hollywood started to wonder what was happening to this once-prolific actress. A spokesman at Fox said, "We haven't seen or heard from Jean for months." Friends and studio executives were worried. Jean was known to have taken trips alone before, but never for such a long time and never without leaving details of where she could be found. In spite of her disappearance, Fox announced Jean as the female lead first in *The View from Pompey's Head* (1955), starring Richard Egan, and then in *The Bottom of the Bottle* (1955) opposite Van Johnson and Joseph Cotten. However, her lack of communication with the studio and her reluctance to return to work led to her immediate suspension, followed by the cancellation of her contract.

Hollywood reporters, desperate for an explanation behind Jean's disappearance, telephoned her mother's house in East Canton, but an unidentified female speaker refused to be drawn into giving away any information. The only person privy to Jean's whereabouts was Hughes, who also seemed to have vanished. After Jean's divorce had become public news, journalists searched through marriage licenses registered in California and Nevada in an attempt to see if the two had married but found nothing.

Thirty-year-old Jean and fifty-one-year-old Howard Hughes married on January 12, 1957, in Tonopah, Nevada, an abandoned silver mining town located midway between Las Vegas and Reno. In a bid to keep it out of the press, Hughes enlisted the help of Los Angeles attorney James Ardito, who arranged for the couple to be married at the unusual location using assumed names. Howard Robard Hughes was G. A. Johnson of Las Vegas, and Elizabeth Jean Peters was Marian Evans of Los Angeles.

The ceremony took place in utmost secrecy in a local hotel room. Some reported it as the Mitzpa Hotel, others as the L&L Motel. Jean was dressed in a suit with high-heeled pumps. While she had made concessions to Hughes about the secrecy of the location and marrying under an assumed name, she told him she would not be married in disguise.[5]

The service was conducted by Justice of the Peace Walter Bowler. Attorney D. Martin Cook, who was a Hughes employee, and an unknown named James Perry were registered as witnesses. The brief ceremony ended after Hughes slipped a ruby ring on Jean's finger.

Jean had never heard of Tonopah and claimed she had "no idea" why the ceremony was held there. Years later, she could not even remember all the names of the men at the wedding. "I know Marty Cook was there and [George] Francom, and I think Roy Crawford [and] perhaps Levar Myler,"[6] she said, referring to four of Hughes's personal aides. No women were in attendance.

Once the ceremony was over, the small group returned to an abandoned airfield, boarded the same Constellation plane they had disembarked from an hour earlier, and flew back to Los Angeles. The entire operation took three hours. Not one photograph was taken to immortalize the happy event.

The newlyweds spent their first night at Jean's house on Strada Vecchia Road in Bel Air. Then, after spending a few days at the Beverly Hills Hotel, they flew to Palm Springs.

Two months after the wedding, Hughes feared that the news could not be kept secret any longer and personally informed Louella Parsons that he had married Jean. The columnist was excited to get such an exclusive scoop and was ready to make it the front page of every American newspaper in which her syndicated column appeared. But Hughes told her he had given her the news on the condition it was handled his way, with no sensationalism, no front pages—just a few lines, very short and simple, and limited to Parsons's column.

She agreed and wrote a few paragraphs, but even that was too much for the famously reclusive Hughes, who felt too much information had been given away. She had to write five drafts in order to get his approval. And even then, he didn't trust her. To make sure she was printing the article his way, he called Parsons's publisher, William Randolph Hearst Jr., in New York and asked him to supervise the columnist personally to ensure she was following his guidelines.

Meanwhile, as Hughes spent time tweaking the article, news that Parsons was about to print a story about his marriage to Jean leaked, and another Hollywood columnist, Florabel Muir, beat them to it, breaking the story in the *Los Angeles Mirror-News* on March 16. It carried all the sensationalism he had been trying to avoid, and the headline screamed: "Howard Hughes, Hollywood's most eligible bachelor for more than twenty-five years, has secretly married Jean Peters." But without Hughes on site to give her the facts, much of the article was wrong, including the date and location of the wedding. The story claimed that the couple had married at sea on Hughes's yacht off Miami Beach on March 12.

Muir's incorrect news was picked up and reported by all national and international newspapers, but when journalists could not find evidence of a marriage certificate, speculation arose that it was a ruse. This was put right when, shortly after the news broke, friends of the couple began to receive thank-you notes and occasion cards all signed "Jean and Howard Hughes."

Jean and Howard spent the first month of marriage together on a secluded ranch near Palm Springs, rarely leaving the property, which was surrounded by security guards. Hughes had sold his Los Angeles house in 1945 because he did not want to be taxed as a California resident. Therefore, in March, the couple settled at the Beverly Hills Hotel, where four bungalows and several rooms were rented. Bungalow number 9 was for Jean, while Howard stayed in bungalow number 4, his old "bachelor quarters."

Another bungalow was for his eight Mormon security guards, and a fourth bungalow was kept empty. In addition, several suites were kept reserved for guests or for people in Hughes's entourage, which consisted of several secretaries and assistants.

In her three-bedroom bungalow, Jean kept the hotel furniture but brought in her sewing machine, her dress dummy, and all her fabrics so she could carry on with her sewing. She tried to make the place as homey as possible, planting flowers in old coffee cans, which she placed on her porch and veranda.

Although husband and wife lived in separate bungalows that sprawled out into the lush imperial garden, Howard kept strict control of Jean's movements and even her food. He gave his staff of personal chefs precise instructions on how her food had to be prepared and delivered. Everything his wife ate or drank had to be indexed in a surveillance report that was presented to him daily. Jean and Hughes ate separately in their own bungalows.

Although they lived only fifty yards apart, conversations between husband and wife were made mostly by phone via the hotel receptionist or by handwritten notes they scribbled on yellow pads. Hughes obsessively annotated everything they said to each other with dates and times. Rather than speaking, he would write Jean messages for his aides to read to her, and she would answer the same way. Most of those notes and memos were destroyed on his orders to shred and burn all personal papers. However, a few were spared destruction and, in recent years, have resurfaced and were sold by several auction houses. They were jotted notes about planned meetings, films, business, and opinions in general. Although they are not revealing, those little yellow pieces of paper are proof of how difficult and frustrating Jean's marriage must have been from the very beginning. Yet they are also testimony of the deep love and devotion they both had for each other despite their abnormal marriage. A moving example is a short poem handwritten in pencil in which Jean professed her love to Hughes. The poem was posted on the internet, and the original was sold at a public auction.

> *I am like a fragile plant—whose roots are strong,*
> *but whose head's vacant.*
> *I need a strong and able arm*
> *To shield and keep me from earthly harm.*
> *And so I deem myself most blest—*
> *to have Sir Hughes at my behest.*

Each night I thank the Lord above—
That Howard Robard
is my Love.

About four months after their wedding, a popular fan magazine published a dramatic story about Jean and Hughes (although his name was never mentioned) after he allegedly "imprisoned" her and forced her to give up her Hollywood career. The entire first page was dialogue exchanged in block letters.

HE: "I LOVE YOU. AND YOU BELONG TO ME, BUT I WON'T
    MARRY YOU."
SHE: "I TRY TO RUN AND I CAN'T. I WANT TO SEE YOU ON
    ANY TERMS. I CAN'T HELP IT."[7]

In subsequent years as Jean disappeared from the screen and from any kind of social life, stories and articles like this would appear with greater frequency.

• • •

In June 1957, Jean's beloved sister Shirley got married, and the bride was given away by her uncle, Nelson Doss. The Episcopalian ceremony was followed by a four-hundred-guest reception held at the Polo Loggia and patio of the Beverly Hills Hotel.[8] The local press that covered the event did not mention Jean's name among the guests (maybe Hughes had ordered them not to), but according to his biographer, Richard Mathison, Jean attended the wedding alone. It was there that the disturbing way in which Hughes controlled her every move became apparent.

At the reception, Jean was said to have been in a tense mood as in each corner of the room, a Mormon security guard, sent by Hughes, stood in a dark suit holding a glass of milk. If she was thirsty, she had to walk over to one of the guards and take a sip of milk.

Hughes was a Mormon, and his faith did not allow him to drink or smoke. Jean, who was a smoker and liked to drink, had been a cause of concern among Hughes's Mormon circle of friends. Hughes demanded she follow his rules, especially in public, even though she was an Episcopalian.

According to actress Terry Moore, the maître d' at the Beverly Hills Hotel told her that he was under strict orders from Hughes not to serve Jean any liquor except for half a bottle of champagne on her birthday.[9]

Nevertheless, during the reception, Jean drank a few glasses of champagne in the company of Hughes's private investigator, Chouinard. The guards signaled to the detective that this transgression was not allowed, but he ignored them. He was then approached by a guard who told him Hughes had ordered his wife not to drink. Chouinard was outraged by how Jean was being treated in public and how humiliated she was made to feel.[10]

Over the next three years, Jean and Hughes experienced several long periods of separation. His psychological problems (he battled obsessive-compulsive disorder all his life, which worsened following a number of plane and car accidents) forced him to be treated in a medical center, whose location he did not disclose—not even to Jean. He wrote to her to say he had an undiagnosed illness and that if she were to visit him, she could be contaminated. Jean did not see her husband for months before he finally returned to the Beverly Hills Hotel in the spring of 1958 and locked himself in his bungalow.

Finally, in December 1960, the couple left the hotel and moved into a rented house at Rancho Santa Fe, an exclusive community located north of San Diego, where Jean had space for a ceramics kiln and a room for sewing and handwork. Hughes's mental health was deteriorating, and his seclusion deepened at Rancho Santa Fe.

Jean slept next to him, although now that they were living under the same roof, his phobias sometimes upset her—notably the clicking of his overlong toenails, which he refused to cut, and which disrupted her sleep. (From an early age, Jean had been a light sleeper, resting no more than five hours per night.) She overcame the problem by inserting tissues between his toes every night. Fearful of dust, Hughes refused to let her clean their bedroom. Jean complied by cleaning the rest of the house thoroughly except for their room.

Despite his behavior, Hughes was not insensitive to Jean's emotional crises. Once, when her cat was missing and she became distraught, he got very angry with his assistants who had failed to find the missing feline. Two days later, Jean's cat returned to the house by himself.[11]

In November 1961, after some pipes broke at the Santa Fe residence, Hughes left after believing the house was contaminated with sewage. He and Jean moved to another luxurious rental property at 1001 Bel Air Road atop a peak of the Santa Monica mountains. Hughes settled into a separate area of the mansion while Jean stayed in the master bedroom.

Nobody really knew much about Jean's matrimonial life with Hughes, although there was much speculation. Rumors swirled about his weakening physical condition, his lack of personal hygiene and grooming, and the fact that he conducted all his business from his bedroom. Yet in spite of his supposedly precarious health, Hughes began an odd life of jetting from country to country and wandering from hotel to hotel, leaving Jean alone at home and communicating with her only over the telephone.

He finally settled into a penthouse on the top of the Desert Inn in Las Vegas. Jean joined him for a short time, settling in separate accommodations, but she never enjoyed living in Las Vegas due to its lack of cultural events. Her visits to Los Angeles became longer and more frequent as she attended the ballet, the opera, and art exhibitions.

On one occasion, after she saw a performance by the Comédie Française at the Greek Theatre in Griffith Park, Los Angeles, she talked briefly with a reporter. "I haven't been ducking the press," she admitted. "It's just that they aren't interested in an old married woman anymore." She smiled. "My husband and I don't go out very often," she said, as if to explain her attendance alone at the theater. She added that she was confident her husband would regain control of his aerial dominions.

"No," she said as she walked toward a black Cadillac limousine where two guards waited; she did not believe she would return to acting. "Not unless it was a dream role. And those don't come along anymore."[12]

In 1966, Hughes made a mysterious train trip to Boston. Some affirmed that it was for surgery at a famous clinic there; others believed he was trying to decide whether to move to Canada or the Bahamas. Years later, Jean revealed that she was not told by Hughes's aides where her husband was going. "I stayed in my room," she recalled, "but I heard them leave. I knew he was leaving." She only found out it was Boston "the next day when I read the newspaper."[13]

Jean flew to Boston for a three-day visit, but Hughes kept her at an across-the-room distance because of his fear of germs. According to columnist Jack Anderson, once Jean returned to California, she was so furious that she found a pistol and petulantly began shooting holes through her mansion's copper roof at 2 a.m.[14]

Boston would be the last time she would see Hughes in person, and the trip marked the end of their marriage. Later, he told her that he had bought a nine-thousand-square-foot home for her near the upscale Rancho Circle area in Las Vegas. Yet she reaffirmed her intention of living in Los Angeles and her disinterest in moving anywhere else, especially Vegas. Since Hughes preferred her to live in her own house and not stay at a hotel, he bought her a new home located at 507 North Palm Drive in Beverly Hills.

She told him she did not want security guards near the Spanish-style house and ordered them to stay outside the fence and park their black cars on the street. Hughes was unhappy with this as he was reportedly afraid that Jean could be kidnapped and held for a huge ransom. The security around the property was so high that a Beverly Hills police officer said, "One of the safest streets in this town is the one Mrs. Hughes lives on. We hardly bother to send patrol cars past that block, it's so well protected by the Hughes people."[15]

After settling in her new house, Jean communicated with her husband in Las Vegas only over the telephone or via mail. Each time they spoke, Hughes tried to convince her to move back to Nevada. Eventually, Jean agreed on the condition that Hughes leave his hideout hotel penthouse and move into one of the properties he had bought there, which included a five-hundred-acre ranch located on the outskirts of Las Vegas. He never did. Instead, he leased a house across the street from Jean's home in Beverly Hills to keep her under "secret surveillance."[16]

At the end of the year, Jean tried to visit her husband in the penthouse of the Desert Inn, Las Vegas, but he was heavily medicated and refused to see her. Finally, in the spring of 1967, she received a desperate note: "Dearest, I'm ill but very, very ill yet confident I'll feel better soon. You will hear from me the minute I feel even a little better. My very most love."[17] Communications resumed a few months later via telephone and letter until 1970, when Jean finally filed for divorce.

CHAPTER 12

A Brief Comeback

My life with Howard Hughes was and shall remain a matter
on which I will have no comment.

—JEAN PETERS

JEAN'S DISAPPEARANCE FROM THE SCREEN HAD NOT AFFECTED HER POPULARITY.
Her marriage to Howard Hughes had continued to fascinate and puzzle
the media, which had tried in vain to catch a glimpse of the pair together.
This ensured she was as in-demand off-screen as on. Yet she did not live
the life of a hermit, and she laughed as she read stories about her apparent
isolation and loneliness. She had a small group of friends whom she met
regularly, but they were protective of her private life even though they
were often hounded for information about Jean and her bizarre marriage.

Jeanne Crain, who had been one of Jean's closest friends for years,
was quoted as saying: "Jean hasn't changed much. Her basic personality
is almost the same. She doesn't like to have her friends discuss her with
anyone. So, I don't even tell Paul [husband Paul Brinkman] what we do.
She wants to protect her husband, and if that's the way she wants to live,
why should anyone object?"[1]

While Hughes rarely, if ever, ventured out in public, Jean moved freely.
Throughout their marriage, she attended the opera, the ballet, concerts,
and sports events, always unrecognized. Without makeup and expensive
clothes, Jean was able to remain anonymous; no one thought she was a
famous film star.

In the earlier years of her marriage when she wanted a new dress, shops
would send garments to her home so she could choose them without
going into the store. Eventually, when she lived separately from Hughes,
Jean rediscovered the pleasure of browsing and shopping in department
stores and boutiques around Beverly Hills. Once a week, she would drive
her vintage Chevrolet or an ordinary station wagon to a popular beauty

salon in the center of the Beverly Hills shopping district to have her hair done. She would call the parlor an hour before to announce her visit to avoid the possibility of setting a regular routine that could be discovered by reporters. She was also seen in a box at the Hollywood Bowl during a few classical music concerts and spotted at several baseball games around Los Angeles.

Nevertheless, whether she was alone or in the company of female companions, when she was married to Hughes, Jean was constantly but discreetly followed by his security men.

Besides her usual hobbies, Jean had kept herself busy with charitable work. One of her favorites was volunteering for the Braille Institute in Los Angeles. Using the alias Jean Smith, she regularly read to Sunday classes for blind children. She also made a few records of *Talking Books* ("until I couldn't stand the sound of my own voice anymore"),[2] spending long hours a week making technical material for young collegegoers with sight loss. She also developed a method of self-taught swimming for children.

From 1966 to 1968, Jean studied at UCLA for a bachelor's degree program, majoring in psychology, to continue what she had abandoned twenty-two years earlier at OSU as an honor student. In her early days in Hollywood, she had attended several classes, but only for her own intellectual fulfillment, and had never completed the program studies.

As a student, she had engaged in many extracurricular activities and spent much of her time conducting door-to-door surveys for UCLA labor relations schools on subjects such as the four-day work week and compiling material on the IUD birth control device for university research development. "Nobody ever recognized me," she commented in an interview.[3] Only when she conducted an opinion survey for the Los Angeles mayoral candidate was she recognized by an actor who said he had seen her on television in an old film.

Her cover was blown on only one occasion. Columnist Vernon Scott (who later wrote an article under the pseudonym D. L. Lyons) spotted her at an anthropology night class and wrote a long article titled "America's Richest Wife," published in the *Ladies' Home Journal*. The journalist was fascinated by how Jean walked around campus unrecognized. He described her in a rather derogatory fashion as looking like a "drab Hausfrau." He continued:

> Friends could pass Jean Peters Hughes on campus and fail to recognize her; her disguise is that flawless. She wears her medium-brown hair short and loosely waved above her high forehead. Clear, plastic-rimmed glasses perched on her up-tilted nose. She wears no makeup,

not even a hint of lipstick. Her dress . . . was an inexpensive red, purple, lavender, and orange print, the type available on the rack at Ohrbach's for $12. Simple black patent-leather bag and low-heeled shoes completed the disguise. Her only jewelry was a plain gold wedding band and a large, nondescript wristwatch.[4]

Jean had become defensive when she realized that the man who approached her at UCLA was not a student but a reporter who knew her real identity. Nevertheless, she made small talk with him and explained that her professors and classmates thought she was a schoolteacher picking up some extra credits. It turned out that according to her outstanding grades, Elizabeth Hughes (Jean used her real first name to enroll) was one of the best students in her program. Despite this, she never took a psychological statistics course—which was the last class required to complete the degree.

In March 1969, *Esquire* magazine put on its cover a few Kodak frames of a man and a woman standing near a swimming pool who looked strikingly like Jean and Hughes. Spotting the camera, the angry man ordered an aide to pursue the photographer. The title screamed, "Howard Hughes. We see you! We see you!"

The magazine sold out instantly on newsstands across America before it was revealed that the man and the woman were models. The photographs, shot in Fort Lauderdale, were to draw attention to a story on Hughes by a reporter who had spent two months on the assignment but never got a glimpse of Hughes or Jean.[5]

On June 16, 1970, Jean announced her separation from Hughes and said, "This is not a decision made in haste, and is done only with the greatest regret. Our marriage had endured for thirteen years, which is long by present standards. Any property settlement will be resolved privately between us."[6]

Six months earlier, shortly before Christmas 1969, Jean had attended the Hollywood gala premiere of *Hello Dolly!* and was escorted by Stanley Hough, Fox's vice president of production operations, whom she had been dating for a few weeks. The event marked their first official public appearance together, even though reports failed to recognize them, and the studio photographers were notified not to snap them.

Fifty-one-year-old Stanley "Stan" Lee Hough, a Los Angeles native, was the son of Robert E. Lee "Lefty" Hough, a longtime production executive and assistant director, first at Universal and later at Fox. In his youth, the athletic Stan had played professional baseball with the Seattle Rainiers of the Old Pacific Coast League team before starting his showbusiness career.

He joined Fox in 1937, then left to serve in the US Navy during the Second World War. He returned to work at Fox as assistant director in 1946.

A year later, he met Jean when she was filming *Captain from Castile*, as he was one of Henry King's many assistant directors. "A very tough assistant director," Jean recalled of her beau. "He used to pound on my dressing room door and yell, 'All right, Peters, get it out here and get to work.' And I have a feeling he'd treat me just the same if I worked for him today."[7] At that time, their relationship was thought to have been exclusively professional, although Jean's friend Robert Slatzer indicated they had "a brief relationship on the *Captain from Castile* location."[8]

Hough had been widowed twice and had four children: two daughters, Melinda and Christina; one stepdaughter, Shelly; and a son, Mark. In 1967, Hough's second wife died of a heart attack while they were on a trip to Europe. Two years later, Jean and Stanley met again, by chance, at the home of a mutual friend. They spent the evening reminiscing about their time on *Castile*. After a few dates, their acquaintance struck a new spark and transformed into a discreet relationship. Interviewed by columnist Earl Wilson, Stan said, "Jean is an old friend. We went to the Rose Bowl twenty years ago; we went again two years ago. . . . She is still married to Mr. Hughes, whom I've never met. At this point, it is not a romance. It would not help anyone to say anything. About the future, I don't know."[9]

One of the first trips the newly rekindled Jean and Stan took together was to Pittsburgh. There she met his oldest daughter Melinda and her husband, Frank Hoffman. A few days later, they rented a car and drove to East Canton to spend Thanksgiving with Jean's mother Mary on her farm.

In April 1971, Jean attended the 43rd Academy Awards Ceremony in an elegant 1940s-style white wool dinner suit created exclusively for the occasion by her friend, Hollywood costume designer Bill Travilla. She arrived at the Dorothy Chandler Pavilion with Stan. The couple stole the attention of the press, especially at the supper dance following the telecast when she was photographed with Stan's daughter Christina. Speculation of an upcoming wedding began to circulate and strengthened when Jean did not deny the possibility. As she was still legally married to Hughes, she refused to comment, even though a spokesman for her husband had come forward saying that the billionaire had "given his blessing."

Her appearance at the Oscars signified that she might be interested in resuming her acting career, which had grounded to a halt. Three months before filing for divorce, Jean had been investigated by the Internal Revenue Service, which asked her questions about her tax return, specifically why she had not filed one while married to Hughes. She answered that during those years, she had not worked at all, and that her income was such that no return was required.

On June 18, 1971, Jean's fourteen-year marriage to Howard Hughes ended in a near-empty courtroom in Hawthorne, Nevada. Jean, who was represented by Hughes's attorney, was granted an uncontested divorce by State District Court Judge Kenneth Mann after she said she had lived apart from her husband for more than one year, which was grounds for divorce in Nevada. Hughes, who had then moved to the Bahamas, was not present, and his attorney offered no objection to the divorce. There was no property settlement included in the divorce filings. Jean listed her address as Crystal Bay, Nevada, a fancy resort in the North Lake Tahoe area, where she had lived in one of Hughes's houses for a few weeks to establish divorce residency.

When the divorce settlement was eventually disclosed, it emerged that Jean had kept her North Palm Drive home in Beverly Hills, and Hughes had agreed to pay her between $70,000 and $140,000 a year for twenty years, with the actual amount determined by the yearly consumer index. It was an amount that was regarded by many as trifling, considering Hughes's $4 billion net worth. Yet Jean stuck to her principles and proved, once again, that she was never interested in her former husband's money.

Interestingly, considering her ex-husband's reclusive nature, the settlement did not contain any prohibition against Jean talking or writing about her life with him.

In the summer, reports of Jean's imminent wedding plans with Stan spread in the press. A friend of the couple revealed that Alaska was the location picked for their ceremony and that Hughes had offered to loan one of his planes to have the couple jetted anywhere they wanted to get married.

On August 25, 1971, the couple appeared in the Santa Monica courthouse to apply for a wedding license. Jean gave her occupation as research interviewer. Two days later, Jean and Stan got married in a private ceremony witnessed by only seven people at Westwood United Methodist Church. After a short honeymoon, the couple lived in two Beverly Hills homes—the ones they had each occupied before they were married. They retained Hughes's home because it was close to Stan's younger daughter's school. Jean didn't return to the screen but once again resumed her life as a housewife, away from the limelight. She redecorated her Spanish Mexican-style house, adding a room near the swimming pool for her teenage stepdaughter Christina.

Although Jean was denied motherhood (some claimed that Hughes had hidden from her a vasectomy he had in 1955, secretly denying her dream of having a child with him), her maternal instinct was very strong. She loved Christina and loved to babysit Shirley's children and the children of her friends. In discussing motherhood, Jean had a very clear opinion:

> I considered the feminists groups simply terrible who put down ... motherhood. Women's Lib groups sometimes just ignored the fact that females are biologically different than men. If we're lucky, we have babies. If we're not lucky, we don't. The maternal instinct is something we're born with, and the role of motherhood should be the most rewarding of our lives. To resent that role is sad, as sad as all those women who sit about complaining about their troubles, doing nothing to correct them.[10]

Although Jean had, at this point, stopped attending UCLA, she kept working on behalf of several charities. She served as honorary chairman of the National Society for Autistic Children, appearing on posters throughout the country with a five-year-old autistic boy, appealing for support of the society's research and education program. She was also a board member of the Screen Smart Set, a women's auxiliary of the Motion Picture and Television Relief Fund that operated the Cinema Glamour Shop in Hollywood. Jean devoted one day a week to volunteering as a salesperson in the thrift shop and, in 1974, became the store manager. "I suppose it's the old Protestant work ethic that still influences me," she said in an interview. "Women have so many opportunities to find fulfillment, if only they don't allow themselves to be stopped."[11]

During the New Year's holiday of 1972, Jean, Stan, and Christina flew to the Bahamas for a vacation. According to a report, the Houghs stayed at the Grand Britannia Beach Hotel as guests of Howard Hughes, who made available his yacht for sightseeing and watersports. "Elizabeth [as Stan called Jean] and I were invited, and we went," Stan said to the press, who were intrigued at the family's relationship with Jean's formerly domineering ex.[12]

The Houghs' visit coincided with a press conference Hughes held on January 7 to discuss a lawsuit he had recently filed against an author of an upcoming unauthorized biography and the warning he had given to the publishing house to stop its publication. According to an unconfirmed report, just a few hours before the press conference, Hughes had a brief meeting with Jean in his closely guarded suite at the Britannia Beach Hotel. At that short reunion, she confirmed that she had nothing to do with the book.

Some doubt the meeting actually took place because, after Hughes's death, Jean testified in a sworn statement about his will that the last time she had seen him in the flesh was in a Boston hotel in 1966.

The unauthorized biography never materialized after it was revealed to be a hoax concocted by the author and his wife.

Stan, Jean, Christina, and Stan's niece Carol spent the summer of 1972 on location in Cottage Grove, Oregon, a tiny village where Hough was producing *Emperor of the North Pole* (1973), directed by Robert Aldrich and starring Lee Marvin and Ernest Borgnine. The Houghs rented a house for three months, and while Stan worked most of the time on the set, Jean and the two girls took long rides into the countryside, often in the company of Aldrich and Marvin's wives.

In a far cry from married life with Hughes, Jean spent the evenings attending parties and get-togethers with Stan and members of the crew, including a weekly bowling competition. She also paid regular visits to the set to watch Marvin and Borgnine act, and this rekindled her interest in acting. "It was very exciting," Jean recalled. "If I hadn't gone along with him [Stan], I wouldn't have sat on the sidelines watching Bob Aldrich direct the picture. I felt like a football player wanting to get back in the game."[13] Jean's fascination with the film increased as the shoot went on, and by the time it was complete, she was ready to return to acting with full support from Stan.

When rumors circulated about her possible return to work, Jean received a few offers of films, but she was reluctant to do anything that required her to be separated from Stan. Fortunately, the perfect opportunity arose when she was approached by Norman Lloyd. Lloyd was a producer of the *Hollywood Television Theatre* series (1970–78) and asked her to star in *Winesburg, Ohio*, a teleplay that was to be filmed in Los Angeles for three weeks the following December. *Winesburg, Ohio* was based on Sherwood Anderson's 1919 classic novel of loneliness, sex, and frustration and was adapted for television by Christopher Sergel and directed by Ralph Senensky.

In an interview released as the play was broadcast, Lloyd explained why Jean was considered for the female lead:

We had to have a woman from a certain era . . . Dorothy McGuire and Eva Marie Saint were ruled out because they had both played it before on the stage. Jean's name was mentioned, and I said: "Jean Peters? I haven't heard that name in years." We didn't know if, since her divorce, she was planning to come back. But we felt if she did, this was the way to do it.[14]

Jean enjoyed reading Sherwood Anderson's novels because he was an Ohio author. Being a theater lover and a fan of televised plays, she liked the script, especially because her age matched her character's, and she would not have to pretend to be younger or glamorous. The role of Elizabeth Willard—a mother struggling to save her son from the despair and emptiness of feeling trapped in a small town—struck a chord with Jean. It appealed not only for the emotional depth of the character but because its settings evoked her own childhood in East Canton. "I liked my small town," Jean revealed to *TV Guide*. "I often wondered what my life would have been like if I had remained there."[15]

No official announcement was made about Jean's comeback, which suited her as she had hoped to do the teleplay without clamor. Yet when the media learned the news, she was overwhelmed with requests for interviews and photoshoots. She was advised to hold a press conference and pose for photographs to get it all over with at once.

The event took place in a small theater packed with newsmen in early December 1972, three months before *Winesburg, Ohio* aired on television. Never a fan of interviews, Jean, now forty-five, appeared in front of the press in amazing shape, albeit nervous, often biting her lower lip. A long time had passed since she had talked with a group of reporters, and she felt intimidated by the large crowd. She was fully aware that they were there not to ask about the TV movie or her resurrected career but about her life with Howard Hughes.

She responded with candor to all the questions about her comeback, but when someone fired the first question about her ex-husband, Jean said, "I'm not so naïve as to think that the only reason for being here is your interest in my career, but my life with Howard Hughes was and shall remain a matter on which I will have no comment."

Asked if she had missed acting, she replied, "Not acting. Actors. The camaraderie on the set. I missed the world of actors. That's why I wanted to get back."[16]

Winesburg, Ohio was taped in four days at KCET in Los Angeles and was preceded by two weeks of rehearsals. It was Jean's first television experience, and she was surprised by how it differed from films. "When I worked in films, we chopped up the scenes more," she said. "In this, we did complete scenes at once. . . . They work you to death."[17] She found it awkward performing in front of three or four TV cameras shooting simultaneously. "I was a little nervous when we first began shooting because it seemed so new to me," she admitted. "As we went along, it all came back to me."[18]

Acting in *Winesburg, Ohio* was a trip down memory lane for Jean despite it being set in 1890. In an interview, she said, "I returned home a year ago to visit my mother, and I didn't want to return to Beverly Hills. I'm basically a country girl; I love land and long strolls down country lanes through the woods. I guess that's what I like about the play I'm in. I can see Ohio from Anderson's writings with its isolated farmhouses way off the road and trains running through the towns." Nevertheless, the character of neurotic and bitter Elizabeth Willard was a demanding role for Jean, as they had nothing in common. As she explained:

> For one reason, I'm quite different from the woman in the story. She's a complainer, a bellyacher, a nonrealist. I'm a hardline realist. I don't like complaining or worrying about what might have been.... She is tragic and sick, but there is a flaw in her character. She doesn't really know what she wants or should do. She just feels that someplace out there, there is something she missed, and she cries out against everything and complains about her life.[19]

Jean based the character on two embittered women she had known as a girl in Ohio. Producer Lloyd explained that "Miss Peters was 'a bull's eye choice' for the role of a forty-six-year-old woman who hates her environment but doesn't have the courage to get out of it. She comes from Ohio, she knows these kinds of people, and she understands the background and this kind of woman."[20]

Costar William Windom described Jean as "warm, friendly, and charming on the set, and quite naturally, a bit guarded about attendant publicity."[21] Like the rest of the cast, Jean accepted union minimum wages for the chance to do a *Hollywood Television Theatre* show. Once again, she proved that she wasn't motivated by money, and the paltry wage was the least of her worries. After seeing herself in a partial rough cut, she said:

> I couldn't look any worse than I do in this play. I've never worked with tape before, and I found it a whole new experience. You can think the camera is far away from you in a long shot, and you find out you've been in a choking closeup. I've seen some parts of it I like very much, but I haven't seen the final version. It was a new experience for me, and I have a lot to learn about the technique of tape.[22]

Winesburg, Ohio was aired across America on March 5, 1973. The *Hollywood Reporter* called the production "outstanding, underscored by a sensitive and moving performance by Miss Peters."[23] Reviews were generally positive, but as a perfectionist, Jean was critical of her work. "I'm not pleased with the show or my performance in it," she commented. "I found it rather dull."[24] She reiterated this on a different occasion: "I'm a little disappointed in the outcome of *Winesburg*," she said. "It's a little drab and slow-moving, but then that's what it's all about. I hope my next role will be a little more upbeat, something a little happier."[25]

Having indicated that she was to continue acting, Jean was asked about her future on screen. She replied, "I don't envision myself going back on a full-time basis. There are too many interesting things to do and not enough good scripts for women. If only my husband would produce a picture with a woman in it. I'd like to do a picture with him, but then I'm not sure we wouldn't kill each other."[26]

A few days later, two hundred celebrities, government officials, and civic leaders paid tribute to director Henry Hathaway at the Beverly Hills Hotel on the occasion of his seventy-fifth birthday. Jean, who had worked with Hathaway in *Niagara*, was among the guests. The event reunited her with many colleagues she had not seen since her days at Fox, and she found catching up with old friends very moving.

Once the buzz of Jean's comeback started to fade, she returned to her life as Mrs. Stanley Hough. However, she did still attend movie previews and social functions and was often seen with her husband dining in fancy restaurants. She still devoted one day a week to raising money for the Motion Picture Country House and Hospital for aging showbusiness people, selling used clothes in the organization's shop and gathering things for auctions. She was determined to keep busy as she waited to see what acting opportunities would come her way. She had a while to wait.

CHAPTER 13

Tranquility

The inspiring spirit of my mother gave me so little desire to
become the victim of my possessions.
—JEAN PETERS

IN JANUARY 1975, THE BRITISH PRESS REPORTED THAT JEAN WAS PLANNING
to resume her career, this time as host of a daytime talk show on American television, and was negotiating with three major TV networks over a
salary of £75,000 a year. Jean, however, denied that any network had ever
approached her. By this point, more than two years after making *Winesburg,
Ohio*, Jean confessed she had no intention of returning to work and was
happy filling her days as a Beverly Hills housewife.

A year and a half later, she changed her mind, and after an absence of
almost four years from a set, she returned to acting in *The Moneychangers* (1976), a six-and-a-half-hour TV miniseries based on Arthur Hailey's
bestselling novel.

The Moneychangers was produced by Ross Hunter and Jacques Mapes for
NBC-TV. It marked the first time a novel that was *still* on the bestseller's
list had been filmed for television. The story focused on the struggle for
power in a banking establishment, the criminal elements that threatened
its collapse, and the lethal rivalries of two vice presidents struggling to
win the bank's presidency. Jean joined an impressive cast headed by Kirk
Douglas, Christopher Plummer, Helen Hayes, Susan Flannery, Anne Baxter,
Timothy Bottoms, Joan Collins, and Robert Loggia.

Jean chose *The Moneychangers* to return to work because the offer came
directly from her old friend, Paramount TV's producer Ross Hunter, who
explained that her role required just two full working days and only in Los
Angeles. It was a dream job that would not have interfered with her daily
routine. Jean told the press:

I was afraid to come back and try to handle a whole vehicle. I play a well-to-do Bel Air matron in the story, the wife of Christopher Plummer. It's a good part and one I could feel comfortable with. . . . During my eleven years in movies, I didn't take my work seriously. When I was younger, I didn't think acting was very important—just something to have fun with. Now I feel differently. We need people to personify our dreams. In that respect, actors serve an important function. Now I take my work seriously, and I find I enjoy it more.[1]

She added, "My part did not require a character change. It was a sympathetic character, a little sharp-tongued, and that was easy to bring off. It's a cameo role. I'm older now and not as adventurous. A small part satisfies me."[2]

Jean's role was filmed in June 1976. After completing the final sequence, she received a round of applause from coworkers. At this point, her trepidation about being away from a set for so long had faded, thanks also to her costar Christopher Plummer, whom she called "a super actor and a warm and friendly person."[3] For his role, Plummer won an Emmy award as Outstanding Lead Actor in a limited series.

The Moneychangers aired on NBC in four segments in December 1976. Despite the stellar cast, it was dismissed by critics as too soap opera-ish and only mildly entertaining, but the audience disagreed. TV ratings were so high that the series grossed a record $1.25 million in overseas sales, where it was released in a much shorter version.

• • •

On April 5, 1976, two months before Jean's return to work in front of a camera, Howard Hughes died onboard an aircraft. (When she filmed *The Moneychangers*, she asked Paramount to bar visitors from the set, as people bombarded her asking for stories about him).

Painfully thin, he was at this stage addicted to prescription painkillers to alleviate injuries sustained from numerous plane crashes, and his cause of death was listed as kidney failure, almost certainly as a result of his drug abuse.

"Tell her I love her to the end . . . that I've always loved her," was allegedly Hughes's last message sent to Jean from the Acapulco Princess Hotel via his guard and aide Gordon Margulis days before his death. When Jean heard the tragic news, her only comment to the swarm of reporters that besieged her residence was, "I'm sorry, and I'm sad that he's dead." The funeral home where Hughes's body was embalmed reported that not one person came to pay their final respects to him. Only one call came in inquiring about Hughes's body, and that was from Jean.

A will dated March 19, 1968, was found on the desk of an official at the Church of Jesus Christ of Latter-day Saints in Salt Lake City, Utah. The so-called "Mormon will" gave $1.56 billion to various charitable organizations including the Howard Hughes Medical Institute, almost $470 million to the upper management in Hughes's companies and to his aides, $156 million to his first cousin William Lummis, and $156 million (equal to one-sixteenth of Hughes's estate) to be divided equally between his two ex-wives, Ella Rice and Jean Peters.

A trial in Las Vegas was set to determine the will's authenticity, while a second trial took place in Houston, where the Texas attorney general was attempting to prove that Hughes considered Texas his legal residence. If successful, the state would have collected millions of dollars in inheritance taxes. In the meantime, the temporary administrators of the estate claimed Nevada, which had no inheritance tax, was Hughes's legal residence.

On January 31, 1978, Jean was summoned to Houston to testify before a probate court jury to determine her former husband's legal residence at the time of his death. The court deposition shed some light on Jean's marriage with Hughes for the first time. Jean testified that Hughes never mentioned anything to her about returning to Texas. She stated that in 1960, he told her he planned to spend the rest of his life in Nevada. Over the next few years, she and Hughes had discussed the possibility of him opening offices in Las Vegas and finding a ranch where they could live. Jean admitted in court that she discovered he had moved to Las Vegas in 1966 only by reading about it in the papers.

Jean added that in the early 1960s, when they were living in Rancho Santa Fe, Hughes did not want her to register to vote. "He didn't want me to state I was, we were, residents of California," she said.[4] Later, she claimed, Hughes "wanted to be out of the state of California when the TWA matter was settled [he had sold the airline he owned for $566 million and did not want to pay state taxes]. I felt my whole life was being controlled by a bunch of tax lawyers. I argued with him. I said, 'Pay the tax. Life is too short.'"

Jean said the last time she saw him in person was in a Boston hotel in 1966, where they discussed several locations for building a home, none of which were in Texas.

Three months later, Jean was summoned to appear in the Las Vegas court. She did not testify in person, but her sworn statement was introduced as evidence. Jean affirmed that her billionaire ex-husband discussed updating his will with her shortly after they met in 1946, and in the 1950s, said in a telephone conversation that he was in the process of revising the document. Jean stated that they never discussed a will after that. "He said his fortune was to go to medical research,"[5] added Jean. This was the Hughes Medical Institute, a Miami-based, tax-free charitable foundation Hughes had created years earlier that he funded through profits from the Hughes Aircraft Company. Jean testified that Hughes never told her whether she would be a beneficiary. She said she had never seen a legally drawn will and never asked to.

Over the years, Jean never commented on her marriage, but she did reveal reasons for it ending:

> I eventually realized that he was a sociopath, a man utterly incapable of understanding the needs of another person. I believe it is a very appropriate definition of the man I was with for twenty years. He was very manipulative, even though he was just darling and charming at the same time. And even though he was affectionate in some ways ... and totally persuasive, it was a charade, I guess. I'll just say that my faith in him was eroded.[6]

In June 1978, the Nevada court officially ruled that Hughes's will was a forgery and that Hughes had died intestate (without a valid will). Eventually, when his estate was divided among his relatives, Jean did not get anything but continued to receive her monthly alimony payments under the divorce agreement. In March 1980, the Nevada Supreme Court dismissed a suit filed by the heirs of Howard Hughes that, among other things, objected to these monthly alimony payments of more than $8,000 to Jean. At the time, under the divorce agreement, Jean was receiving $8,086 a month—a payment that had been readjusted during the last nine years with the cost-of-living index.

• • •

On May 29, 1979, Jean appeared on *Dinah!*, a popular talk show hosted by singer and actress Dinah Shore. The other guests were four legendary Hollywood celebrities: Diahann Carroll, Debbie Reynolds, Jane Russell, and Jane Powell who, together with fashion designer Bill Travilla, discussed what being glamorous meant. Jean looked radiant in a stylish long black dress and a new chic short haircut. She explained that her idea of glamour was connected mostly to someone's personality rather than their looks. She also named Tyrone Power as the sexiest costar she had worked with.

At the end of December, Hollywood paid its final respects to Darryl F. Zanuck, the man who had built Jean's career at 20th Century Fox. The producer had died suddenly of pneumonia in Palm Springs at age seventy-seven. At the funeral, Jean and Stan were among the several hundred mourners who filed quietly into the United Methodist Church of Westwood. Two months later, Jean participated in a Zanuck tribute on the USC campus in Los Angeles hosted by director Hal Kanter. It was an evening of memories and anecdotes shared by those who worked with the Fox chief. Among the 450 guests, those who spoke included Philip Dunne, David Brown, Frank McCarthy, Mary Anita Loos, Jane Withers, John Payne, Cesar Romero, Sammy Cahn, Roddy McDowall, and Richard Widmark. Jean talked briefly about her Zanuck days and how pleasant it had been for her working under "Darryl's dukedom."[7]

The following summer, the *Hollywood Reporter* wrote, "Though the offers get bigger and bigger, Jean Peters is keeping her promise not to talk or write about her life as Mrs. Howard Hughes. Latest turn-down by Jean is a publisher's offer up front of two million bucks!"[8]

Jean steadfastly refused to write a memoir, although she did decide to go back to work.

After a four-year absence from acting, she took on a small but key role in *Peter and Paul* (1981), a four-hour miniseries directed by Robert Day and starring Robert Foxworth as Peter and Anthony Hopkins as Paul. After reading Christopher Knopf's script, Stan had agreed to produce the series, and he thought that the character of Priscilla, a wealthy Roman who was one of Paul's converters to Christianity, was perfect for his wife. Jean loved the role that was part of the biblical account of the early days of Christianity. *Peter and Paul* chronicled the two apostles' journey of faith from Christ's crucifixion until they sacrificed their own lives for their beliefs.

Filmed on the Greek island of Rhodes and in Athens rather than Israel for security reasons, the cast was made up of international actors, including Eddie Albert, Raymond Burr, José Ferrer, and Herbert Lom. More than two thousand actors and extras were used during the fifty-three-day shoot. Some of the costumes brought from the States were used previously in epic films, such as *Quo Vadis* (1951), *Ben-Hur* (1959), *Spartacus* (1960), and *Cleopatra* (1963).

Jean and Stan flew to Greece and spent a few weeks there in the fall of 1980. *Peter and Paul* aired in two parts in April 1981 on the CBS network as the annual Easter special. Reviews of the $8 million epic production were generally disappointing. The teleplay was accused of lacking the sweep and grandeur of the 1977 TV hit *Jesus of Nazareth*. Still, Jean was able to make her role memorable, as some of the critics remarked.

In 1986, eighty-eight-year-old Mary Peters passed away, and Jean returned to Ohio for her funeral. Her strong-willed mother had inspired her to keep her feet on the ground and ignore the trappings of wealth and movie stardom. "It's my mother's influence," she had said while discussing Mary a few years earlier. "She is an extraordinary woman, still active and self-sufficient. When I was in a position to send her money, she invested in real estate in my name. . . . It was . . . the inspiring spirit of my mother that gave me so little desire to become the victim of my possessions."[9] And it was in her mother's memory that, two years later, she returned to acting in what would be the final role of her career.

Jean was astounded when casting director Ron Stephenson called to ask her to be a guest star in an episode of *Murder, She Wrote* (1984–1996), a popular television series starring Angela Lansbury as Jessica Fletcher, a shrewd mystery writer and amateur detective. Jean agreed mostly for sentimental reasons, as she told the *Los Angeles Times*: "It was my mother's very favorite program. She passed away two years ago, and I figured she'd be very angry if I didn't do it. Angela is such an angel. She's wonderful to work with. They sure work longer hours than *we* used to. It's the first acting I've done in some time, but I'd do it again if it was something I liked."[10]

"Wearing of the Green" was the name of the episode that Jean taped in September 1988, and it was broadcast the following November. She played Siobhan O'Dea, a reclusive legendary former actress involved in a murder connected to the theft of a priceless tiara. It was a notable guest appearance and an intriguing character that suggested a few parallels with Jean's real life out of the limelight when she was married to Howard Hughes.

In February 1990, seventy-two-year-old Stan died of a cardiac arrest in Crans-Montana, Switzerland, while on a ski holiday with Jean and his family. Stan's brother Richard and his adult children attempted CPR in vain. Jean was devastated. The funeral service was held at Westwood United Methodist Church, the same church in which Jean and Stan had married nineteen years earlier.

In October, the 22nd Annual Screen Smart Set Auction and Fashion Show marked Jean's first public appearance after Stan's death. Just like in previous years, she agreed to walk the runway of a catwalk show held at the Regent Beverly Wilshire Hotel to support the Motion Picture and Television Fund; it was an event Jean had never missed.

After Stan's death, Jean felt lonely as she had no children of her own and spent most of her time at home. Once again, her public appearances became increasingly rare. She decided that it was time to leave Beverly Hills and move close to her sister's family, and in 1993, Jean bought a house at 2409 Buena Vista Circle in Carlsbad, a coastal town in the North County region of San Diego, three doors down from Shirley's home.

She spent her last years in complete retirement under the name of Elizabeth (as Stan always called her) J. Hough. She enjoyed her free time reading, planting flowers in her large garden, and taking long walks with her dog. As Shirley would say, "She was very happy here. It's a small town like East Canton."

Jean seemed to be in good health until August 2000, when she was diagnosed with leukemia. Two months later, on October 13, she died at La Jolla Hospital, two days before her seventy-fourth birthday. As per Jean's wishes, a small graveyard service was held at the Holy Cross Cemetery in Culver City, attended by a few family members and no celebrities. She was buried next to Stan, and they shared a simple headstone.

Except for Shirley and a few close relatives, no one knew about Jean's leukemia. Walt Sigler, her old friend from East Canton High School, told the press, "I am in shock because I had no idea. Even though I was in touch with her from time to time, she hadn't informed me of her illness."[11] Shirley respected her sister's wishes and informed the media of Jean's death only after the funeral. She told the press that throughout her life, Jean had maintained a great fondness for her Ohioan rural roots, saying, "She loved East Canton . . . she was tied to the area. She corresponded with several people there."

In September 2016, sixteen years after her death, Jean was officially remembered in East Canton with a special event hosted by the Osnaburg Historical Society, a nonprofit organization preserving the history of the town. A few of her films were shown, along with an exhibition of various items from Jean's memorabilia, including scrapbooks, yearbooks, and other photographs. The society also put on display a piece of scenery that Jean had painted for a local friend.

Nowadays, Jean Peters's legacy as an actress is seldom remembered. She is mostly unknown to the younger generations and almost forgotten by the old ones. Her filmography is unfairly overlooked by historians and film critics. On those rare occasions when her name does appear in the news, it is mostly connected to Howard Hughes and those mysterious years they shared together.

Once, Jean was asked if she found being the ex-Mrs. Hughes a help or a hindrance to her career. "I just try to ignore it," she replied with a sigh, "and I wish everyone else would."[12]

Peters with James A. Rhodes, mayor of Columbus, Ohio (left), as she is presented with the Miss Ohio State cup (1945).

Peters at age six (1932).

Peters seducing Michael Dunne in her first screen test at 20th Century Fox (1945).

Peters in a publicity shot (1947).

Peters at home
in Brentwood,
California (1948).

Cesar Romero, Tyrone Power, and Peters in a scene from *Captain from Castile* (1947).

Peters as Catana in *Captain from Castile* (1947).

Dana Andrews, Anne Revere, and Peters in a scene from *Deep Waters* (1948).

Peters in a publicity still (1950).

Peters and Ray Milland in *It Happens Every Spring* (1948).

Paul Douglas and Peters in *Love That Brute* (1950).

Peters lip-syncing "You Took Advantage of Me" in *Love That Brute* (1950).

Peters and David Wayne in a scene from *As Young as You Feel* (1951).

Jeffrey Hunter, Lenka Peterson, and Peters in *Take Care of My Little Girl* (1951).

Peters as Dallas Pruitt in a publicity shot for *Take Care of My Little Girl* (1951).

Peters as Anne in *Anne of the Indies* (1951).

Marlon Brando and Peters in a publicity shot for *Viva Zapata!* (1952).

Peters and David Wayne in a scene from *Wait Till the Sun Shines, Nellie* (1952).

Walter Brennan, Jeffrey Hunter, and Peters in *Lure of the Wilderness* (1952).

Peters in a publicity still for
Lure of the Wilderness (1952).

Peters and Gregory Ratoff in a scene from *O. Henry's Full House* (1952).

Richard Widmark and Peters in *Pickup on South Street* (1953).

Russell Collins, Marilyn Monroe, Peters, and Casey Adams in *Niagara* (1952).

Casey Adams, Peters, Dennis O'Dea, and Marilyn Monroe in *Niagara* (1952).

Peters and Marilyn Monroe in a *Niagara* advertising shot (1952).

Charlton Heston and Peters on a lunch break from the *Lux Radio Theatre* broadcast of *Viva Zapata!* (November 1952).

Joseph Cotten and Peters in a dramatic publicity shot for *A Blueprint for Murder* (1953).

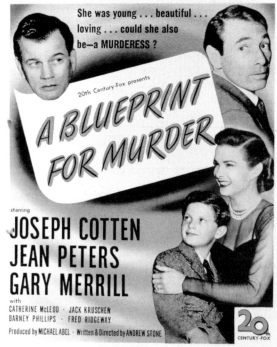

An advertising bill for *A Blueprint for Murder* (1953).

Jeanne Crain, Elliott Reid, and Peters in a scene from *Vicki* (1953).

Peters, Louis Jourdan, Maggie McNamara, and Dorothy McGuire in *Three Coins in the Fountain* (1954).

Peters as Nalinle
in *Apache* (1954).

Peters and Robert Wagner
in a publicity shot of
Broken Lance (1954).

Peters and Stuart W. Cramer III the day of their wedding, May 29, 1954.

Peters and Richard Todd in
A Man Called Peter (1955).

Peters in one of her last
publicity shots (1954).

Peters with Richard Todd in *A Man Called Peter* (1955).

Peters and William Windom in a publicity shot for the TV movie *Winesburg, Ohio* (1973).

A publicity shot for miniseries *The Moneychangers* (1976).

ACKNOWLEDGMENTS

In writing this book, I have benefited from the help of many individuals and institutions and from the assistance and support of friends, without whom its completion would have been impossible. I would like to thank my husband Yaakov Perry; the helpful staff of the British Film Institute Library in London, in particular Anastasia Kerameos, Sarah Currant, and Victoria Crabbe for their kind help; the amazing staff of the New York Public Library for the Performing Arts at Lincoln Center in New York, particularly Jeremy Megraw; Genevieve Maxwell from the Margaret Herrick Library of the Academy of Motion Picture Arts and Sciences in Beverly Hills; Jill Fleck from the Milwaukee Public Library; the staff of the Bibliothèque du Cinéma François Truffaut in Paris; the staff of the British Library's Humanities Reading Room in London; Biblioteca Renzo Renzi—Cineteca di Bologna.

Most of all, my deepest gratitude goes to my editors, the amazing Kate Bohdanowicz and my longtime friend Stuart Williams—without their invaluable help, completing this book would have been almost impossible.

NOTES

CHAPTER 1: FARM GIRL

1. Lydia Lane, "Surmounting the Materialism," *Los Angeles Times*, December 10, 1976, G7.
2. Eleanor Harris, "The Girl Who Didn't Go Hollywood," *Collier's*, November 5, 1949, 60.
3. Myrtle Gebhart, "Farm Girl Is Promising Film Star," *Boston Sunday Post*, June 15, 1947, 4.
4. Jack Holland, "Cinderella from Ohio," *Screenland*, October 1947, 82.
5. Gladys Hall, "Exploding the Myth of the Mysterious Jean Peters," *Photoplay*, October 1954, 106.
6. Robert F. Slatzer, *The Life and Curious Death of Marilyn Monroe* (London: W. H. Allen, 1975), 100.
7. Gebhart, "Farm Girl Is Promising Film Star," 4.
8. Harris, "The Girl Who Didn't Go Hollywood," 61.
9. Holland, "Cinderella from Ohio," 81.
10. Mary E. Peters, "She Never Left Home," *Modern Screen*, June 1949, 35.
11. Peters, "She Never Left Home," 102.
12. Cecil Smith, "Jean Peters Back After 18 Years," *Los Angeles Times*, March 5, 1977, F13.
13. Richard Buskin, *Blonde Heat: The Sizzling Career of Marilyn Monroe* (New York: Billboard Books, 2001), 24.
14. Buskin, *Blonde Heat*, 14.
15. Hedda Hopper, "Hollywood's Mystery Girl," *Photoplay*, March 1953, 101.
16. Charles Whiting, *American Hero: The Life and Death of Audie Murphy* (York, UK: Eskdale Publishing, 2000), 310.
17. Richard Hack, *Hughes, the Private Diaries, Memos and Letters* (Waterville, ME: Thorndike Press, 2001), 277.
18. Peter Harry Brown and Pat H. Broeske, *Howard Hughes: The Untold Story* (New York: Warner Books, 1997), 210-11.
19. Sheilah Graham, "Whatta Gal!," *St. Louis Globe-Democrat*, April 28, 1947, 11.
20. Sheilah Graham, "Chasing Howard Hughes," *Ladies' Home Journal*, August 1974, 76.
21. Hack, *Hughes*, 277.

22. Charles Higham, *Howard Hughes: The Secret Life* (New York: Putnam, 1993), 126.

23. Whiting, *American Hero*, 311.

CHAPTER 2: CANTANA

1. *Zanuck* (Los Angeles: Friends of the USC Libraries, University of Southern California, 1981), 33.

2. Rudy Behlmer, *Memo from Darryl F. Zanuck: The Golden Years of 20th Century Fox* (New York: Grove Press, 1994), 112–13.

3. Tom Stempel, *An Oral History Interview with Henry King* (Los Angeles: American Film Institute, 1972), 143.

4. Frank Thompson, *Henry King Director: From Silent to 'Scope* (Los Angeles: Directors Guild of America, 1995), 146.

5. Reba Churchill and Bonnie Churchill, "Better Than Red Apples," *Silver Screen*, December 1947, 56.

6. Holland, "Cinderella from Ohio," 82.

7. Raymond Strait, *Mrs. Howard Hughes* (Los Angeles: Holloway House Publishing, 1970), 69.

8. *Dinah!* CBS-TV Network, May 29, 1979.

9. Lowell E. Redelings, "Hollywood Scene," *Los Angeles Hollywood Citizen News*, December 13, 1946, 6.

10. Arnold Mann, "Top of the Line Design," *Emmy Magazine*, March/April 1984, 6–7.

11. John Franceschina, *Hermes Pan: The Man Who Danced with Fred Astaire* (Oxford: Oxford University Press, 2012), 149.

12. Jean Peters, "He Kissed Me!," *Movieland*, November 1947, 64–65.

13. Donald Dewey, *Lee J. Cobb: Characters of an Actor* (Lanham, MD: Rowman & Littlefield Publishers, 2014), 113.

14. *Charlotte Observer*, August 3, 1947, 56.

15. Henry King, "Try and Stop Me!," *Modern Screen*, December 1947, 90.

16. *Hollywood Reporter*, November 26, 1947, 3.

17. *Newsweek*, January 5, 1948, 68.

18. Strait, *Mrs. Howard Hughes*, 111.

19. Behlmer, *Memo from Darryl F. Zanuck*, 164–65.

CHAPTER 3: SENSE AND SENSIBILITY

1. William R. Wilkerson, "Tradeviews," *Hollywood Reporter*, December 3, 1947, 1.

2. "Jean Peters Wears Rings of Millionaire Hughes," *Pittsburgh Post-Gazette*, March 14, 1947, 2.

3. Graham, "Whatta Gal!," 11.

4. Higham, *Howard Hughes*, 126–27.

5. Louella Parsons, "In Hollywood with Jean Peters," *Los Angeles Examiner*, October 12, 1947.

6. Arthur Millier, "Unknown 20-Year-Old Wins Prize Screen Role," *Los Angeles Times* November 10, 1946, B1.

7. Behlmer, *Memo from Darryl F. Zanuck*, 148.

8. Harris, "The Girl Who Didn't Go Hollywood," 61.

9. John L. Scott, "Change to Svelte Becomes Jean Peters," *Los Angeles Times*, April 24, 1949, D1.

10. Scott, "Change to Svelte Becomes Jean Peters," D3.

11. Jessie Royce Landis, *You Won't Be So Pretty* (London: W. H. Allen, 1954), 226.

CHAPTER 4: DALLAS PRUITT

1. Harrison Carroll, "Behind the Scenes in Hollywood," *Lancaster Eagle-Gazette*, August 5, 1949, 6.

2. *Charlotte Observer*, October 5, 1949, 33.

3. *Variety*, May 10, 1950.

4. Thomas M. Pryor, *New York Times*, May 27, 1950, II, 27.

5. Lowell E. Redelings, "Hollywood Scene," *Los Angeles Evening Citizen News*, June 24, 1949, 18.

6. Peters, "She Never Left Home," 103.

7. "Pressure on 20th to Forego Pic on College Frat Evils," *Variety*, December 13, 1950. 1.

8. Patricia Clary, "Hollywood Film Shop," *Bakersfield Californian*, January 3, 1951, 18.

9. Clary, "Hollywood Film Shop," 18.

10. "Vital Statistics," *Take Care of My Little Girl*, 20th Century Fox Press Release, 2.

11. "Vital Statistics," 2.

12. "When Hollywood Calls: It's About Face for Jean Peters," *The 7th Hollywood Album* (London: Sampson Low Marston & Co., Ltd., 1953), 138.

13. Jean Peters, "The Role I Liked the Best," *Saturday Evening Post*, September 27, 1952, 57.

14. *Hollywood Reporter*, June 12, 1951, 3.

15. Harold V. Cohen, "The New Film," *Pittsburgh Post-Gazette* July 2, 1951.

CHAPTER 5: LADY PIRATE

1. John Brady, *The Craft of the Screenwriter* (New York: Simon & Schuster, 1981), 47.

2. Hedda Hopper, "Study in Contradiction—That's Jean Peters' Life," *Los Angeles Times*, March 25, 1951, D1.

3. Buskin, *Blonde Heat*, 77.

4. Buskin, *Blonde Heat*, 78–79.

5. Hedda Hopper, "Jean Peters Wanted to Be a School Marm," *Hartford Courant*, March 25, 1951, SM10.

6. Elia Kazan, *A Life* (New York: Knopf, 1988), 404.

7. Gene Handsaker, "Hollywood," *Times Munster*, February 12, 1951, 9.

8. "When Hollywood Calls: It's About Face for Jean Peters," 140.

9. Philip Dunne, *Take Two: A Life in Movie and Politics* (New York: Limelight Editions, 1992), 71.

10. Hedda Hopper, "Looking at Hollywood with Hedda Hopper," *Chicago Sunday Tribune*, March 25, 1951, 6.

11. "Tattoos Taboos in the Movie," *Baltimore Evening Sun*, March 20, 1951, 26.

12. Olivier Minne, *Louis Jourdan: Le Dernier French Lover d'Hollywood* (Paris: Séguier, 2017), 375.

13. Hopper, "Hollywood's Mystery Girl," 101.

14. "Top Grossers of 1951," *Variety*, January 2, 1952, 2.

15. Otis L. Guernsey Jr., "On the Screen," *New York Herald Tribune*, August 10, 1951.

16. Jean Negulesco, *Things I Did . . . and Things I Think I Did* (New York: Linden Press/Simon & Schuster, 1984), 181.

CHAPTER 6: KAZAN AND BRANDO

1. *Hollywood Reporter*, November 11, 1948, 3.

2. Jeff Young, *Kazan: The Master Director Discusses His Films* (New York: Newmarket Press, 1999), 93.

3. Edwin Schallert, "Jean Peters, Weary of Ragged Roles, Wants Finery in Films," *Los Angeles Times*, March 2, 1952, 7.

4. "When Hollywood Calls: It's About Face for Jean Peters," 140.

5. Marlon Brando, *Songs My Mother Taught Me* (New York: Random House, 1994), 172.

6. Charles Higham, *Brando: The Unauthorized Biography* (New York: New American Library, 1988), 121.

7. Darwin Porter, *Brando Unzipped* (New York: Blood Moon Production, 2004), 361.

8. Hedda Hopper, "Hollywood's New Sex-Boat," *Photoplay*, July 1952, 63.

9. Brando, *Songs My Mother Thought Me*, 172.

10. Higham, *Brando*, 122.

11. Ron Offen, *Brando* (Chicago: Henry Regnery Company, 1973), 69.

12. *Hollywood Reporter*, February 6, 1952, 3.

13. *Saturday Review,* March 1, 1942, 6.

14. Thomas R. Dash, *Women's Wear Daily*, February 8, 1952, 48.

15. Behlmer, *Memo from Darryl F. Zanuck*, 179.

16. Buskin, *Blonde Heat*, 90.

17. Lowell E. Redelings, "Hollywood Scene," *Los Angeles Evening Citizen News*, September 21, 1951, 16.

18. Stuart Awbrey, "Last of Nellie Is Filmed in Hollywood," *Hutchinson News*, October 8, 1951, 6.

CHAPTER 7: NEGULESCO'S MUSE

1. "Starlet Jean Peters Cheered at Waycross," *Atlanta Constitution*, October 26, 1951, 26.

2. Sidney Skolsky, *Los Angeles Evening Citizen News*, December 12, 1951, 13.

3. Edith K. Roosevelt, "Long Tresses Seen Key to Caresses," *Salt Lake Tribune*, July 7, 1952.

4. Erskine Johnson, "In Hollywood," *Fitchburg Sentinel*, January 30, 1952, 6.

5. Erskine Johnson, "Lost Horizon Sequel Planned," *Rhinelander Daily News*, February 27, 1952.

6. "When Hollywood Calls: It's About Face for Jean Peters," 140.

7. Inez Wallace, "Lure of the Wilderness," *Cleveland Plain Dealer Pictorial Magazine*, September 1952, 22.

8. "Actress Freezes Making Summer Scenes for Film," *Hartford Courant*, July 6, 1952, D6.

9. Hedda Hopper, "Widmark to Play Ex-Con," *Salt Lake Tribune*, December 4, 1951, 15.

10. *Photoplay*, October 1952, 26.

11. *Variety*, July 30, 1952, 6.

12. *Hollywood Reporter*, July 24, 1952, 4.

13. "Jean Negulesco: Dossier," *Positif*, October 1986, 53.

14. Charles Higham and Joel Greenberg, *The Celluloid Muse: Hollywood Directors Speak* (London: Angus & Robertson, 1969), 196.

15. Buskin, *Blonde Heat*, 118.

16. Michelangelo Capua, *Jean Negulesco. The Life and Films* (Jefferson, NC: McFarland & Co., 2017), 75.

17. Pat McGilligan, *Backstory 2: Interviews with Screenwriters of the 1940s and 1950s* (Berkeley: University of California Press, 1991), 237.

18. Mike Connolly, "Rambling Reporter," *Hollywood Reporter*, May 14, 1952, 2.

19. Adam Victor, *Marilyn Encyclopedia*, Woodstock (NY: The Overlook Press, 1999), 137.

20. R. F. Slatzer, *The Life and Curious Death of Marilyn Monroe* (Pinnacle House, 1974), 106.

21. Tom Weaver, *Science Fiction and Fantasy Film Flashback* (Jefferson, NC: McFarland & Co., 1998), 9.

22. *Hollywood Reporter*, January 20, 1953, 3.

23. *Variety*, January 21, 1953, 6.

CHAPTER 8: FEMME NOIR

1. Samuel Fuller, *A Third Face: My Tale of Writing, Fighting, and Filmmaking* (New York: Applause, 2002), 301.

2. *Rocky Mount Evening Telegram*, September 22, 1952.

3. Bob Thomas, "Jean Peters Turns Down Sexy Buildup, Goes Against Trend," *Sedalia Democrat*, October 5, 1952, 19.

4. *Présence du Cinéma*, December 1963–January 1964, 11–12.

5. Hedda Hopper, "Hollywood's Gorgeous Jean," *Chicago Tribune Magazine*, July 11, 1954, 19.

6. Michael Buckley, *Films in Review*, May 1986, 270.

7. Samuel Fuller, *A Third Face*, 303.

8. *Hollywood Reporter*, May 13, 1953, 3.

9. Richard. L. Coe, *Washington Post*, May 30, 1953, 16.

10. Bosley Crowther, *New York Times*, June 18, 1953, 38.

11. Sidney Skolsky, *Los Angeles Evening Citizen News*, December 12, 1952, 21.

12. Karen Burroughs Hannsberry, *Femme Noir: Bad Girls of Film* (Jefferson, NC: McFarland & Co., 2009), 392.

13. Frederick Worden, "Why I've No Time for Love!," *Screenland*, February 1954, 60.

14. Strait, *Mrs. Howard Hughes*, 114.

15. Hedda Hopper, "Goldstein Will Star Jean Peters as Siren," *Los Angeles Times*, December 26, 1952, B4.

16. Strait, *Mrs. Howard Hughes*, 159.

17. Lowell E. Redelings, "Hollywood Scene," *Los Angeles Evening Citizen News*, April 9, 1953, 18.

18. *Brazil Daily Times*, April 9, 1953, 23.

19. *Hollywood Reporter*, September 8, 1953, 3.

CHAPTER 9: NO TIME FOR LOVE

1. Capua, *Jean Negulesco*, 89.

2. Henry Toby, "Italy Finds a New Heart-Throb," *Picturegoer*, March 5, 1955, 15.

3. Hopper, "Hollywood's Gorgeous Jean," 19.

4. 20th Century Fox, *Vital Statistics* on *Three Coins in the Fountain*, New York, 1953, 2–3.

5. Mike Connolly, "Rambling Reporter," *Hollywood Reporter*, September 3, 1953, 2.

6. Richard Mathison, *His Weird and Wanton Ways: The Secret Life of Howard Hughes* (London, Hale, 1978), 192.

7. Erskine Johnson, "You'll Remember," *Binghamton Press*, October 29, 1953, 28.

8. Hopper, "Hollywood's Gorgeous Jean," 19.

9. Worden, "Why I've No Time for Love!," 58–59.

10. *Variety*, May 12, 1954, 6.

11. Hopper, "Hollywood's Gorgeous Jean," 19.

12. Worden, "Why I've No Time for Love!," 59–60.

13. Richard Combs, *Robert Aldrich* (London, BFI, 1978), 52.

14. Higham and Greenberg, *The Celluloid Muse*, 27.

15. Strait, *Mrs. Howard Hughes*, 70.

16. Hopper, "Hollywood's Gorgeous Jean," 19.

17. Eugene L. Miller and Edwin T. Arnold, *Robert Aldrich: Interviews* (Jackson: University Press of Mississippi, 2004), 23.

18. Higham and Greenberg, *The Celluloid Muse*, 27.

19. *Monthly Film Bulletin*, September 1954, 126.

20. Hopper, "Hollywood's Gorgeous Jean," 19.

CHAPTER 10: SURPRISING GIRL IN SURPRISE WEDDING

1. Robert Wagner, *Pieces of My Heart: A Life* (London: Hutchinson, 2008), 83.

2. Jean Peters, "What I Like About Bob Wagner," *Movie Life*, 1953, 18.

3. D. P., "Wagner Learns to Love," *Picturegoer*, September 11, 1954, 10.

4. Edward Dmytryk, *It's a Hell of a Life but Not a Bad Living* (New York: New York Times Books, 1978), 183–84.

5. John Campbell, "On the Range with *Broken Lance*," *New York Times*, May 2, 1954, X5.

6. Jack Moffitt, *Hollywood Reporter*, July 23, 1954, 3.

7. K. Burroughs Hannsberry, *Femme Noir: Bad Girls of Film*, 394.

8. *Valley Times*, June 11, 1954, 12.

9. Louella Parsons, *San Francisco Examiner*, June 1, 1954, 37.

10. Hedda Hopper, "Actress Jean Peters Weds Oil Man," *New York Daily News*, May 30, 1954, 27.

11. Hall, "Exploding the Myth of the Mysterious Jean Peters," 107.

12. Alin Mosby, "Quiet Actress, Jean Peters, to Live with Hubby in East," *Vidette-Messenger of Porter County*, November 3, 1954, 7.

13. Hall, "Exploding the Myth of the Mysterious Jean Peters," 107.

14. Hedda Hopper, "Jean Peters Missing on Eve of Film Role," *Los Angeles Times*, September 14, 1954, 5.

15. Richard Todd, *In Camera: An Autobiography Continued* (London: Hutchinson, 1989), 78.

16. Erskine Johnson, "In Hollywood; Jean Peters Falls Victim to LA Smog," *Fitchburg Sentinel*, October 1954.

17. *Vital Statistics on A Man Called Peter*, 20th Century Fox's Press Release, 1954.

18. Jack Moffitt, "A Man Called Peter is a Great Inspirational Film," *Hollywood Reporter*, March 23, 1955, 3.

19. Arthur Gratz, *Films in Review*, April 1955, 188.

CHAPTER 11: BYE-BYE HOLLYWOOD

1. Peter Harry Brown, "Howard's End," *Vanity Fair*, April 1996, 299.

2. Noah Dietrich and Bob Thomas, *Howard, the Amazing Mr. Hughes* (Greenwich, CT: Coronet: 1972), 279–80.

3. D. L. Lyons, "America's Richest Wife," *Ladies' Home Journal*, November 1968, 164.

4. Lyons, "America's Richest Wife," 164.

5. Ronald L. Bartlett and James B. Steele, *Empire: The Life, Legend and Madness of Howard Hughes* (New York: Norton, 1979), 227.

6. *Deposition of Elizabeth Jean Peters Hough*, Hughes Estate Texas, July 26, 1977, 23.

7. "The Jean Peters Mystery," *Modern Screen*, May 1957, 60.

8. "Indies Destination," *Pasadena Independent*, June 17, 1956, 59.

9. Terry Moore, *The Beauty and the Billionaire* (New York: Pocket Books, 1984), 299.

10. Mathison, *His Weird and Wanton Ways*, 227–28.

11. Ronald L. Bartlett and J. B. Steele, *Howard Hughes: His Life and Madness* (New York: Norton, 2004), 262–63.

12. John Keats, *Hughes* (London: MacGibbon & Kee, 1967), 300–301.

13. *Deposition of Elizabeth Jean Peters Hough*, January 31, 1978.

14. Jack Anderson "Hughes' Personal Life Suffered," *San Angelo Standard-Times*, April 14, 1976, 4.

15. Vernon Scott, "Secluded Life Not for Howard Hughes' Mate," *Pittsburgh Press*, December 12, 1969, 21.

16. Dietrich and Thomas, *Howard the Amazing Hughes*, 62.

17. Darwin Porter, *Howard Hughes: Hell's Angel* (New York: Blood Moon, 2005), 780.

CHAPTER 12: A BRIEF COMEBACK

1. Lyons, "America's Richest Wife," 160.
2. *Time*, "People," December 18, 1972, 45.
3. Kay Gardella, "Hughes' Ex-Wife Makes TV Debut," *Sunday News*, March 4, 1973, 20.
4. Gardella, "Hughes' Ex-Wife Makes TV Debut," 164.
5. Ovid Demaris, "Howard Hughes, We See You! We See You!," *Esquire*, March 1969.
6. D. L. Lyons, "The Liberation of Mrs. Howard Hughes," *Ladies' Home Journal*, March 1971, 112.
7. Vernon Scott, "Jean Peters Returns to Work, but Still Likes Housewife Role," *Bridgeport Post*, October 17, 1976, 65.
8. Robert Slatzer, "Jean Peters: 1926–2000," *Classic Image*, December 2000, 45.
9. Earl Wilson, "It Happened Last Night," *New York Post*, January 19, 1970.
10. Marilyn Beck, "Mrs. Howard Hughes Rejoins the World," *Sunday Examiner*, February 25, 1973.
11. Beck, "Mrs. Howard Hughes Rejoins the World," 1973.
12. Haber, "Hughes, Jean Talk," *Victoria Advocate*, January 22, 1972, 9.
13. D. L. Lyons, "Jean Peters: Howard Hughes's Ex-Wife Speaks Out," *Ladies' Home Journal*, March 1973, 70.
14. Barbara Holsopple, "Jean Peters Returns to Acting in Winesburg, Ohio," *Pittsburgh Press*, March 2, 1973, 42.
15. "Change of Address," *TV Guide*, March 3, 1973, 26.
16. Smith, "Jean Peters Back After 18 Years," F13.
17. Beth Slocum, "Isolation Haunts Jean Peters in Ohio," *Milwaukee Journal*, March 4, 1973, 4.
18. Lyons, "Hughes' Ex-Wife Speaks Out," 71.
19. Slocum, "Isolation Haunts Jean Peters in Ohio," 4.
20. Holsopple, "Jean Peters Returns to Acting in Winesburg, Ohio," 42.
21. Charles Witbeck, "TV Keynotes: Winesburg Revisited," *Morning Call*, March 2, 1973, 39.
22. Gardella, "Hughes' Ex-Wife Makes TV Debut," 20.
23. Ron Pennington, *Hollywood Reporter*, March 5, 1973, 6.
24. Cindy Howell, "Jean Peters Returns to Acting in Winesburg, Ohio," *Des Moines Register & Tribune*, March 4, 1973, 11-TV.
25. Slocum, "Isolation Haunts Jean Peters in Ohio," 4.
26. Norma Lee Browning, "The Magic Made Her Come Back," *Chicago Tribune TV Week*, March 4, 1973, 7.

CHAPTER 13: TRANQUILITY

1. Vernon Scott, "Jean Peters in Mini-Series," *Lubbock Avalanche-Journal*, November 21, 1976, 102.
2. *Time*, September 6, 1976, 71.
3. "Jean Peters in TV Role; Won't Discuss Hughes," *Chicago Tribune*, August 23, 1976, A6.
4. "Nevada Hughes' Home, Jean Peters Says," *Los Angeles Times*, February 1, 1978, A1.
5. "Hughes Reported Wanting Money to Aid Research," *Los Angeles Times*, April 23, 1978, A24.

6. Brown and Broeske, *Howard Hughes. The Untold Story*, 334.

7. *Zanuck*, University of Southern California, 33.

8. Hank Grant, "The Rambling Reporter," *Hollywood Reporter*, July 16, 1980, 2.

9. Lane, "Surmounting the Materialism," G7.

10. Isobel Silden, "It's No Crime When Yesterday's Stars Get into 'Murder,'" *Los Angeles Times*, August 17, 1989, VI, 12K.

11. Mark J. Price, "Actress Jean Peters Dies of Leukemia," *Akron Beacon Journal*, October 20, 2000, 15.

12. Joyce Wagner, "Actress in a New Role After Years as Wife of Recluse," *Kansas City Star TV*, March 4, 1973, 4G.

FILMOGRAPHY

Captain from Castile

20th Century Fox Film Corporation—Darryl F. Zanuck
USA Technicolor 140 minutes
Premiered in New York City and Los Angeles, December 25, 1947

CREDITS: *Producer*: Lamar Trotti; *Director*: Henry King; *Assistant Directors*: William Eckhardt, Henry Weinberger; *Screenplay*: Lamar Trotti, from the novel by Samuel Shellabarger; *Technicolor Director*: Natalie Kalmus; *Associate Technicolor Consultant*: Richard Mueller; *Directors of Photography*: Charles G. Clarke, ASC, Arthur E. Arling, ASC; *Music*: Alfred Newman; *Orchestral Arrangements*: Edward Powell; *Art Directors*: Richard Day, James Basevi; *Set Decorator*: Thomas Little; *Film Editor*: Barbara McLean, ACE; *Costumes*: Charles LeMaire; *Director of Second Unit*: Robert D. Webb; *Makeup Artist*: Ben Nye; *Special Photographic Effects*: Fred Sersen; *Sound*: Winston H. Leverett, Roger Heman, *Choreographer*: Hermes Pan

CAST: Tyrone Power (Pedro De Vargas), Jean Peters (Catana Pérez), Cesar Romero (Hernàn Cortéz), Lee J. Cobb (Juan Garcia), John Sutton (Diego de Silva), Antonio Moreno (Don Francisco De Vargas), Thomas Gomez (Father Bartolome Romero), Alan Mowbray (Professor Botello), Barbara Lawrence (Luiza de Carvajal), George Zucco (Marquis de Carvajal), Roy Roberts (Capt. Alvarado), Marc Lawrence (Corio), Robert Karnes (Manuel Perez), Fred Libby (Soler), John Laurenz (Diego Cermeno), Virginia Brissac (Doña

Maria De Vargas), Dolly Arriaga (Mercedes De Vargas), Jay Silverheels (Coatl), Reed Hadley (Juan Escudero), Estela Inda (Doña Marina), Mimi Aguglia (Hernandez), Chris-Pin Martin (Sancho Lopez), Ed Mundy (Crier), Robert Adler (Reyes), Gilberto Gonzales (Aztec Ambassador), Harry Carter (Capt. Sandoval), Willie Calles (Aztec), Ramon Sanchez (Aztec), Bud Wolfe (Sailor), David Cato (Singer), Julian Rivero (Servant), John Burton (De Lora)

PLOT: Spain, 1518, the time of the Inquisition, is a country where people live in dread. Diego de Silva, the callous inquisitor-general, has quarreled with Pedro de Vargas and has ordered Pedro, his father, mother, and little sister to be brought before him as heretics. The little girl is tortured to death and the others imprisoned. Catana, a poor peasant girl in love with Pedro, induces her brother to take a job as a turnkey at the prison, and through the good offices of the jailer and Pedro's friend, Juan Garcia, acquires a key and a sword. When de Silva comes to mock him, Pedro turns on him and they fight a duel. Pedro is the conqueror, and he leaves de Silva stretched on the floor, believing him to be mortally wounded. The prison alarm is sounded but not before Pedro and Juan, followed by Catana, have made good their escape. Pedro's father and mother have been released and escorted out of the country. While Pedro, Juan, and Catana are discussing plans for the future, Juan suggests that they join Cortez, who is planning to go to the New World, where there are reputed to be boundless riches. Arriving in Cuba, Pedro and Juan decide to enlist in Cortez's army, which is about to invade Mexico to gather a fortune in jewels and gold. Instructed by Cortez to guard a treasure store, Pedro temporarily leaves his post to go to the aid of Juan, who has gone berserk. When he returns, the jewels are gone. Cortez furiously demands the return of the fortune within twenty-four hours, or else Pedro will pay with his life. Pedro traces the thieves to one of the ships of Cortez's fleet anchored off the coast. These traitors are some of Cortez's own men who have planned to sell their leader to the governor of Cuba. Pedro retrieves the jewels and returns them to Cortez. He is badly wounded in the process but is rewarded with a promotion to the rank of captain. To Pedro's horror, de Silva, whom he thought to be dead, arrives to extend the power of the Inquisition. Cortez deliberately gives Pedro the responsibility, under threat of execution, of seeing that no harm comes to their visitor. De Silva is later found dead, and Pedro is to die. To spare Pedro any further suffering, Catana plunges a knife into his breast just as Cortez enters to tell Pedro he is free, as an Indian has already confessed to the murder. Pedro recovers, and Cortez and his men renew their march across Mexico. Bringing up the rear is Catana with her newborn son.

REVIEWS:
"As a massive spectacle alone, this Technicolor production deserves [a] big rating, but it has an interesting story as well, with plentiful action, considerable human interest, and [a] generous share of romance." *Harrison's Reports*, November 29, 1947

"Readers of Samuel Shellabarger's spectacular *Captain from Castile* will be distressed to discover a rather pastel reflection of the book in 20th Century Fox's film version." *New York Times*, December 26, 1947

"*Captain from Castile* is a bountiful but confusing entertainment." *New York Herald Tribune*, December 26, 1947

REVIEWS for Jean Peters:
"Miss Peters is a flashy looker who handles the thesping needs competently." *Variety*, November 26, 1947

"Jean Peters, an attractive newcomer, shows herself to be [an] appealing and most convincing actress." *Hollywood Reporter*, November 26, 1947

"Romance plays its part, with a newcomer, Jean Peters, creating a very favorable impression as Catana, the tavern maid who follows the hero to the New World." *Los Angeles Times*, December 26, 1947

ADDITIONAL REVIEWS and ARTICLES:
Boxoffice Barometer, 1946; *Hollywood Reporter*, November 15, 1946, p. 9; *New York Times*, December 15, 1946, p. X5; *Newsweek*, January 31, 1947, p. 68; *Boxoffice*, May 7, 1947; *Photoplay*, May 1947, pp. 46–47; *American Cinematographer*, November 1947, p. 389; *Motion Picture Daily*, November 6, 1947, pp. 1, 8; *Film Daily*, November 26, 1947, p. 6; *Hollywood Reporter*, November 26, 1947, p. 3; *Variety*, November 26, 1947, p. 11; *Motion Picture Herald*, November 29, 1947, p. 3,953; *Showmen's Trade Review*, November 29, 1947, p. 20; *Modern Screen*, December 1947; *Boxoffice*, December 6, 1947, p. 880; *Pix* (Australia), December 13, 1947; *Commonweal*, December 19, 1947, p. 256; *New York Times*, December 21, 1947, p. X5; *Women's Wear Daily*, December 26, 1947, p. 41; *New York Daily Mirror*, December 28, 1947, p. 20; *This Year of Films* (UK), 1947; *Modern Screen*, January 1948, p. 18; *Movie Makers*, January 1948, p. 24; *Hollywood* (Italy), January 3, 1948, p. 10; *Daily Graphic* (UK), January 3, 1948, p. 5; *New Republic*, January 5, 1948, p. 32; *Time*, January 5, 1948, p. 71; *Scholastic*, January 12, 1948 p. 36; *Picturegoer* (UK), January 17, 1948, pp.

8–9; *Photoplay*, March 1948, p. 20; *American Cinematographer*, March 1948, pp. 80–81, 103; *Hollywood Reporter*, October 17, 1948 p. 1; *Hollywood* (Italy), January 29, 1949, pp. 11, 14; *Cinémonde* (France), January 24, 1949, p. 13; *Cinémonde* (France), January 31, 1949, p. 14; *L'Écran Français* (France), February 1, 1949, p. 12; *Today's Cinema*, April 8, 1949, p. 8; *The Times* (UK), April 11, 1949, p. 7; *Picturegoer* (UK), May 7, 1949, p. 17; *Focus*, June 1949, p. 149; *Mon Film* (France), October 5, 1949 p. 3; *Il Corriere della Sera* (Italy), October 1949, p. 2; *Photoplay* (UK), April 1982, p. 20; *American Cinematographer*, March 1998, pp. 98–104; *Music from the Movies*, February-March 2001, p. 49; *Film Score Monthly*, July 2003, p. 44

AWARDS and HONORS:
Academy Awards USA 1948; Nominated: Best Music, Scoring of a Dramatic or Comedy Picture: Alfred Newman

FILM NOTES: Composer Alfred Newman gave the rights to the film's stirring march to the University of Southern California to serve as the theme music for the football team.

Deep Waters

20th Century Fox Film Corporation—Darryl F. Zanuck
USA B&W 85 minutes
Premiered in New York City, July 22, 1948

CREDITS: *Producer*: Samuel G. Engel; *Director*: Henry King; *Screenplay*: Richard Murphy based on the novel *Spoonhandle* by Ruth Moore; *Director of Photography*: Joseph LaShelle, ASC; *Film Editors*: Barbara McLean, ACE, Gilbert Hackforth-Jones; *Music*: Cyril J. Mockridge; *Musical Direction*: Lionel Newman; *Orchestral Arrangements*: Maurice De Packh; *Art Direction*: Lyle Wheeler, George Davis; *Set Decorations*: Thomas Little; *Wardrobe Direction*: Charles LeMaire; *Make-up Artist*: Ben Naye; *Special Photographic Effects*: Fred Sersen; *Sound*: Bernard Freericks, Roger Heman Sr; *Assistant Director*: Joseph Behm

CAST: Dana Andrews (Hod Stillwell), Jean Peters (Ann Freeman), Cesar Romero (Joe Sangor), Dean Stockwell (Danny Mitchell), Anne Revere (Mary McKay), Ed Begley (Josh Hovey), Leona Powers (Mrs. Freeman), Mae Marsh (Molly Thatcher), Will Geer (Nick Driver), Bruno Wick (Druggist), Cliff

Clark (Harris), Harry Tyler (Hopkins), Raymond Greenleaf (Judge Tate), Eleanor Moore (Secretary), Harry Cooke (Bus Station Operator)

PLOT: Danny Mitchell, a twelve-year-old ward of the state who had run away from three homes, is taken by Ann Freeman to the home of Mary McKay, who agrees to take him on probation. The youngster makes friends with Hod Stillwell who, understanding the boy's love for the sea, hires him to work on his boat on Saturdays in an effort to rehabilitate him. The joy Danny feels after a day at sea with Hod soon turns into dejection when Ann, whose fear of the sea had caused her to break her engagement to Hod, forbids the lad to go to sea again on the grounds that it is too dangerous. The dispirited youngster decides to run away to Boston. He steals a camera and sells it to a pawn shop to obtain enough funds for the fare. But a mistaken belief that the robbery had been discovered causes him to panic, and he steals a motorboat and heads out to sea in the midst of a storm. He is spotted by Hod and Joe, who set off in pursuit and rescue him when the boat capsizes. Heeding Hod's advice, Ann agrees to permit Danny to work on the boat to keep him happy. But this time, the robbery is discovered and traced to Danny. The lad confesses and is taken to a reform school. Realizing that the boy has had a rough time in life and believing that there is much good in him, Hod enlists the aid of a local politician to secure his release and offers to adopt him. At a hearing before a judge, Ann and Mrs. McKay agree with Hod that he should be allowed to adopt the boy, with Ann explaining that she had made a mistake in trying to condition him for an island occupation when his love for the sea was so strong. The judge grants the petition, and Hod and Ann reconcile.

REVIEWS:
"*Deep Waters* . . . is a basically silly picture even though it was meant seriously." *New York Times*, July 23, 1948

"As a pure entertainment, [the] film is too somber-toned, and the subject presented doesn't always lend itself to more than average appeal." *Variety*, June 30, 1948

"Henry King's direction is solid though slow-paced." *Los Angeles Times*, July 17, 1948

REVIEWS for Jean Peters:
"Jean Peters [is] lovely to look at, plays the part of the social worker with utmost finesse." *Hollywood Reporter*, June 30, 1948

"Jean Peters . . . is natural and pleasing." *Harrison's Reports*, July 3, 1948

"Jean Peters is pleasant but unspectacular in the role of Ann." *Modern Screen*, September 1948

ADDITIONAL REVIEWS and ARTICLES:
Hollywood Reporter, December 24, 1946, p. 1; *Boxoffice*, September 13, 1947, p. 114; *Hollywood Reporter*, September 15, 1947, p. 9; *Hollywood Reporter*, September 17, 1947, p. 11; *Hollywood Reporter*, September 25, 1947, p. 12; *Hollywood Reporter*, October 15, 1947, pp. 1–2; *Hollywood Reporter*, October 27, 1947, p. 7; *Hollywood Reporter*, October 28, 1947, p. 2; *Hollywood Reporter*, December 3, 1947, p. 1; *Boxoffice*, December 27, 1947, p. 20; *Motion Picture Herald*, January 31, 1948, p. 4,039; *Daily Variety*, June 30, 1948, p. 3; *Motion Picture Herald*, July 3, 1948; *Boxoffice*, July 3, 1948 p. 948; *Motion Picture Herald*, July 3, 1948, p. 4,225; *Showmen's Trade Review*, July 3, 1948, pp. 31, 33; *Film Daily*, July 7, 1948, p. 14; *Newsweek*, July 12, 1948, p. 82; *Time*, July 12, 1948, p. 82; *Los Angeles Examiner*, July 17, 1948; *New York Herald Tribune*, July 23, 1948; *Cue*, July 24, 1948; *Hollywood Reporter*, July 27, 1948, p. 6; *New Yorker*, July 31, 1948, p. 40; *Photoplay*, September 1948, p. 24; *The Cinema* (UK), September 20, 1948, p. 6; *Today's Cinema* (UK), October 1, 1948; *Screenland*, October 1948, p. 14; *Monthly Film Bulletin* (UK), November 1948, p. 157; *Picturegoer* (UK), February 12, 1949, pp. 14–15; *Hollywood Reporter*, February 17, 1949, p. 9.

AWARDS and HONORS:
Academy Awards USA 1949; Nominated: Best Effects, Special Visual Effects: Ralph Hammeras, Fred Sersen, Edward Snyder; Special Audible Effects: Roger Heman

FILM NOTES: Alternative titles were *Spoonhandle, Fisherman Takes a Wife*, and *Deep Water*. Actress Donna Reed took Jean Peters's role in a *Lux Radio Theater* adaptation.

It Happens Every Spring

20th Century Fox Film Corporation
USA B&W 87 minutes
Premiered in St. Louis, MO, May 26, 1949
Opened in New York City, June 10, 1949

CREDITS: *Director*: Lloyd Bacon; *Producer*: William Perlberg; *Screenplay*: Valentine Davies from a story by Shirley W. Smith and Valentine Davis;

Director of Photography: Joe MacDonald, ASC; *Film Editor*: Bruce Pierce; *Art Direction*: Lyle Wheeler, J. Russell Spencer; *Set Decorations*: Thomas Little, Stuart Reiss; *Wardrobe Direction*; Charles LeMaire; *Costume Designer*: Bonnie Cashin; *Music*: Leigh Harline; *Musical Direction*: Lionel Newman; *Orchestration*: Edward Powell, Herbert Spencer; *Makeup Artist*: Ben Nye; *Special Photographic Effects*: Fred Sersen; *Sound*: Eugene Grossman, Harry M. Leonard

CAST: Ray Milland (Vernon Simpson aka King Kelly), Jean Peters (Deborah Greenleaf), Ray Collins (Prof. Greenleaf), Paul Douglas (Monk Lanigan), Ed Begley (Edgar Stone), Ted de Corsia (Manager Jimmy Dolan), Jessie Royce Landis (Mrs. Greenleaf), Alan Hale Jr. (Schmidt), Bill Murphy (Tommy Isbell), William E. Green (Prof. Forsythe), Debra Paget (Alice - College Coed), Robert Patten (Can Driver), Mae Marsh (Greenleaf's Maid), Gene Evans (Batter Mueller), Robert Adler (Reporter), Robert B. Williams (Reporter), Max Wagner (Umpire)

PLOT: A brilliant but penniless chemistry professor, Vernon Simpson, is in love with Debbie Greenleaf, daughter of the college president. He is working on an important experiment which, if successful, would bring him sufficient money to enable him to marry. One day, a baseball crashes through a window in the laboratory and smashes the beaker containing his precious fluid. But Vernon discovers an extraordinary fact—the mixture that has soaked into the leather has the effect of making the baseball repellent to wood. A wood-repellent baseball, thinks Vernon, would be a godsend to a pitcher in a season noted for its dearth of pitchers. Obtaining from the president an indefinite leave of absence to devote to "important experiments," Vernon goes to the St. Louis baseball team for a job as a pitcher. He receives short shrift until he prevails upon the manager to let him have a trial. Sure enough, nobody is able to hit his pitches as he's applied the fluid to the ball. Signing under the name of "Kelly," Vernon and his friend and roommate Monk Lanigan, who is the team's catcher, are a great success. Every match is won. A big diamond ring he sends to Debbie convinces Mrs. Greenleaf that Vernon has joined a gang of jewel thieves. Debbie runs into Vernon in St. Louis and will not believe him when he tells her that he is the St. Louis pitcher. Only when she goes to watch the team does she discover that he was telling the truth. In the World Series games, Vernon is dumbfounded to discover that his precious fluid has been used as a hair restorer by two of the team, and the remainder has been accidentally spilled into a wash basin. In the final innings, Vernon, with the magic formula gone, is hit all over the ground but wins the game with a brilliant catch, which breaks a bone in his hand. An X-ray reveals that his hand is so badly damaged that he will never be able to pitch again. Returning rather fearfully to college, he finds that the president, his wife, and Debbie have become ardent "Kelly" fans and Vernon is given a lucrative job as head of a new science laboratory.

REVIEWS:
"A highly amusing comedy." *Harrison's Reports*, May 7, 1949

"Like a pitcher who has but one fastball or one curve in his pitching repertoire, *It Happens Every Spring* . . . has but one cute idea." *New York Times*, June 11, 1949

"*It Happens Every Spring* is timely and antic." *New York Herald Tribune*, June 11, 1949

REVIEWS for Jean Peters:
"Jean Peters is . . . well cast as the girl." *Hollywood Reporter*, May 5, 1949

"Miss Peters demonstrates little thesping ability as Milland's vis-à-vis, but the part doesn't call for much, so she gets by." *Variety*, May 11, 1949.

"Miss Peters is decorative and efficient as the heroine." *Los Angeles Times*, June 18, 1949

ADDITIONAL REVIEWS and ARTICLES:
Los Angeles Times, November 13, 1948, p. 9; *Hollywood Reporter*, December 10, 1948, p. 15; *Motion Picture Daily*, March 17, 1949, p. 2; *Daily Variety*, May 5, 1949, p. 3; *Film Daily*, May 5, 1949, p. 6; *Women's Wear Daily*, May 5, 1949, p. 3; *Motion Picture Herald*, May 7, 1949, p. 4,597; *Motion Picture Daily*, May 13, 1949, p. 2; *Boxoffice*, May 14, 1949, p. 1,035; *Motion Picture Daily*, May 20, 1949, p. 3; *Motion Picture Daily*, May 26, 1949, p. 4; *Motion Picture Daily*, May 31, 1949, p. 3; *Time*, June 6, 1949, p. 97; *New Republic*, June 11, 1949, p. 22; *Cue*, June 11, 1949; *New York Journal of Commerce*, June 13, 1949; *Newsweek*, June 13, 1949, p. 85; *Women's Wear Daily*, June 13, 1949, p. 42; *Los Angeles Times*, June 14, 1949, p. A5; *New Yorker*, June 18, 1949, p. 52; *Michigan Today Summer*, 1949, p. 14; *Commonweal*, June 24, 1949, p. 272; *Seventeen*, July 1949, p. 20; *Christian Century*, July 20, 1949, p. 879; *Good Housekeeping*, August 1949, pp. 10–11; *Silver Screen*, August 1949, p. 13; *Screenland*, August 1949, p. 74; *Photoplay*, August 1949, p. 25; *Boxoffice*, August 20, 1949, p. 31; *Rotarian*,

September 1949, pp. 36–37; *Monthly Film Bulletin* (UK), December 1949, p. 217; *Kinematograph Weekly* (UK), December 15, 1949, p. 182; *Il Corriere della Sera* (Italy), June 28, 1950, p. 2; *Premiere*, March 1993, p. 97

AWARDS and HONORS:
Academy Awards USA 1950; Nominated: Best Writing, Motion Picture Story: Shirley W. Smith, Valentine Davies

Writers Guild of America; USA 1950; Nominated: Best Written American Comedy: Valentine Davies

FILM NOTES: Actress Colleen Townsend played Jean Peters's picture part in a *Lux Radio Theater* adaptation (10/3/49). Another version was broadcast on *Screen Directors' Playhouse* (4/14/50).

Love That Brute

20th Century Fox Film Corporation
USA B&W 85 minutes
Premiered in New York City, May 26, 1950

CREDITS: *Director*: Alexander Hall; *Producer*: Fred Kohlmar; *Screenplay*: Karl Tunberg, Darrell Ware, John Lee Mahin; *Director of Photography*: Lloyd Ahern, ASC; *Film Editor*: Nick DeMaggio; *Art Direction*: Lyle Wheeler, Richard Irvine; *Set Decorations*: Thomas Little, Stuart Reiss; *Wardrobe Direction*: Charles LeMaire; *Costume Designer*: Rene Hubert; *Music*: Cyril J. Mockridge; *Musical Direction*: Lionel Newman; *Orchestration*: Earle Hagen; *Choreography*: Billy Daniel; *Makeup Artist*: Ben Nye; *Special Photographic Effects*: Fred Sersen; *Sound*: Arthur Kirbach, Harry M. Leonard. *Songs*: "You Took Advantage of Me," sung by Jeri Sullavan, music by Richard Rodgers, lyrics by Lorenz Hart; "Lucky Day," music by Ray Henderson, lyrics by Buddy DeSylva and Lew Brown

CAST: Paul Douglas (Big Ed Hanley), Jean Peters (Ruth Manning), Cesar Romero (Pretty Willie Wetzchahofsky), Keenan Wynn (Bugs Welch), Joan Davis (Mamie Sage), Arthur Treacher (Quentin), Peter Price (Harry Jr. the Kid), Jay C. Flippen (Biff Sage), Barry Kelley (Detective Charlie "Burly"), Leon Belasco, (François Ducray "Frenchy"), Leif Erickson (Elmdale Military Academy Captain), Charles Evans (Ex-Governor Logan), Richard Allan (Backup Chorus Man, Paradise Club)

PLOT: In 1928, Big Ed Hanley, boss of a Chicago gang and racketeers, has money and power, but he's bored. Watching some kids in the park, he spots lovely Ruth Manning, who is in charge of the youngsters. Interested at once, he pretends he has a kid and gives her the job of taking care of him. He hires Harry, a pint-sized mobster, as his son and his friend Mamie as housekeeper. One night, a couple of boys sent by his archrival Pretty Willie show up to put Ed out of his misery, but Quentin, Ed's butler, and Bugs, his right-hand man, relieve them of their guns and send them down a stairway that supposedly leads to the river—but actually leads to a jail in the cellar where Ed keeps the guys he's supposed to have rubbed out. Ruth has by now taken quite a shine to Ed, but when Willie and his henchmen drop in, she finally realizes Ed is a gang leader. Ed convinces Willie that there's no need for bloodshed and agrees to split up the city into two areas—his and Willie's. Ruth leaves in a huff. But Ed, who knows she has singing ambitions, gets his Paradise Club to hire her. There's a party at Ed's place after Ruth's debut to celebrate the truce. In the middle of it, Ruth rushes in with the news that Harry has run away from school. Bugs tries to square things between Ruth and Ed by showing her the cellar full of Ed's unharmed victims. Ruth now realizes she's been mistaken, but Bugs has let Pretty Willie's boys escape, and with these new additions, Willie dissolves the partnership by taking Ed for a ride. However, the two henchmen, who are there to dispatch Big Ed, remember the gangster's past kindness and only pretend to kill him. Ed now shows up disguised at his own funeral. Willie is one of the pallbearers, but the cops come for him, accusing him of murdering Big Ed. Ruth is also a tearful spectator, but Ed sees her, tells her everything, and asks her to meet him at the lake boat that evening. He then talks Willie's henchmen into giving their boss away to the district attorney and as Willie is being escorted to jail, he shows himself to the unfortunate mobster when the detectives aren't around. Willie pleads not to go to jail for a murder he didn't commit, but Ed waves a cheery goodbye. Then he hurries to meet Ruth and start the new life they will lead together.

REVIEWS:
"A farce with plenty of sparkle and speed." *Variety*, May 10, 1950

"Not a world-beater by any means, [*Love That Brute*] is bright and breezy entertainment through most of its eighty-odd minutes' running time." *New York Times*, May 27, 1950

"Apart from a few macabre touches of humor . . . this burlesque of the gangster tradition falls flat." *Monthly Film Bulletin* (UK), October 1950

REVIEWS for Jean Peters:
"Jean Peters . . . matches her beauty with a smart, professional performance." *Hollywood Reporter*, May 10, 1950

"Miss Peters' wholesome charm and beauty are well exploited." *Los Angeles Times*, June 10, 1950

"Jean Peters is a ravishing Ruth." *Picturegoer* (UK), October 28, 1950

ADDITIONAL REVIEWS and ARTICLES:
Los Angeles Times, April 8, 1949, p. A6; *Hollywood Reporter*, June 17, 1949, p. 17; *Hollywood Reporter*, July 22, 1949, p. 13; *Silver Screen*, March 1950 p. 29; *Boxoffice*, April 26, 1950, p. 6; *Daily Variety*, May 10, 1950, p. 3; *Film Daily*, May 10, 1950, p. 7; *Motion Picture Herald*, May 13, 1950, p. 293; *Boxoffice*, May 13, 1950; *Harrison's Reports*, May 13, 1950, p. 6; *New York Daily News*, May 27, 1950, p. 26; *New York Herald Tribune*, May 27, 1950, p. 7; *Chicago Daily Tribune*, May 2, 1950; *Women's Wear Daily*, May 29, 1950, p. 32; *New York Times*, June 4, 1950, p. 1 sec. II; *Seventeen*, June 19, 1950, p. 89; *Newsweek*, June 19, 1950, 89; *Time*, June 26, 1950, p. 95; *Christian Century*, June 28, 1950; p. 800; *Rotarian*, June 1950, p. 44; *Good Housekeeping*, July 1950, p. 98; *Photoplay*, August 1950, p. 28; *Il Corriere della Sera* (Italy), August 27, 1950, p. 2; *Screenland*, September 1950, p. 15; *Modern Screen* September 1950, p. 20; Today's Cinema (UK), September 7, 1950; *L'Écran Français* (France), January 10, 1951, p. 8; *Focus*, March 1951, p. 89

FILM NOTES: *Love That Brute* was a remake of the 20th Century Fox film *Tall, Dark and Handsome* (1941). The picture's original title was *Turned Up Toes*.

Take Care of My Little Girl

20th Century Fox Film Corporation
USA Technicolor 93 minutes
Premiered in Los Angeles, July 6, 1951

CREDITS: *Producer*: Julian Blaustein; *Director*: Jean Negulesco; *Screenplay*: Julius J., Philip G. Epstein based on the novel *Take Care of My Little Girl* by Peggy Goodin; *Director of Photography*: Harry Jackson, ASC; *Art Direction*: Lyle Wheeler, Joseph C. Wright; *Set Decorations*: Thomas Little, Claude Carpenter; *Film Editor*: William Reynolds; *Wardrobe Direction*: Charles LeMaire; *Costumes*: Bill Travilla; *Music*: Alfred Newman; *Associate Music*

Director: Ken Darby; Orchestration: Edward Powell; *Makeup*: Ben Nye; *Special Photographic Effects*: Fred Sersen; *Sound*: George Leverett, Harry M. Leonard; *Assistant Director*: Art Lurker; *Technical Advisor*: Peggy Goodin; *Color Consultant*: Monroe W. Burbank; *Songs*: "The Lambs Are Coming," "The Old Maine Bell," "Here's to Our Lizzie," "Nighty Night, Delta Mu," "Sweet Dreams to You, Tri-U," "The Clasp of Hands," "Crown Us Gently, Gently," "To You, Sweetheart," "Lambs Are in the Clover," "Goodnight, Chi Eta, Goodnight," and "My Prince Will Come Riding," lyrics by Ken Darby

CAST: Jeanne Crain (Elizabeth Erickson), Dale Robertson (Joe Blake), Mitzi Gaynor (Adelaide Swanson), Jean Peters (Dallas Pruitt), Jeffrey Hunter (Chad Carnes), Betty Lynn (Marge Colby), Helen Westcott (Merry Coombs), Lenka Peterson (Ruth Gates), Carol Brannon (Casey Krause), Natalie Schafer (Mother Clark), Beverly Dennis (Janet Shaw), Kathleen Hughes (Jenny Barker), Peggy O'Connor (June), Marjorie Crosland (Olive Erickson), John Litel (John Erickson), Charlene Hardey (Ellie Stokes), Janet Stewart (Polly), Gail Davis (Thelma), Judy Walsh (Justine), Irene Martin (Marcia), Penny McGuiggan (Helen), Pattee Chapman (Paula), Mary Thomas (Vivian Brooks), Palma Shard (Georgette), Jean Romaine (Rosalyn), Margia Dean (Claire), William A. Mahan (Pete Grayson), June Alden (Girl in Gym), Billy Lechner (Bellboy), George Nader (Jack Gruber), Grandon Rhodes (Professor Benson), Harry Harvey (Clerk), Virginia Hunt (Lyn Hippenstahl), Eleanor Lawson (Freshman), Shirley Tegge (Freshman), Charles Conrad (Ticket Agent), Margaret Field (Girl), King Donovan (Cab Driver), Pat Goldin (Porter)

PLOT: Lovely Liz Erickson and her hometown friend Janet Shaw, who is plain-looking and from humbler stock, are deeply impressed with Midwestern University on their arrival as freshmen. At the hotel in town, they meet Adelaide Swanson, the breezy daughter of a wealthy Western businessman. Liz soon gets an invitation from Marge Colby to visit her at Tri U House. The Tri U president, snobbish Dallas Pruitt, greets the freshmen with an eye to weeding out the girls they want to pledge. Liz is accepted, but not Janet, who is brokenhearted and goes home. Meanwhile, Liz has been taken out by Joe Blake, a senior undergraduate who fought in the war and doesn't belong to a fraternity. Liz then meets Chad Carnes, an undergraduate with a reputation, but she loyally asks Joe to be her partner at the Christmas dance. One day, Chad asks for Liz's help. It is important for him to graduate, and he finds he is unable to do justice to the French paper. Through Liz's intervention and help, he manages to switch examination papers.

Chad, deeply grateful, gives her his fraternity pin. When the initiation week comes along, the pledges have to go through many embarrassing ordeals. One evening Liz, who is given a task, meets Joe, who persuades her to drop into a non-fraternity gathering where a party is taking place. Chad crashes in and accuses Liz of being unfaithful to her sorority. Chad and Joe come to blows. Chad is knocked down by Joe and leaves. Liz takes off the fraternity pin Chad has given her and leaves it on the mantelpiece. When she arrives home, Liz discovers that there is some concern about Ruth, a shy, plain girl who had been asked to renounce her pledge to Tri U. Liz and Joe find her in the street trying to fulfill her pledge duties. She is in a state of collapse. When they get Ruth home and a doctor is sent for, it is found that she has pneumonia. Liz threatens to turn in her sorority pin, but Dallas and the president promise that if she agrees not to do this, Ruth will be welcomed back when she recovers. But Liz has had enough of sororities. She shakes her head, gives up her pin, and joins Joe, who is waiting for her outside. (Original press release source)

REVIEWS:
"Although the story is treated in a serious vein, it does have its light touches throughout and is further enhanced by a pleasant romantic interest . . . a diverting entertainment." *Harrison's Reports*, June 16, 1951

"Lightweight story has a script, however, that has fresh situations and some good dialog; plus an engaging cast of attractive youngsters . . . enhanced by Technicolor." *Variety*, July 13, 1951

REVIEWS for Jean Peters:
"Jean Peters, a gorgeous beauty, plays the top snob of the bunch to near perfection." *Hollywood Reporter*, June 12, 1951

"Miss Jean Peters looks and acts the parts." *Pittsburgh Post-Gazette*, July 2, 1951

"Jean Peters is familiarly top-lofty as the coldest and meanest sorority girl. *New York Times*, July 19, 1951

ADDITIONAL REVIEWS and ARTICLES:
Hollywood Reporter, February 28, 1950 p. 2; *New York Herald Tribune*, September 25, 1950; *Hollywood Reporter*, October 12, 1950, p. 6; *Hollywood Reporter*, October 13, 1950, p. 13, *Hollywood Reporter*, November 10, 1950,

p. 13; *Hollywood Reporter*, November 13, 1950, p. 6; *Daily Variety*, December 13, 1950; *Hollywood Reporter*, December 26, 1950, p. 7; *Screenland*, April 1951, p. 28; *McCall's*, May 1951, pp. 28–29; *Modern Screen*, May 1951, p. 104; *Scholastic*, May 2 1951; *Hollywood Reporter*, May 2, 1951, p. 2; *Saturday Review*, June 2, 1951; *Look*, June 5, 1951, p. 40–43; *Film Daily*, June 13, 1951, p. 7; *Daily Boston Globe*, June 16, 1951; *Boxoffice*, June 16, 1951, p. 1,269; *Motion Picture Herald*, June 16, 1951, p. 887; *Photoplay*, July 1951, p. 25; *Screenland*, July 1951, p. 16; *Los Angeles Examiner*, July 7, 1951; *Los Angeles Times*, July 7, 1951; *Hollywood Citizen-News*, July 10, 1951; *Chicago Daily Tribune*, July 16, 1951, p. A4; *Newsweek*, July 16, 1951, p. 85; *New York Times*, July 18, 1951, p. 20; *Hollywood Reporter*, July 19, 1951, p. 1; *Motion Picture Daily*, July 19, 1951, p. 2; *New York Herald Tribune*, July 19, 1951; *Time*, July 23, 1951, p. 84; *Commonweal*, July 27, 1951; *New Yorker*, July 28, 1951, p. 74; *The Nation*, August 11, 1951 p. 118; *Picturegoer* (UK), February 9, 1952; *Modern Screen*, June 1952, p. 56; *Saturday Evening Post*, September 27, 1952; *Modern Screen*, January 1953, p. 47

FILM NOTES: Jeanne Crain and Dale Robertson reprised their roles for a *Lux Radio Theater* broadcast of the story (2/4/52).

As Young as You Feel

20th Century Fox Film Corporation
USA B&W 70 minutes
Premiered in Los Angeles, June 15, 1951
Premiered in New York City, August 2, 1951

CREDITS: *Director*: Harmon Jones; *Producer*: Lamar Trotti; *Screenwriter*: Lamar Trotti, based on an original story by Paddy Chayefsky; *Director of Photography*: Joseph MacDonald, ASC; *Film Editor*: Robert Simpson; *Art Direction*, Lyle Wheeler, Maurice Ransford; *Set Decorations*: Thomas Little, Bruce MacDonald; *Wardrobe Direction*: Charles LeMaire; *Costume Designer*: Renié; *Music*: Cyril J. Mockridge; *Musical Direction*: Lionel Newman; *Orchestration*; Maurice De Packh; *Makeup Artist*: Ben Nye; *Special Photographic Effects*: Fred Sersen; *Sound*: W. D. Flick, Roger Heman

CAST: Monty Wooley (John Hodges), Thelma Ritter (Della Hodges), David Wayne (Joe Elliot), Jean Peters (Alice Hodges), Constance Bennett (Lucille McKinley), Marilyn Monroe (Harriet), Allyn Joslyn (George Hodges), Albert Dekker (Louis McKinley), Clinton Sundberg (Frank Erickson), Minor Watson (Harold P. Cleveland), Wally Brown (Horace Gallagher), Rusty Tamblyn (Willie McKinley)

PLOT: John Hodges enjoys working as a hand printer in a factory and is upset when, on turning sixty-five, he learns that the company policy obliges him to retire. Dying his beard, he poses as the head of the corporation that owns the company he works for. (He has established that nobody knows what the real corporation head looks like.) He is received by his own company boss, Mr. McKinley, and during his tour of the premises, he impresses everyone with his shrewd comments, but he has one complaint to make and that is about the mandatory retirement age. He is assured this will be changed. He is taken to a lunch given in his honor at the chamber of commerce and his speech there, championing the older workforce, is met with approval by industry, the press and the public. Finally, he dines at McKinley's house and goes out with McKinley and his unhappily married wife, whom Hodges dances with, admires, and charms. The consequences of his deception soon mount up. The man he is imitating faces a dilemma, as the sentiments about valuing the expertise of senior workers have proven popular and vastly beneficial for the corporation, even resolving its problems with the unions, so he is reluctant to admit they were not really his idea. Members of the Personnel department at Hodges's company are torn between revealing that they have been duped and keeping it a shameful secret. The police try to track down the impostor. Mrs. McKinley leaves her unromantic husband and declares her love for Hodges. Amidst all the hullabaloo, Hodges just wants to go back to work and see everything settle down.

REVIEWS:
"[As Young as You Feel] is a family-type comedy that keeps one chuckling throughout for the situations, though not hilarious, are amusing." *Harrison's Reports*, June 9, 1951

"Superior cast fails to save comedy." *Chicago Daily Tribune*, June 19, 1951

"A few sparks of humor fly off on its erratic course, but *As Young as You Feel* [is] a mildly diverting nonsense that is disappointing only because it misses by such a narrow margin." *New York Herald Tribune*, August 3, 1951

REVIEWS for Jean Peters:
"Jean Peters is charming as Thelma [Ritter]'s daughter." *Hollywood Reporter*, June 5, 1951

"Faring better are David Wayne and Jean Peters." *Variety*, June 6, 1951

"Jean Peter is nice as [the] granddaughter." *New York Times*, August 3, 1951

ADDITIONAL REVIEWS and ARTICLES:
Los Angeles Examiner, October 27, 1950; *Hollywood Reporter*, October 31, 1950, p. 1; *Hollywood Reporter*, November 10, 1950, p. 6; *Hollywood Reporter*, December 15, 1950, p. 10; *Hollywood Reporter*, January 19, 1951, p. 13; *Library Journal*, June 1, 1951, p. 972; *Daily Variety*, June 5, 1951, p. 3; *Motion Picture Daily*, June 5, 1951, p. 6; *Boxoffice*, June 9, 1951, p. 1,297; *Motion Picture Herald*, June 9, 1951, p. 878; *Chicago Daily Tribune*, June 11, 1951, p. D4; *Chicago Daily Tribune*, June 12, 1951, p. A5; *Film Daily*, June 13, 1951, p. 6; *Chicago Daily Tribune*, June 13, 1951, p. B5; *Los Angeles Examiner*, June 16, 1951; *Los Angeles Times*, June 16, 1951, p. 9; *Photoplay*, July 1951, p. 30; *Today's Cinema* (UK), July 5, 1951 p. 6; *Christian Century*, July 11, 1951, p. 831; *Newsweek*, July 23, 1951, p. 84; *The Times* (UK), July 23, 1951, p. 2; *Hollywood Reporter*, July 26, 1951, p. 5; *The New Statesman and Nation*, July 28, 1951, pp. 97–98; *Monthly Film Bulletin* (UK), August 1951, p. 310; *Screenland*, August 1951, p. 73; *Modern Screen*, August 1951, p. 16; *New York Daily News*, August 3, 1951, p. 13C; *Picturegoer* (UK), August 18, 1951, p. 17; *Washington Post*, August 31, 1951, p. 21; *Focus*, September 1951, p. 257; *Cinémonde* (France), April 18, 1952, p. 13; *Films in Review*, November 1987, p. 527

FILM NOTES: Working titles were *The Great American Hoax* and *Will You Love Me in December?* The story was later filmed for TV as *The Great American Hoax* (1957).

Anne of the Indies

20th Century Fox Film Corporation
USA Technicolor 81 minutes
Premiered in New York City, October 24, 1951

CREDITS: *Director*: Jacques Tourneur; *Producer*: George Jessel; *Screenplay*: Philip Dunne, Arthur Caesar, based on an original short story in *The Saturday Evening Post* by Herbert Ravenel Sass; *Director of Photography*: Harry Jackson; *Film Editor*: Robert Fritch; *Art Directors*: Lyle Wheeler, Albert Hogsett; *Set Decorations*: Thomas Little, Claude Carpenter; *Music*: Franz Waxman; *Orchestration*: Edward Powell; *Wardrobe Direction*: Charles LeMaire; *Costume Designer*: Edward Stevenson; *Makeup Artist*: Ben Nye; *Special Photographic Effects*: Fred Sersen; *Sound*: E. Clayton Ward, Harry M. Leonard; *Technicolor Color Consultant*: Leonard Doss; *Assistant Director*: Horace Hough

CAST: Jean Peters (Capt. Anne Providence), Louis Jourdan (Capt. Pierre Francois LaRochelle), Debra Paget (Molly LaRochelle), Herbert Marshall (Dr. Jameson), Thomas Gomez (Capt. Edward Teach aka Blackbeard), James Robertson Justice (Red Dougal), Francis Pierlot (Herkimer), Sean McClory (Hackett), Holmes Herbert (British Sea Captain), Byron Nelson (Bear Handler), Douglas Bennett (Bear Wrestler), Marco Siletti (Slave Market Auctioneer), Bob Stephenson (Tavern Host), Carleton Young (Pirate Mate)

PLOT: Captain Anne Providence helms one of the most dreaded pirate vessels in the Caribbean, the *Sheba Queen*. The French Navy is determined to destroy her and devises a scheme whereby an officer, Pierre LaRochelle, is signed on as a member of her crew. Blackbeard, Anne's instructor since childhood, suspects him and falls out with Anne over it since she is by now in love with Pierre. Intrigue, adventure, love, and betrayal follow, ending in a spectacular sea battle in which Anne, disappointed in love and loyalty, engages the mighty Blackbeard's vessel and goes down in flames.

REVIEWS:
"A handy package of escapism filled with good commercial value . . . a lot of action into that comparatively brief space . . . casting also is top-notch, particularly in the title role." *Variety*, October 17, 1951

"Despite all the axioms about the female being deadlier than the male, the script puts too great a strain on adult credulity." *New York Herald Tribune*, August 10, 1951

"The action is swift and continuous so that it can be said there is never a dull moment." *Focus*, March 1952

REVIEWS for Jean Peters:
"Miss Peters, as tough as Long John Silver and as agile with the sword as Monte Cristo, is almost the whole show, and her performance surely establishes her as an actress about to enter the big box-office leagues." *Hollywood Reporter*, October 15, 1951

"Jean Peters is surprisingly convincing in the title role of the lady—if the term may be used a bit loosely—buccaneer." *Boxoffice*, October 20, 1951

"Jean Peters, who plays her part without adornments or makeup, almost indeed excels Gregory Peck in the ability to command, fight, and frown with horrid asperity." *Monthly Film Bulletin* (UK), November 1951

ADDITIONAL REVIEWS and ARTICLES:
New York Times, February 27, 1948, p. 26; *New York Times*, August 10, 1948, p. 18; *Hollywood Reporter*, January 31, 1951, p. 6; *Hollywood Reporter*, February 23, 1951, p. 13; *Hollywood Reporter*, February 27, 1951, p. 13; *Hollywood Reporter*, April 6, 1951, p. 11; *Hollywood Reporter*, May 2, 1951, p. 2; *Today's Cinema*, October 12, 1951, p. 1; *Daily Variety*, October 15, 1951, p. 3; *Film Daily*, October 18, 1951 p. 10; *Motion Picture Daily*, October 19, 1951; *Motion Picture Herald*, October 20, 1951, p. 1,065; *Harrison's Reports*, October 20, 1951, p. 166; *Women's Wear Daily*, October 22, 1951, p. 43; *New York Times*, October 25, 1951 p. 36; *Picturegoer* (UK), November 3, 1951, p. 5; *Chicago Daily Tribune*, November 5, 1951, p. D4; *Chicago Daily Tribune*, November 6, 1951, p. A5; *Chicago Daily Tribune*, November 7, 1951, p. B3; *Los Angeles Times*, November 8, 1951, p. A10; *Sunday News*, November 11, 1951, p. 32; *Los Angeles Times*, November 15, 1951, p. A11; *Chicago Daily Tribune*, November 23, 1951, p. D4; *Film Bulletin*, December 3, 1951, p. 15; *Christian Century*, December 26, 1951, p. 152; *The Times* (UK), February 4, 1951, p. 8; *Daily Express* (UK), February 6, 1952; *Picture Show* (UK), February 16, 1952, pp. 9–10; *Picturegoer* (UK), February 16, 1952, p. 13; *Il Corriere della Sera* (Italy), May 7, 1952, p. 2; *Cinémonde* (France), July 4, 1952, p. 26; *Cinémonde* (Italy), September 19, 1952, p. 16; *Positif* (France), January 2004, pp. 78–79; *CinémAction* (France), June 2006, pp. 168–17, 172–80; *Positif* (France), July 2010, pp. 50–51; *Positif* (France), November 2019, p. 81

FILM NOTES: Patricia Neal and Valentina Cortese were also screen tested for the title role.

Viva Zapata!

20th Century Fox Film Corporation
USA B&W 113 minutes
Premiered in New York City, February 7, 1952
Premiered in Los Angeles, March 12, 1952
Premiered in London, April 3, 1952

CREDITS: *Director*: Elia Kazan; *Producer*: Darryl F. Zanuck; *Screenplay*: John Steinbeck, based on the book *Zapata the Unconquerable* by Edgcomb Pinchon; *Director of Photography*: Joseph MacDonald, ASC; *Special Photographic Effects*: Fred Sersen; *Film Editor*: Barbara McLean, ACE; *Art Directors*: Lyle Wheeler, Leland Fuller; *Set Decorators*: Claude Carpenter, Thomas Little; *Costume Design*: Bill Travilla; *Wardrobe Director*: Charles LeMaire; *Makeup Artist*: Ben Nye; *Music*: Alex North; *Music Director*: Alfred Newman;

Orchestrations: Maurice De Packh; *Sound*: Roger Heman, W. D. Flick; *Technical Advisers*: Prof. Sologuren, Juan José Segura; *Interpreter*: Tina Menard; *2nd Unit Director*: Robert Snody; *Assistant Director*: Horace Hough; *Assistant to Mr. Kazan*: Guy Thomajan; *Script Supervisor*: Stanley Scheuer

CAST: Marlon Brando (Emiliano Zapata), Jean Peters (Josefa Espejo Zapata), Anthony Quinn (Eufemio Zapata), Joseph Wiseman (Fernando Aguirre), Arnold Moss (Don Nacio), Alan Reed (Pancho Villa), Margo (Soldarera), Harold Gordon (Francisco Indalecio Madero), Lou Gilbert (Pablo), Frank Silvera (Victoriano Huerta), Florenz Ames (Señor Espejo), Richard Garrick (Old General), Fay Roope (Porfirio Díaz), Mildred Dunnock (Señora Espejo), Nina Varela (Aunt), Bernie Gozier (Zapatista), Will Kuluva (Lazaro), Frank De Kova (Colonel Jesús Guajardo), Pedro Regas (Innocente), Ross Bagdasarian (Officer), Leonard George (Husband), Abner Biberman (Captain), Philip Van Zandt (C.O.), Guy Thomas (Eduardo), Fernanda Eliscu (Fuente's Wife), Lisa Fusaro (Garcia's Wife), Belle Mitchell (Nacio's Wife), Henry Silva (Hernandez)

PLOT: At the turn of the century, a delegation of Mexican peons, led by Emiliano Zapata, protests to President Diaz about the seizure of their lands by "the big estates." Diaz, a tyrant ruler for thirty-four years, refuses to remedy the injustice. Realizing they must take matters into their own hands, Zapata and his brother Eufemio lead the Morelos villagers in cutting fences to restore their rightful property. The peons are met by soldiers, and a bloody battle ensues. Now a hunted man, Emiliano is urged by his aides, Pablo and Fernando Aguirre, to join up with Francisco Madero, the revolutionary leader of the north, who is in Texas plotting the overthrow of Diaz's corrupt government. Meanwhile, Senorita Josefa Espejo, the girl with whom Emiliano is in love, refutes his ideas of revolution and tells him that she will only marry a man of wealth and social position. Open rebellion, however, leaves him no choice. For days, soldiers are ambushed, their guns are taken, and ammunition trains are wrecked and looted. Madero names Zapata as the general of the Armies of the South. With the prestige of such a title, Emiliano calls on Josefa and, at last, she realizes her love for him. Their wedding takes place, and word comes that Diaz has fled the country. As abuses continue, Emiliano realizes that Madero is not a better ruler than Diaz. Madero, however, rules only for a short time as political intrigue sends him to his doom. Pancho Villa, another of Madero's generals, enters Mexico City and appoints Zapata president. Convinced that there is no one else, Emiliano reluctantly assumes office. The semi-educated Zapata soon discovers that he cannot endure the devilry of political dealings and returns to Morelos despite Fernando's warning that his enemies will take over once he leaves. Fernando's words ring true as federal soldiers begin to pillage the countryside. The peons flee to the hills to join Zapata's guerrilla army, and his name becomes synonymous with freedom. Emiliano, however, is betrayed by Fernando. He is lured to an old hacienda to meet a general who promises to aid his cause. In the courtyard, a volley of bullets splits the silence, and he falls dead. For years afterward, the oppressed peons of Mexico believed that Zapata was still alive; for some, he would never die.

REVIEWS:
"A stirring and thrilling historical melodrama." *Harrison's Reports*, February 9, 1952

"Authentically staged, finely directed, and acted convincingly. It has plenty of action, a fair measure of romance." *Motion Picture Daily*, February 6, 1952

"John Steinbeck's script for this interesting but unsuccessful film is scrappily constructed and often confusing." *Monthly Film Bulletin* (UK), April 1952

REVIEWS for Jean Peters
"Jean Peters is warm and appealing in the romantic lead." *Hollywood Reporter*, February 6, 1952

"Miss Peters, although costarring, hasn't too much opportunity to inject warmth and feeling into the footage." *Variety*, February 6, 1952

"Jean Peters is as good as she can be as the proper young lady of the village who hooks up with the wild man of the hills." *New York Times*, February 8, 1952

ADDITIONAL REVIEWS and ARTICLES:
New York Times, September 25, 1940, p. 41; *Hollywood Reporter*, March 17, 1941, p. 1; *Saturday Review*, March 1, 1942, p. 6; *New York Times*, August 31, 1947, p. X3; *Hollywood Reporter*, September 22, 1947, p. 1; *Hollywood Reporter*, November 11, 1948, p. 3; *Los Angeles Times*, November 11, 1948, p. 25; *Hollywood Reporter*, January 12, 1949, p. 1; *New York Times*, January 12, 1949; *Los Angeles Examiner*, January 13, 1949; *Hollywood Reporter*, February 27, 1950, p. 4; *Hollywood Reporter*, March 2, 1951, p. 4; *Hollywood Reporter*, March 19, 1951, p. 2; *Hollywood Reporter*, March 27, 1951, p. 2; *Hollywood Reporter*, March 30,

1951, p. 2; *Hollywood Reporter*, April 23, 1951, p. 2; *Hollywood Reporter*, April 30, 1951, p. 2; *Hollywood Reporter*, May 10, 1951, p. 3; *Hollywood Reporter*, May 21, 1951, pp. 3, 8; *Hollywood Reporter*, May 28, 1951, p. 4; *Hollywood Reporter*, May 31, 1951, p. 4; *Hollywood Reporter*, June 6, 1951, p. 4; *New York Times*, June 17, 1951, sec. II p. 5; *Hollywood Reporter*, June 19, 1951, p. 4; *Hollywood Reporter*, July 2, 1951, p. 3; *Hollywood Reporter*, July 5, 1951, p. 4; *Los Angeles Daily News*, July 5, 1951; *Hollywood Reporter*, July 17, 1951, p. 4; *Hollywood Reporter*, July 18, 1951, p. 6; *Hollywood Reporter*, July 23, 1951, p. 6; *Hollywood Reporter*, July 27, 1951, pp. 5, 11; *Hollywood Reporter*, August 3, 1951 p. 6; *Hollywood Reporter*, January 23, 1952, p. 1; *Argosy*, February 1952; *Hollywood Reporter*, February 1, 1952 p. 1; *New York Times*, February 3, 1952, sec. VI pp. 46, 47; *New York Herald Tribune*, February 3, 1952, p. D3; *Newsweek*, February 4, 1952, p. 78; *Daily Variety*, February 6, 1952, p. 3; *Film Daily*, February 6, 1952, p. 6; *New York Times*, February 7, 1952 p. 3; *Hollywood Reporter*, February 8, 1952, p. 1; *Women's Wear Daily*, February 8, 1952, p. 48; *New York Herald Tribune*, February 8, 1952, p. 15; *Boxoffice*, February 9, 1952, pp. 24, 1,341; *Motion Picture Herald*, February 9, 1952, p. 1,229; *Saturday Review*, February 9, 1952, p. 25; *Cue*, February 9, 1952, p. 16; *Time*, February 11, 1952, pp. 92, 97; *Hollywood Reporter*, February 12, 1952, p. 5; *Library Journal*, February 15, 1952, p. 311; *Saturday Review*, February 16, 1952, p. 6; *New Yorker*, February 16, 1952, p. 105; *New York Times*, February 17, 1952, sec. II p. 1; *Washington Post*, February 23, 1952, p. 8; *New Republic*, February 25, 1952, p. 21; *Hollywood Reporter*, February 25, 1952, p. 2; *Life*, February 25, 1952, p. 61; *Film Bulletin*, February 25, 1952, p. 10; *Commonweal*, February 29, 1952, p. 517; *Catholic World*, March 1952, p. 459; *Seventeen*, March 1, 1952, p. 16; *Films in Review*, March 1952, p. 132; *Hollywood Reporter*, March 3, 1952 p. 6; *Scholastic*, March 5, 1952, p. 26; *Variety*, March 5, 1952, p. 9; *Hollywood Reporter*, March 6, 1952, p. 2; *Today's Cinema* (UK), March 6, 1952, p. 14; *Hollywood Reporter*, March 12, 1952, p. 6; *Hollywood Citizen-News*, March 13, 1952; *The Times* (UK), March 31, 1952, p. 311; *American Cinematographer*, April 1, 1952, pp. 154–55, 183; *Cosmopolitan*, April 1952, p. 129; *Photoplay*, April 1952, p. 33; *Modern Screen*, April 1952, p. 93; *Picturegoer* (UK), April 5, 1952, p. 16; *Saturday Review*, April 5, 1952, p. 22; *The Tatler* (UK), April 9, 1952, p. 82; *Illustrated London News* (UK), April 19, 1952, p. 676; *Christian Century*, April 23, 1952, p. 510; *Picturegoer* (UK), April 26, 1952, pp. 12–13; *Holiday*, May 1952, p. 105; *Focus*, May 1952, p. 113; *Hollywood Reporter*, May 13, 1952, p. 4; *Saturday Review*, May 24, 1952, p. 25; *Sight and Sound* (UK), April/June 1952, p. 170; *Hollywood Reporter*, August 13, 1952 p. 2; *Variety*, September 3, 1952, p. 2; *Il Corriere della Sera* (Italy), September 13, 1952, p. 2; *Cahiers du Cinéma* (France), January 1953; *Hollywood Reporter*, March 13, 1953, p. 3; *Saturday Evening Post*, June 6, 1953, pp. 16–30;

New York Times, December 16, 1956, p. X7; *Image et Son* (France), July 1958, p. 48; *Image et Son* (France), April 1959, p. 11; *Movie Winter*, 1972, pp. 19–20; *Cinéaste*, February 1976, pp. 10–17; *Positif* (France), February 1976, pp. 49–53; *Film and History*, May 1977, pp. 25–33, 45; *Positif* (France), April 1981, pp. 15–18; *The Listener* (UK), March 30, 1989, p. 36; *Film History Summer*, 1996, pp. 109–30; *DGA Quarterly*, Autumn 2010, pp. 62–69

AWARDS and HONORS:
Academy Awards USA 1953; winner: Best Actor in a Supporting Role: Anthony Quinn; nominated: Best Actor in a Leading Role: Marlon Brando; Best Writing, Story and Screenplay: John Steinbeck; Best Art Direction/ Set Decoration, Black and White: Lyle R. Wheeler, Leland Fuller, Thomas Little, Claude E. Carpenter; Best Music, Scoring of a Dramatic or Comedy Picture: Alex North

BAFTA Awards; UK 1953; winner: Best Foreign Actor: Marlon Brando, USA; Nominated: Best Film from Any Source USA

Cannes Film Festival; France 1952; winner: Best Actor: Marlon Brando; Nominated: Grand Prize of the Festival: Elia Kazan

Directors Guild of America; USA 1953, nominated: Outstanding Directorial Achievement in Motion Pictures: Elia Kazan

Golden Globes; USA 1953: nominated: Best Supporting Actress: Mildred Dunnock

International Film Music Critics Award, USA 1998
Nominee, Best New Recording of a Previously Existing Score: Alex North, conducted by Jerry Goldsmith/Royal Scottish National Orchestra

FILM NOTES: *Viva Zapata!* had several different working titles, including *Emiliano Zapata, The Beloved Tiger; The Life of Emiliano Zapata; Zapata, The Little Tiger; The Tiger;* and *Zapata.*

Wait 'Till the Sun Shines, Nellie

20th Century Fox Film Corporation
USA Technicolor 108 minutes
World premiere in Hutchinson, Kansas, May 14, 1952

Premiered in New York City, June 27, 1952

CREDITS: *Director*: Henry King; *Producer*: George Jessel; *Screenplay*: Allan Scott; *Adaptation*: Allan Scott, Maxwell Shane, based on the novel *I Heard Them Sing* by Ferdinand Reyher; *Director of Photography*: Leon Shamroy, ASC; *Technicolor Color Consultant:* Leonard Doss; *Special Photographic Effects*: Ray Kellogg; *Film Editor*: Barbara McLean, ACE; *Art Directors*: Lyle Wheeler, Maurice Ransford; *Set Decorators*: Thomas Little, Claude Carpenter; *Costume Designer*: Renié; *Wardrobe Director*: Charles LeMaire; *Makeup Artist*: Ben Nye; *Music*: Alfred Newman; *Orchestrations*: Edward B. Powell; *Vocal Director*: Eliot Daniel; *Sound*: E. Clayton Ward, Roger Heman; *Assistant Director*: Henry Weinberger

CAST: Jean Peters (Nellie Jordan Halper), David Wayne (Ben Halper), Hugh Marlowe (Ed Jordan), Albert Dekker (Lloyd Slocum), Helene Stanley (Eadie Jordan), Tommy Morton (Benny Halper Jr., age twenty), Joyce Mackenzie (Bessie Jordan), Alan Hale Jr. (George Oliphant), Richard Karlan (Mike Kava), Jim Maloney (Austin Burdge), Merry Anders (Adeline Halper), Warren Stevens (McCauley), Charles Watts (Mr. Burdge), David Wolfe (Sam Eichenbogen), Dan White (Doc Thomas), Erik Nielsen (Ben Halper, age eight), Jerrylyn Flannery (Nellie Foster Halper, age five), Noreen Corcoran (Adeline Halper, age six), William Walker ("Trooper" Robert Waverly), James Griffith (Ollie), Tony Barr (Broidy), Kermit Echols (Hotel Clerk), Eugene Mazola (Ben Jr., ages two to four), Maude Pickett (Mrs. Burdge), Mary Hain (Adeline, age two)

PLOT: As the town of Sevillinois celebrates its fiftieth anniversary, Ben Halper, who is sitting in a barbershop being shaved, carries his mind back over the past half-century. He had married a pretty spirited girl, Nellie, who could not hide her disappointment when they first moved to Sevillinois, a place as small as their hometown. There, Ben acquires his own barbershop without her knowledge. When business prospers, Ben buys a picturesque little house. Nellie disapproves of the purchase since she has never given up the idea of moving to Chicago. However, all is forgiven when she announces her pregnancy. Meanwhile, Ed Jordan, who runs the local hardware store, shows his interest in Nellie. When Ben enlists in the US Army in the Spanish-American war, Ed tries his best to comfort Nellie, who agrees to accompany him on a trip to Chicago. Ben, in camp, is notified that his wife has been killed in a train accident in Chicago. Immediately released from the Army, Ben returns home, where he is told that Nellie has gone away with Ed, who also lost his life. Left with his son, Benny, and Adeline, his daughter born to Nellie while he was in the Army, Ben starts to drink heavily, but helped by his friends, he pulls himself together. One day, Ben's barbershop is burnt to the ground, but with a bank loan, he is able to build a bigger, more modern shop. When 1917 comes, Benny, who is now a wild young man, much to Ben's annoyance, starts dating Eddie, Ed Jordan's daughter. Knowing that his father does not approve, Benny runs away with Eddie to be married. The two become a successful variety act, but it is only after Benny joins the Army in the First World War and they become parents that Ben forgives them. Upon his return from the war, Benny joins his father's barbershop but he's unhappy and later gets involved in a shady insurance company run by a gangster named Kava. Eventually, Kava and Benny are both killed by a rival gang. Grief-stricken, Ben finds comfort in his granddaughter and spends the following years caring for her. Now, fifty years have passed, and reporters come around for reminiscences; Ben and other old inhabitants of Sevillinois lead the anniversary parade.

REVIEWS:
"A sincere and unpretentious picture." *Picturegoer* (UK), July 13, 1952

"A surprisingly nice little film." *Washington Post*, July 26, 1952

"*Wait 'Till the Sun Shines, Nellie* is long on nostalgia and even longer in running time." *Newsweek*, June 23, 1952

REVIEWS for Jean Peters:
"Miss Peters is appealing and effectively fiery as Nellie." *Hollywood Reporter*, May 26, 1952

"Miss Peters gives a satisfactory account of herself as the wife, although with shorter footage than that allotted her costar." *Variety*, May 28, 1952

"Jean Peters is pouty and pretentious as the unfaithful wife." *New York Times*, June 28, 1952

ADDITIONAL REVIEWS and ARTICLES:
Daily Variety, October 16, 1946; *Daily Variety*, December 4, 1946; *Hollywood Reporter*, October 2, 1950, p. 2; *Hollywood Reporter*, December 21, 1950, p. 1; *Hollywood Reporter*, July 6, 1951, p. 8; *Hollywood Reporter*, July 10, 1951, p. 4;

Hollywood Reporter, August 3, 1951, p. 7; *Hollywood Reporter*, August 8, 1951, p. 4; *Hollywood Reporter*, August 15, 1951 p. 5; *Hollywood Reporter*, August 17, 1951, p. 19; *Hollywood Reporter*, August 30, 1951, p. 8; *Hollywood Reporter*, September 17, 1951, p. 7; *Hollywood Reporter*, September 24, 1951, pp. 10, 12; *Hollywood Reporter*, October 10, 1951, p. 4; *Hollywood Reporter*, March 26, 1952, p. 3; *Boxoffice*, April 12, 1952, p. 33; *Motion Picture Herald*, April 12, 1952, p. 51; *Motion Picture Herald*, April 19, 1952, p. 1,322; *Women's Wear Daily*, May 14, 1952, p. 2; *Hollywood Reporter*, May 15, 1952, p. 3; *Film Bulletin*, May 19, 1952, p. 19; *Motion Picture Daily*, May 26, 1952, p. 6; *Daily Variety*, May 27, 1952, p. 3; *Film Daily*, May 27, 1952, p. 6; *Daily Film Renter*, May 29, 1952, p. 5; *Today's Cinema* (UK), May 29, 1952, p. 7; *Boxoffice*, May 31, 1952, p. 1,379; *Motion Picture Herald*, May 31, 1952, pp. 40, 1,381; *Harrison's Reports*, May 31, 1952, p. 86; *Motion Picture Herald*, June 7, 1952, p. 46; *The Times* (UK), June 9, 1952, p. 9; *The Globe and Mail* (Canada), June 13, 1952, p. 13; *New York Daily News*, June 28, 1952, p. C12; *New York Herald Tribune*, June 28, 1952, p. 6; *Monthly Film Bulletin* (UK), July 1952, p. 98; *Focus*, July 1952, pp. 162–63; *Photoplay*, July 1952, p. 23; *Los Angeles Examiner*, July 3, 1952; *Los Angeles Times*, July 3, 1952, p. A7; *New Yorker*, July 5, 1952, pp. 51–52; *Pictureshow* (UK), July 5, 1952, p. 2; *Chicago Daily Tribune*, July 16, 1952, p. A4; *Time*, July 21, 1952, p. 99; *Positif* (France), March 1980, pp. 26–32

FILM NOTES: In many advertisements, the title *Wait 'Till the Sun Shines, Nellie* is shown with an apostrophe, but it is omitted in the actual film's main credits. *See Nellie Home* was the working title.

Lure of the Wilderness

20th Century Fox Film Corporation
USA Technicolor 93 minutes
World premiere in Waycross, Georgia, July 16, 1952

CREDITS: *Producer*: Robert L. Jacks; *Associate Producer*: Robert D. Webb; *Director*: Jean Negulesco; *Screenplay*: Louis Lantz based on the novel *Swamp Water* by Vereen Bell; *Director of Photography*: Edward Cronjager; ASC; *Art Direction*: Lyle Wheeler; Addison Hehr; *Set Decorations*: Thomas Little; Fred J. Rode; *Film Editor*: Barbara McLean, ACE; *Wardrobe Direction*: Charles LeMaire; *Costumes*: Dorothy Jeakins; *Music*: Franz Waxman; *Orchestration*: Leonid Raab; *Makeup*: Ben Nye; *Special Photographic Effects*: Ray Kellogg; *Sound*: Alfred Bruzlin; Harry M. Leonard; *Assistant Directors*: Joe Rickards; Robert D. Webb; *Color Consultant*: Leonard Doss; *Song*: "Starry Hill"; music and lyrics by Ken Darby

CAST: Jean Peters (Laurie Harper), Jeffrey Hunter (Ben Tyler), Constance Smith (Noreen McGowan), Walter Brennan (Jim Harper), Tom Tully (Zack Tyler), Harry Shannon (Pat McGowan), Will Wright (Sheriff Clem Brink), Jack Elam (Dave Longden), Harry Carter (Ned Tyler), Pat Hogan (Harry Longden), Al Thompson (Shep Rigby), Robert Adler (Will Stone), Sherman Sanders (Square Dance Caller), Robert Karnes (Jack Doran), George Spaulding (Sloane), Walter Taylor (Sheriff Jepson), Ted Jordan (Young Man), Danny Borage (Musician), Norman Field (Deputy Sheriff), George Spaulding (Sloan), Dale Robertson (Opening Off-Screen Narrator)

PLOT: The year is 1910, and the Okefenokee Swamp in Georgia is considered a death trap to those living on its outskirts. Young Ben Tyler and his father are searching for two trappers lost in the swamp when Ben's dog, Careless, spots a deer, swims ashore and does not reappear. Ben's father tries to dissuade him from returning to the swamp to find the dog, as does his fiancée Noreen and the two shiftless Longden brothers, Dave and Harry. But Ben does return and that night is clubbed into unconsciousness. On waking in the morning, he finds himself a prisoner of Jim Harper and his daughter Laurie. Careless is with them. Laurie wants to kill Ben, but Jim stops her. Jim explains that eight years ago, he'd been unjustly accused by Dave and Harry Longden of the murder of their brother Bill and a man named Sam Black. Actually, Jim had shot Bill in self-defense and the Longdens had murdered Black. When the sheriff allowed a lynch party to get out of hand, Jim fled to the swamp with his wife and daughter. Mrs. Harper died, but Jim and Laurie had been there ever since. Jim is willing to return if he is given a fair trial. Ben promises to arrange this, although Laurie is distrustful of everyone, including Ben. Jim gives a bundle of skins to pay for the legal costs of the trial and shows him the way out of the swamp. On returning home, Ben is turned out of the house by his father when he learns that his son intends to go back to the swamp. After selling the skins, Ben finds that the proceeds are not sufficient to pay the lawyer's fees. He buys Laurie a frock, Jim a box of cigars and, with these presents, returns to the swamp to collect enough otter skins to pay for the fees. Laurie, delighted with the frock, is fascinated by Ben's description of a dance to be held on the mainland but fearful that her identity might be discovered, does not accept his invitation. One day, twisting from a snake, Ben falls on a tree root and is knocked unconscious in the water. It's only Jim's quick intervention that saves Ben from being killed by an alligator. At the dance, Ben is furious when he sees Noreen dancing continuously with Jack Doran, but then he sees Laurie, who has been brought ashore by her father. Now Noreen is jealous. She recognizes the dress Laurie is wearing as one that had been displayed in the shop just before Ben returns to the swamp and puts two and two together. Furious, Noreen tells Laurie that Ben told her she and her father were hiding in the swamp. The sheriff and the Longdens challenge Ben, who refuses to lead them to the Harpers. They then subject him to repeated dunking in the creek, and his life is only saved by the appearance of his father. When Ben returns to the swamp with the legal documents, he finds that the Harpers do not trust him. Only when the documents are proven genuine do they relent. The three head out for the mainland, but the Longdens, waiting in an ambush, fire at the party, wounding Jim in the leg. Once again, Laurie and Jim believe that Ben has trapped them. Only when he reveals himself and is fired at do they believe him. Laurie's knowledge of the swamp proves invaluable. She lures the Longdens onto the quicksand, which swallows up Dave. Harry is taken prisoner. At the entrance to the swamp, the sheriff, Ben's father, and the local townspeople welcome the party knowing that justice has been done. (Original press release source)

REVIEWS:
"The fascinating background of the great Okefenokee Swamp in Georgia, enhanced by Technicolor photography, adds much to the entertainment values of this exciting adventure melodrama. . . . The direction and acting are competent, and the color photography is pleasing." *Harrison's Reports*, July 26, 1952

"The basic passions with which the novel was concerned do not run as rampant in this version as they did in the earlier screen treatment." *Variety*, July 30, 1952

"A sound, fast-moving, adventure-packed script was milked for the last drop of its dramatic possibilities by the sterling cast and the skillful direction contributed by Jean Negulesco." *Boxoffice*, August 2, 1952

REVIEWS for Jean Peters:
"[W]ith Miss Peters handling the part of the people-hating, semi-wild swamp girl with sensitivity and appeal." *Hollywood Reporter*, July 24, 1952

"Miss Peters presents an appearance that resembles nothing so much as a Campfire Girl got up for a patriotic pageant in her role of a swamp barbarian." *New York Times*, October 4, 1952

"Last time up on Technicolor film, Miss Peters was observed brandishing a cutlass. This time it is a bow, but the performance is the same: somber, determined, and melting back to feminine type at the sight of a pretty dress." *New York Herald Tribune*, October 4, 1952

ADDITIONAL REVIEWS and ARTICLES:
Los Angeles Times, September 5, 1951; *Hollywood Reporter*, October 9, 1951, p. 1; *Hollywood Reporter*, October 31, 1951 p. 1; *Hollywood Reporter*, November 2, 1951, p. 15; *Hollywood Reporter*, November 16, 1951, p. 8; *Hollywood Reporter*, November 30, 1951, p. 9; *Hollywood Reporter*, January 4, 1952, p. 8; *Hollywood Reporter*, January 7, 1952, p. 2; *Hollywood Reporter*, February 1, 1952, p. 8; *Hollywood Reporter*, February 7, 1952, p. 5; *Hollywood Reporter*, April 17, 1952, p. 4; *Hollywood Reporter*, April 28, 1952, p. 6; *Motion Picture Herald*, April 19, 1952, p. 1,322; *Newsweek*, June 30, 1952, p. 100; *Hollywood Reporter*, July 11, 1952, p. 11; *Motion Picture Herald*, July 26, 1952, pp. 1,461-1,462; *Saturday Review*, July 26, 1952, p. 26; *Motion Picture Daily*, July 29, 1952; *Film Daily* (UK), August 4, 1952, p. 10; *Daily Film Renter* (UK), August 20, 1952, p. 6; *Today's Cinema* (UK), August 20, 1952, p. 7; *Kinematograph Weekly* (UK), August 21, 1952, p. 20; *Cosmopolitan*, September 1952, pp. 15-17; *Time*, September 8, 1952, p. 108; *Los Angeles Mirror*, September 11, 1952; *Los Angeles Times*, September 12, 1952; *Los Angeles Examiner*, September 12, 1952; *Cleveland Plain Dealer Pictorial Magazine*, September 28, 1952, p. 22; *Photoplay*, October 1952, p. 26; *Picturegoer* (UK), October 11, 1952, p. 23; *Picturegoer* (UK), November 1, 1952, p. 21; *Monthly Film Bulletin* (UK), May 1952; *Il Corriere della Sera* (Italy), January 9, 1953, p. 2; *Film Complet* (France), July 30, 1953

FILM NOTES: *Lure of the Wilderness* is a close remake of the 20th Century Fox 1941 film *Swamp Water*, which was directed by Jean Renoir and starred Anne Baxter, Dana Andrews, and Walter Brennan.

The working titles were *Cry of the Swamp*, *Swamp Girl*, and *The Land of the Trembling Earth*. Twentieth Century Fox originally announced Debra Paget as the film's star and Robert Wise as director.

O. Henry's Full House, aka Full House

20th Century Fox Film Corporation
USA B&W; 117 minutes
World premiere held in Greensboro, North Carolina, August 7, 1952

CREDITS: *Producer*: André Hakim; *Directors*: Henry Koster (*The Cop and the Anthem*), Henry Hathaway (*The Clarion Call* [and prologue and narration]), Jean Negulesco (*The Last Leaf*), Howard Hawks (*The Ransom of Red Chief*),

Henry King (*The Gift of the Magi*); *Screenplays*: Lamar Trotti (*The Cop and the Anthem*), Richard Breen (*The Clarion Call*), Ivan Goff and Ben Roberts (*The Last Leaf*), Walter Bullock and Philip Dunne (*The Gift of the Magi*), Nunnally Johnson (*The Ransom of Red Chief*), based on the short stories "The Cop and the Anthem" in *New York World*; "The Clarion Call" in *New York World*; "The Last Leaf" in *New York World*; "The Ransom of Red Chief" in *The Saturday Evening Post*; "The Gift of the Magi" in *New York World* by O. Henry; *Photography*: Lloyd Ahern ("The Cop and the Anthem"), Lucien Ballard ("The Clarion Call"), Joe MacDonald ("The Last Leaf" and "The Gift of the Magi"), Milton Krasner ("The Ransom of Red Chief"); *Art Direction*: Lyle Wheeler, Chester Gore, Addison Hehr, Richard Irvine, Joseph C. Wright; Film Editors: Nick DeMaggio ("The Cop and the Anthem," "The Clarion Call," and "The Last Leaf"), William B. Murphy ("The Ransom of Red Chief"), Barbara McLean ("The Gift of the Magi"); *Music*: Alfred Newman; Vocal Director: Ken Darby; *Orchestrator*: Edward B. Powell; *Sound*: Harry M. Leonard, W. D. Flick, Eugene Grossman, Winston H. Leverett, Alfred Bruzlin; Unit Manager: Abe Steinberg; *Assistant Directors*: Dave Silver ("The Clarion Call"), Henry Weinberger ("The Gift of the Magi"), Jasper Blystone and Erich Von Stroheim Jr. ("The Last Leaf"), Paul Helmick ("The Ransom of Red Chief"), Tom Connors Jr. ("The Ransom of Red Chief"); *Wardrobe*: Sam Benson, Charles LeMaire; *Dialogue Directors*: Lorry Sherwood, Stanley Scheuer; *Unit Manager*: Abe Steinberg; *Songs*: "Bringing in the Sheaves," words by Knowles Shaw; music by George Minor; "De Camptown Races," words and music by Stephen Collins Foster; "O Little Town of Bethlehem," words by Phillips Brooks, music by Lewis M. Redner; "Hark the Herald Angels Sing," words by Charles Wesley; music by Felix Mendelssohn

CAST: John Steinbeck (Narrator)
Prologue: Tyler McVey (O. Henry), Phil Tully (Guard), Carl Betz (Jimmie Valentine), Donna Lee Hickey (Mother), Phil Arnold (Convict)
"The Cop and the Anthem": Charles Laughton (Soapy Throckmorton), Marilyn Monroe (Streetwalker), David Wayne (Horace Truesdale), Thomas Browne Henry (Manager)
"The Clarion Call": Dale Robertson (Barney Woods), Richard Widmark (Johnny Kernan), Joyce MacKenzie (Hazel Woods), Richard Rober (Chief of Detectives), Will Wright (Manager)
"The Ransom of Red Chief": Fred Allen (Sam "Slick" Brown), Oscar Levant (William Smith), Lee Aaker (J. B. Dorset), Irving Bacon (Ebenezer Dorset), Kathleen Freeman (Mrs. Dorset), Gloria Gordon (Ellie Mae).
"The Gift of the Magi": Jeanne Crain (Della Young), Farley Granger (Jim Young), Fred Kelsey (Mr. Schultz "Santa Claus"), Sig Ruman (Menkie),

Harry Hayden (A. J. Crump), Richard Hylton (Bill), Richard Allan (Pete), Fritz Feld (Maurice).

"The Last Leaf": Anne Baxter (Joanna Goodwin), Jean Peters (Susan Goodwin), Gregory Ratoff (Behrman), Richard Garrick (Doctor), Steven Geray (Boris Radolf), Warren Stevens (Druggist), Martha Wentworth (Mrs. O'Brien), Ruth Warren (Neighbor), Bert Hicks (Sheldon Sidney), Don Kohler (Secretary), Beverly Thompson (Girl), Hal J. Smith (Dandy)

PLOT: John Steinbeck introduces each of the five episodes based on short stories by William Sidney Porter: "The Cop and the Anthem," "The Clarion Call," "The Ransom of Red Chief," "The Gift of the Magi," and "The Last Leaf." Negulesco's "The Last Leaf" is the tale of Joanna Goodwin, a jilted girl without the will to live because of an unhappy love affair. She watches the leaves wither in the late fall wind. In her delirious state, she starts to believe that she will die when the last leaf falls from a vine on a wall opposite her window. Winter arrives and the leaves are blown away, one by one, until a single leaf remains, persistently sticking to the wall. It doesn't die, and its reassuring presence gives Joanna hope. She recovers only to find out, upon close inspection, that the leaf is a creation of Behrman, an impoverished artist who had befriended her and her sister Susan. Behrman did it so that Joanna would hang onto life. The sisters learn that the poor painter had died as a result of working in the freezing weather, scaling a ladder and painting the leaf at night when Joanna was sleeping. Susan promises to someday tell Joanna just what a great painter Behrman was.

REVIEWS:

"20th Century Fox has an unbeatable hand in *O. Henry's Full House*, an entrancing collection of five tales by one of America's great storytellers." *Hollywood Reporter*, August 18, 1952

"Being a mixture of comedy, drama, pathos, and melodrama, the picture offers a variety of moods to suit all tastes, although the entertainment quality of the different stories ranges from just fair to good." *Harrison's Reports*, August 23, 1952

"The house is too full. . . . Five unrelated episodes seem too much for one production. And not all of these adaptations of O. Henry's short stories are as sharp and piquant as they might have been." *Picturegoer* (UK), October 11, 1952

REVIEWS for Jean Peters:

"The two femmes [Anne Baxter and Jean Peters] are excellent." *Variety*, August 20, 1952

"Anne Baxter, Jean Peters, and Gregory Ratoff, incidentally, do a competent job of handling the wistful dramatics and the broad humors of 'The Last Leaf.'" *New York Herald Tribune*, October 17, 1952

"Jean Peters and Gregory Ratoff play the charming second tale with feeling." *Monthly Film Bulletin* (UK), October 1952

ADDITIONAL REVIEWS and ARTICLES:
Daily Variety, October 11, 1943; *Hollywood Reporter*, October 14, 1943; *Hollywood Reporter*, February 23, 1945, p. 2; *Hollywood Reporter*, September 17, 1945, p. 3; *Hollywood Reporter*, November 9, 1951, p. 2; *Hollywood Reporter*, November 16, 1951, p. 15; *Hollywood Reporter*, November 21, 1951, p. 15; *Hollywood Reporter*, November 28, 1951, p. 8; *Hollywood Reporter*, November 29, 1951, p. 1; *Motion Picture Herald*, December 1, 1951; *Hollywood Reporter*, January 3, 1952, p. 8; *Hollywood Reporter*, January 4, 1952, p. 8; *Motion Picture Herald*, January 12, 1952; *Hollywood Reporter*, January 11, 1952, p. 14; *Hollywood Reporter*, January 14, 1952, p. 4; *Hollywood Reporter*, January 24, 1952, p. 6; *Hollywood Reporter*, January 27, 1952, p. 7; *Hollywood Reporter*, January 28, 1952, p. 2; *Motion Picture Herald*, February 2, 1952; *Hollywood Reporter*, February 13, 1952, p. 6; *Hollywood Reporter*, February 21, 1952, p. 13; *Hollywood Reporter*, February 22, 1942, p. 18; *Hollywood Reporter*, February 27, 1952, p. 15; *Hollywood Reporter*, March 3, 1952, p. 1; *Hollywood Reporter*, May 20, 1952, p. 2; *Hollywood Reporter*, May 23, 1952, p. 9; *Hollywood Reporter*, May 27, 1952, p. 5; *Motion Picture Herald*, June 14, 1952, p. 42; *Hollywood Reporter*, August 5, 1952, p. 5; *Motion Picture Herald*, August 9, 1952, p. 1,478; *Hollywood Reporter*, August 14, 1952, p. 4; *Motion Picture Daily*, August 18, 1952; *Motion Picture Herald*, August 23, 1952, p. 1,501; *Boxoffice*, August 23, 1952; *Film Daily*, August 26, 1952, p. 6; *Hollywood Reporter*, September 5, 1952, p. 1; *Hollywood Reporter*, September 8, 1952, p. 2; *Today's Cinema* (UK), September 10, 1952, p. 10; *Daily Film Renter* (UK), September 10, 1952, p. 5; *Kinematograph Weekly* (UK), September 11, 1952, p. 16; *Saturday Review*, September 13, 1952, p. 34; *Hollywood Citizen-News*, September 19, 1952; *Los Angeles Times*, September 19, 1952, p. 17; *The Times* (UK), September 22, 1952, p. 2; *Time*, September 22, 1952, p. 102; *Hollywood Reporter*, September 26, 1952, p. 8; *Audio-Visual Guide*, October 1952, p. 31; *Films in Review*, October 1952, p. 416–17; *Sight and Sound* (UK), October-December 1952, p. 77; *The Spectator* (UK), October 3, 1952; *New York Times*, October 5, 1952, p. X5; *Newsweek*, October 6, 1952, p.

113; *Hollywood Reporter*, October 13, 1952, p. 5; *The Tatler* (UK), October 15, 1952, p. 144; *Chicago Daily Tribune*, October 17, 1952, sec. 2 p. 7; *Hollywood Reporter*, October 17, 1952, p. 3; *New York Times*, October 17, 1952, p. 33; *Cue*, October 18, 1952; *New York Times*, October 26, 1952, p. X1; *Audio-Visual Guide*, November 1952, p. 29; *Focus*, November 1952, p. 249; *The Nation*, November 22, 1952, p. 475; *Theatre Arts*, December 1952, p. 86; *Audio-Visual Guide*, January 1953, p. 14; *Movie*, December 1962, pp. 21–22; *Cinéma* (France), February 1963, p. 104; *Positif* (France), January 1975, p. 4

FILM NOTES: The working titles were *The Full House, Bagdad on the Subway*, and *O. Henry's Bagdad on the Subway*. After a sneak preview, critics felt that *The Ransom of Red Chief* episode was weak, forcing Fox to cut it from the final print. The segment was restored in the early 1960s when the film was broadcast on television.

Niagara

20th Century Fox Film Corporation
USA Technicolor 92 minutes
Premiered in New York City, January 21, 1953

CREDITS: *Director*: Henry Hathaway; *Producer*: Charles Brackett; *Screenplay*: Charles Brackett, Walter Reisch, Richard Breen; *Director of Photography*: Joe MacDonald, ASC; *Technicolor Color Consultant*: Leonard Doss; *Special Photographic Effects*: Ray Kellogg; *Film Editor*: Barbara McLean, ACE; *Art Direction*: Lyle Wheeler, Maurice Ransford; *Set Decorations*: Stuart Reiss, *Wardrobe Direction*: Charles LeMaire; *Costume Designer*: Dorothy Jeakins; *Makeup Artist*: Ben Nye; *Music*: Sol Kaplan; *Musical Direction*: Lionel Newman; *Orchestrations*: Edward Powell; *Sound*: W. D. Flick, Roger Heman; *Stunt Double for Jean Peters:* Polly Burson; *Assistant Director*: Gerd Oswald

CAST: Marilyn Monroe (Rose Loomis), Joseph cotton (George Loomis), Jean Peters (Polly Cutler), Casey Adams (Ray Cutler), Denis O'Dea (Inspector Starkey), Richard Allan (Ted Patrick), Don Wilson (Jess C. Kettering), Lurene Tuttle (Mrs. Kettering), Russell Collins (Mr. Qua), Will Wright (Boatman), Neil Fitzgerald (Canadian Customs Officer), Henry Hathaway (Scenic Tunnel Employee), Minerva Urecal (Mrs. McGrand, Landlady), Sean McClory (Sam, Detective), Lester Matthews (Doctor), Gene Baxter (American Guide), Tom Reynolds (Husband), Nina Varela (Wife), George Ives (Carillon Tower Guide), Henry H. Beckman, Willard Sage (Motorcycle

Cop), Harry Carey Jr. (Cab Driver), Norman McKay (Morris), Carleton Young (Policeman), Arch Johnson (Taxi Driver), Patrick O' Moore (Detective), Gloria Gordon (Dancer)

PLOT: In Rainbow Cabins, a motel on the Canadian side of Niagara Falls, honeymooners Ray and Polly Cutler run into George Loomis and his wife, Rose. During a ride on the Maid of the Mist through the scenic Horseshoe Tunnels, Polly discovers Rose kissing Ted Patrick. That evening, George tells Polly that Rose tries to make people believe that he is crazy. Meanwhile, Rose hurries to another date with Ted, and they concoct plans to kill George the following day. The next morning, George, thinking Rose has entered the scenic tunnels to meet Ted, goes in behind her. Rose gives Ted the high sign, and he follows George, intent on murder. The next day, however, it is Ted's body that is pulled from the Niagara River. Polly discovers that George killed Ted in a fight in the tunnel. Meanwhile, Rose, who has been in a state of collapse after seeing her lover's body in the morgue, escapes from the hospital. She sees George and rushes out into the Carillon Tower. He chases her and strangles her with a red silk scarf, escaping without being seen. Rose's body is found by a janitor the next morning, and the chief of police is notified. The Cutlers, who have been out fishing with Mr. and Mrs. Kettering, dock their boat and go ashore for supplies and fuel. Polly returns and discovers George trying to start the engine. He orders her off the boat. She refuses and begs him to surrender to the police. George sends her sprawling on the deck, starts the engine, and the boat moves down the river. He pulls out the red silk scarf and confesses that he murdered Rose. The boat moves swiftly toward the raging rapids of the Niagara. Polly gets into position to jump overboard, but George convinces her that the current will pull her under. George finally scuttles the boat and pushes Polly to a ledge. Just as she reaches safety, the boat breaks loose and whirls over the Falls. George disappears, clutching Rose's red scarf in his hand.

REVIEWS:
"*Niagara* blends sex and melodrama against the scenic grandeur of Niagara Falls . . . [the] story in itself isn't a big enough eyeful for the filmgoer." *Variety*, January 21, 1953

"This is a morbid but fascinating murder thriller that is packed with suspense from start to finish." *Harrison's Reports*, January 24, 1953

"The story's a tightly plotted suspense yarn, but the real accent of the picture is on two natural wonders: Niagara Falls and Marilyn Monroe.... The movie's hers, but Jean Peters shouldn't be overlooked." *Photoplay*, 1953.

REVIEWS for Jean Peters:
"Jean Peters turns in a warm, sensitive performance as the honeymooner drawn into the murder intrigue." *Hollywood Reporter*, January 20, 1953

"Miss Peters is far better in her cool, well-balanced young wife part than into flaming adventure types she has been doing recently." *New York Herald Tribune*, January 22, 1953

"Jean Peters makes a believable honeymooner who is as comely as they come." *New York Times*, January 22, 1953

ADDITIONAL REVIEWS and ARTICLES:
Los Angeles Times, February 1, 1952, p. B6; *Hollywood Reporter*, March 19, 1952, p. 2; *Hollywood Reporter*, April 3, 1952, p. 2; *Hollywood Reporter*, April 24, 1952, p. 4; *Hollywood Reporter*, May 14, 1952, p. 3; *Hollywood Reporter*, May 19, 1952, p. 5; *Hollywood Reporter*, May 20, 1952, p. 12; *Hollywood Reporter*, May 26, 1952, p. 8; *Hollywood Reporter*, May 27, 1952, p. 2; *Hollywood Reporter*, June 2, 1952, p. 3; *Hollywood Reporter*, June 6, 1952, p. 14; *Hollywood Reporter*, June 18, 1952, p. 8; *Hollywood Reporter*, June 23, 1952, p. 9; *Hollywood Reporter*, July 2, 1952, p. 5; *Hollywood Reporter*, July 11, 1952, p. 11; *Today's Cinema*, August 6, 1952, p. 11; *Motion Picture Herald*, December 27, 1952, p. 1,663; *Hollywood Reporter*, January 9, 1953, p. 15; *Daily Variety*, January 20, 1953, p. 3; *Hollywood Reporter*, January 20, 1953, p. 3; *Film Daily*, January 22, 1953, p. 6; *Film Daily*, January 22, 1953, p. 6; *Boxoffice*, January 24, 1953; *Los Angeles Times*, January 24, 1953, p. 11; *Motion Picture Herald*, January 24, 1953, p. 1,693; *Cue*, January 24, 1953; *The Exhibitor*, January 28, 1953, p. 3,456; *Motion Picture Daily*, January 29, 1953, p. 9; *America*, January 31, 1953, p. 494; *New Yorker*, January 31, 1953, p. 53; *Today's Cinema*, February 1953, p. 8; *Newsweek*, February 2, 1953, p. 78; *Saturday Review*, February 7, 1953, p. 26; *Film Bulletin*, February 9, 1953, p. 9; *Variety*, February 11, 1953, p. 1; *Los Angeles Mirror*, February 13, 1953; *Nation*, February 14, 1953, p. 153; *Kinematograph Weekly* (UK), February 26, 1953, p. 22; *Films in Review*, March 1953, p. 150; *Monthly Film Bulletin* (UK), April 1953, p. 55; *Christian Century*, April 1, 1953, p. 339; *National Parent-Teacher*, April 1953, p. 40; *Los Angeles Herald Express*, April 2, 1953; *The Times* (UK), April 27, 1953, p. 2; *Picturegoer* (UK), May 9, 1953, pp. 7, 18; *Pix*, June 13, 1953; Il *Corriere della Sera* (Italy), September 11, 1953, p. 4; *Cinémonde* (France), August

28, 1953, p. 24; *Cinémonde* (France), September 18, 1953, p. 23; *New Yorker*, April 12, 1989, p. 37; *Variety*, May 10, 1993, p. 16; *Cinema Journal*, Summer 2012, pp. 26–43; *Village Voice*, June 26, 2014, p. 28

FILM NOTES: Jean Peters replaced Anne Baxter, who was the first choice for the role of Polly Cutler.

Pickup on South Street

20th Century Fox Film Corporation
USA B&W 81 minutes
Premiered in New York, May 20, 1954

CREDITS: *Director*: Samuel Fuller; *Producer*: Jules Schermer; *Screenplay*: Samuel Fuller from a story by Dwight Taylor; *Director of Photography*: Joe MacDonald, ASC; *Special Photographic Effects*: Ray Kellogg; *Film Editor*: Nick De Maggio; *Art Directors*: Lyle Wheeler, George Patrick; *Set Decorator*: Al Orenbach; *Costume Designer*: Bill Travilla; *Wardrobe Direction*: Charles LeMaire; *Makeup Artist*: Ben Nye; *Music*: Leigh Harline; *Music Director*: Lionel Newman; *Orchestrations*: Edward Powell; *Sound*: Winston H. Leverett, Harry M. Leonard; *Assistant Director*: Ad Schaumer

CAST: Richard Widmark (Skip McCoy), Jean Peters (Candy), Thelma Ritter (Moe Williams), Murvyn Vye (Capt. Dan Tiger), Richard Kiley (Joey), Willis B. Bouchey (Zara), Milburn Stone (Winocki), Henry Slate (MacGregor), George E. Stone (Police Sergeant), George Eldredge (Fenton), Stuart Randall (Police Commissioner), Jerry O'Sullivan (Enyart), Harry Carter (Dietrich), Roger Moore (Mr. Victor), Frank Kumagai (Lum), Victor Perry (Lightning Louie), George Berkeley (Client), Emmett Lynn (Sandwich Man), Maurice Samuels (Peddler), Parley Baer (Peddler), Jay Loftin (Librarian), Victoria Carroll (Nurse)

PLOT: On the subway, a pickpocket named Skip picks the purse of a sultry young girl named Candy. Later, he is puzzled to find among his loot some stolen microfilm of important scientific secrets that are wanted by the Communists. When Candy reports the theft to her employer, Joey, a Communist spy, whom she believes is a patent attorney, he dispatches her via his informers, one of them being Moe, to get the film back. At the same time, the FBI, led by Zara, enlists the aid of the New York Pickpocket Squad headed by Tiger in recovering the film so that Candy, whom the

FBI has been shadowing in hopes of getting to the ringleader, can lead them to him. Skip, divining from all this activity that the film is valuable, plans to use it as a means to hold the spies for ransom. Meanwhile, Candy is falling in love with Skip, and her efforts to prevent him from betraying his country make for a turbulent story of conflicting emotions marked by violent fights between her and Skip and her and Joey.

REVIEWS:
"*Pickup*, for the most part, falls flat on its face and at times even borders on unfunny and presumably unintended comedy." *Variety*, May 13, 1953

"A tense but unpleasant and not too believable melodrama." *Harrison's Reports*, May 16, 1953

"*Pickup on South Street* is an undistinguished but reasonably exciting slap-dash of sex and sadism and of cops and crooks and communist agents." *Newsweek*, June 22, 1953

REVIEWS for Jean Peters:
"[Samuel Fuller] draws superb performances, particularly from Jean Peters, who is brilliant in a change-of-pace role as a sexy, rather slow-witted ex-B girl." *Hollywood Reporter*, May 13, 1953

"Miss Peters is as pretty a waterfront type as the screen has produced and gives a sincere performance." *Los Angeles Times*, May 30, 1953.

"Jean Peters couldn't be more striking as the 'cannon' and the babe." *Washington Post*, May 30, 1953

ADDITIONAL REVIEWS and ARTICLES:
Hollywood Reporter, February 19, 1952, p. 2; *Hollywood Reporter*, September 2, 1952, p. 2; *Hollywood Reporter*, September 11, 1952, p. 1; *Hollywood Reporter*, September 12, 1952, p. 2; *Hollywood Reporter*, September 15, 1952, p. 1; *Hollywood Reporter*, September 19, 1952, p. 15; *Hollywood Reporter*, September 26, 1952, p. 7; *Hollywood Reporter*, October 10, 1952, pp. 6, 11; *Hollywood Reporter*, October 17, 1952, p. 2; *Hollywood Reporter*, November 19, 1952, p. 2; *Hollywood Reporter*, November 20, 1952, p. 6; *Motion Picture Herald*, February 14, 1953, p. 1,718; *Daily Variety*, May 13, 1953, p. 3; *Today's Cinema* (UK), May 15, 1953, p. 13; *Boxoffice*, May 16, 1953; *Motion Picture Herald*, May 16, 1953, p. 1,837; *Motion Picture Daily*, May 18, 1953, p. 6; *The Exhibitor*, May 20, 1953, p. 3,524;

Kinematograph Weekly (UK), May 21, 1953, p. 17; *Film Daily*, May 29, 1953, p. 6; *Film Daily*, May 29, 1953, p. 6; *Theatre Arts*, June 1953, p. 86; *Redbook*, June 1953, p. 8; *Commonweal*, June 12, 1953, p. 249; *Film Bulletin*, June 15, 1953, p. 27; *New York Times*, June 18, 1953, p. 38; *Saturday Review*, June 20, 1953, p. 33; *New Yorker*, June 27, 1953, p. 59; *Time*, June 29, 1953, pp. 92, 95; *Photoplay*, July 1953, p. 16; *Modern Screen*, July 1953, p. 16; *Monthly Film Bulletin* (UK), July 1953, p. 109; *Picturegoer* (UK), July 11, 1953, p. 18; *New York Daily News*, July 18, 1953, p. 17C; *New York Herald Tribune*, July 18, 1953, p. 26; *America*, July 18, 1953, p. 406; *Chicago Tribune*, July 20, 21, 22, 1953, p. A2; *Punch*, July 29, 1953, pp. 161-62 *Chicago Tribune*, July 31, 1953, p. A9; *Picturegoer* (UK), August 8, 1953, p. 14; *Cinémonde* (France), August 21, 1953, p. 7; *Focus*, September 1953, p. 204; *National Parent-Teacher*, September 1953, p. 39; *Il Corriere della Sera* (Italy), September 13, 1953, p. 4; *Hollywood Reporter*, January 8, 1954, p. 1; *Hollywood Reporter*, June 14, 1954, p. 1; *Hollywood Reporter*, December 13, 1954, p. 2; *Cinéma* (France), June 1961, p. 114; *Cahiers du Cinéma* (France), July 1961, p. 47; *Présence du Cinéma* (France), December 1963/January 1964; *Film Heritage*, Spring 1973, pp. 9-18; *Positif* (France), July/August 1981, pp. 57-61; *Village Voice*, June 15, 1982; *Films in Review*, May 1986, p. 270; *Premiere*, May 1991, p. 103; *CineAction!*, August 1991, pp. 6-16; *Literature/Film Quarterly*, 1994, pp. 187-94; *Scenario*, Autumn 1998, pp. 46-84; *New York Observer*, October 11, 1999, p. 21; *Filmfax*, October/November 2002, pp. 101-6,131; *Film Score Monthly*, February 2004, p. 46; *Film Comment*, March/April 2004, p. 76; *Cinéaste*, Summer 2004, pp. 54-55, *American Cinematographer*, July 2004, pp. 20, 22; *Sight & Sound* (UK), October 2015, p. 107

AWARDS and HONORS:
Venice Film Festival, Italy 1953: Winner: Bronze Lion: Samuel Fuller

Academy Awards USA, 1954; Nominated: Best Actress in a Supporting Role: Thelma Ritter

National Film Preservation Board, USA 2018: Winner: National Film Registry National Film Preservation Board

FILM NOTES: The working title was *Blaze of Glory*. Stephen McNally and Terry Moore took the parts played by Richard Widmark and Jean Peters in a *Lux Radio Theater* broadcast of the story (6/21/54). In 1967, 20th Century Fox remade the picture as *The Cape Town Affair*, starring James Brolin and Jacqueline Bisset.

A Blueprint for Murder

20th Century Fox Film Corporation
USA B&W 77 minutes
Premiered in New York, July 24, 1953

CREDITS: *Director*: Andrew L. Stone; *Producer*: Michael Abel, *Screenplay*: Andrew L. Stone; *Director of Photography*: Leo Tover, ASC; *Film Editor*: William B. Murphy, ACE; *Art Directors*: Lyle Wheeler, Albert Hogsett; *Music Director:* Lionel Newman; *Set Decorator*: Fred J. Rode; *Wardrobe Direction*; Charles LeMaire; *Makeup Artist*: Ben Nye; *Sound*: W. D. Flick, Harry M. Leonard; *Assistant Director*: Ad Schaumer

CAST: Joseph Cotten (Whitney Cameron), Jean Peters (Lynne Cameron), Gary Merrill (Fred Sargent), Catherine McLeod (Maggie Sargent), Jack Kruschen (Hal Cole), Barney Phillips (Capt. Pringle), Fred Ridgeway (Doug Jr.), Joyce McCluskey (Miss Brownell), Mae Marsh (Anna), Jonathan Hole (Dr. Stevenson), Harry Carter (Wheeler), Walter Sande (John J. Henderson), Tyler McVey (Technician), Teddy Mangean (Attendant), Aline Towne (File Clerk), Ray Hyke (Pharmacist), Charles Collins (Nursery Clerk), Eugene Borden (Head Waiter), Carleton Young (Frank Connelly), Grandon Rhodes (Judge James), Herb Butterfield (Judge), George Melford (Bailiff)

PLOT: Whitney Cameron is horrified when he learns that his young niece, Polly, his dead brother's daughter, has died suddenly from convulsions. The brother, who by his first marriage had two children, Polly and Doug, had married again, and Lynne Cameron, his second wife, seems equally appalled. Calling on his lawyer and friend Fred Sargent and his wife Maggie, Cameron tells them of his grief, at the same time pointing out that Polly and his brother seem to have the same symptoms. Maggie, who has conducted intensive research into poisons, suggests that these symptoms could possibly have resulted from strychnine poisoning. Cameron refuses to suspect Lynne until he learns that she would inherit the whole of her dead husband's estate only on the death of the two children, and then he remembers that Lynne had wanted Polly's body cremated, but he had opposed it. Fred arranges a post-mortem that reveals that Polly had been given enough strychnine to kill four people. Cameron, fearful that Lynne may now do away with his nephew, Doug, tells her what has been discovered. Meanwhile, an investigation into Polly's death reveals that the only way a person can die from strychnine is during a convulsion, which would have meant that someone must have given Polly the fatal dose at the hospital. On consulting the hospital authorities, Cameron learns that Polly was given her last capsule by Lynne from a prescription made up at an outside chemist and not at the hospital dispensary. Lynne is brought before the court on a preliminary examination, but there is insufficient evidence to sustain the charges, and the accusations are dropped. When Lynne boards a liner for Europe with Doug, Cameron follows her, carrying with him a bottle of insect poison. Fearing that Lynne will murder Doug, Cameron is prepared to kill Lynne first. On their last night at sea, Cameron discovers in Lynne's suitcase aspirins, among which is a different tablet that he recognizes as being poisonous. He extracts it and, later that night, manages to drop it into Lynne's drink. When she has drained the glass, Lynne is momentarily stunned as Cameron tells her what he did. However, she soon regains her composure, telling Cameron of her disgust at his suspicion and ridiculous behavior. Meanwhile, Cameron has voiced his suspicion to the ship's detective, who is hidden in Lynne's cabin, hoping for a confession. Cameron goes up on deck, angered at having made a fool of himself, when a steward tells him he is wanted by the ship's doctor. With minutes to go before the dose becomes lethal, Lynne's life is saved by the doctor who has administered the proper antidote. Back in New York, Lynne is tried for Polly's death, found guilty, and sentenced to life imprisonment.

REVIEWS:
"This lengthy 20th Century Fox item ... offers a few bursts of suspense and a fairly provocative story blueprint." *New York Times*, July 25, 1953

"A good murder mystery drama . . . the direction and acting are highly competent." *Harrison's Reports*, July 25, 1953

"Mighty moving melodrama of solid interest, *A Blueprint for Murder* is entertaining screen material, thanks to all hands, among them a most capable cast." *Motion Picture Daily*, July 28, 1953

REVIEWS for Jean Peters
"Miss Peters does an outstanding job as the conniving stepmother." *Hollywood Reporter*, July 24, 1953

"Jean Peters is gorgeously attired in mink and bare-shouldered black evening dresses, but now and again, she seems to long to burst out of her seams and become the knowing hoyden of *Pick Up* [*sic*] *on South Street*." *Philadelphia Inquirer*, August 24, 1953

"Jean Peters is pleasing as the widow." *Picturegoer* (UK), November 21, 1953

ADDITIONAL REVIEWS and ARTICLES:
Hollywood Reporter, February 9, 1952, p. 2; *Hollywood Reporter*, January 27, 1953, p. 7; *Hollywood Reporter*, January 21, 1953, p. 2; *Chicago Tribune*, February 5, 1953, p. A2; *Chicago Tribune*, February 10, 1953, p. B2; *Hollywood Reporter*, February 10, 1953, p. 2; *Hollywood Reporter*, February 12, 1953, p. 4; *Hollywood Reporter*, February 13, 1953, p. 10; *Hollywood Reporter*, February 19, 1953, p. 6; *Motion Picture Herald*, February 21, 1953, p. 32; *Hollywood Reporter*, February 25, 1953, p. 10; *Hollywood Reporter*, March 9, 1953, p. 6; *Daily Variety*, July 24, 1953, p. 3; *New York Daily News*, July 25, 1953, p. ML18; *Film Daily*, July 27, 1953 p. 6; *Variety*, July 29, 1953, p. 8; *The Exhibitor*, July 29, 1953; *Boxoffice*, August 1, 1953, p. 1,499; *Motion Picture Herald*, August 1, 1953, p. 1,933; *Newsweek*, August 3, 1953, p. 76; *Today's Cinema* (UK), August 7, 1953, p. 8; *America*, August 8, 1953, p. 467; *Time*, August 10, 1953, p. 96; *Film Bulletin*, August 10, 1953, p. 11; *Kinematograph Weekly* (UK), August 13, 1953, p. 14; *Commonweal*, August 14, 1953, p. 467; *Boxoffice*, August 22, 1953, p. 8; *Christian Science Monitor*, August 22, 1953, p. 7; *Boston Globe*, August 22, 1953, p. 8; *Los Angeles Times*, August 29, 1953, p. 11; *Monthly Film Bulletin* (UK), September 1953, p. 131; *Washington Post*, September 25, 1953, p. 37; *Farm Journal*, November 1953, p. 161; *Holiday*, November 1953, p. 99; *Il Corriere della Sera* (Italy), May 12, 1954, p. 5

FILM NOTES: Dan Dailey and Dorothy McGuire reprised Joseph Cotten and Jean Peters's roles in a *Lux Radio Theater* broadcast of the story (3/29/54).

Vicki

20th Century Fox Film Corporation
USA, B&W, 85 minutes
Premiered in New York, September 7, 1953

CREDITS: *Director*: Harry Horner; *Producer*: Leonard Goldstein; *Screenplay*: Dwight Taylor, based on the novel *I Wake Up Screaming* by Steve Fisher; *Director of Photography*: Milton Krasner, ASC; *Film Editor*: Dorothy Spencer, ACE; *Art Directors*: Lyle Wheeler, Richard Irvine; *Set Decorator*:

Claude Carpenter; *Special Photographic Effects*: Kay Kellogg; *Wardrobe Direction*; Charles LeMaire; *Costume Designer*: Renié; *Makeup Artist*: Ben Nye; *Sound*: E. Clayton Ward, Roger Heman; *Music*: Leigh Harline, *Vicki* by Ken Darby and Max Showalter; *Musical Director*: Lionel Newman; *Orchestrations*: Edward Powell; *Songs*: "I Know Why" music by Harry Warren, lyrics by Mack Gordon; "How Many Times Do I Have to Tell You?" music and lyrics by Jimmy McHugh and Harold Adamson

CAST: Jeanne Crain (Jill Lynn), Jean Peters (Vicki Lynn), Elliott Reid (Steve Christopher), Richard Boone (Lt. Ed Cornell), Max Showalter as Casey Adams (Larry Evans), Alexander D'Arcy (Robin Ray), Carl Betz (Detective McDonald), Aaron Spelling (Harry Williams), Robert Adler (Policeman), Russ Conway (Detective), John Dehner (Police Capt. J. "Chief" Donald), Roy Engel 1st Detective), Frank Fenton (Eric), Jack Gargan (Detective), Frank Gerstle (Detective), Helen Hayden (Connie), Irene Seidner (Cleaning Woman), Al Hill (Bum)

PLOT: All of New York is buzzing over the mysterious killing of glamorous Vicki Lynn, who, under the expert tutelage of publicity agent Steve Christopher, has become Gotham's most popular model and nightclub songstress almost overnight. As the most likely suspect, Steve undergoes a severe grilling by a bulldog-like police officer, Lt. Ed Cornell, while his more sympathetic sergeant, McDonald, records. Six months earlier, Steve and his newspaper columnist friend, Larry Evans, had dropped into a cafeteria to discuss one of Steve's clients, actor Robin Ray, and was impressed by their waitress Vicki, whom Steve decided to take on as a client. After careful grooming, Steve introduces Vicki to café society as a songstress at the club Capri where she is a big hit, especially with Robin, Larry, and Steve, each of whom tries to get on the inside track. When police interrogate Vicki's sister, Jill, she discloses that Steve had had an argument with Vicki when she signed a film contract without his knowledge. Jill gets a second shock when she meets and recognizes Cornell as the sinister-looking man who had shadowed Vicki when she was still a waitress. He counters with a lashing accusation that she is secretly in love with Steve, whom she had witnessed standing over her sister's lifeless form. Suddenly the pressure is off Steve when suspicion falls on the moronic-looking youth, Harry Williams, the switchboard operator in her apartment house who has a secret crush on the beauty. But he is soon cleared by Lt. Cornell, and Steve again becomes the chief suspect. Jill is convinced he is innocent and that she is in love with him. She produces a note Vicki wrote that seemingly implicates him when Cornell enters her apartment and handcuffs Steve. Jill manages to knock out the police officer, and Steve makes a getaway. When the police hold Jill, Steve returns to her. Sergeant McDonald gives them time to manage to get a confession out of Williams and to say that Cornell knew he was guilty. Steve and McDonald force their way into Cornell's quarters to find it's a photographic shrine to Vicki. Cornell felt that Steve had deprived him of Vicki's love, and it was revenge that the unbalanced officer wanted.

REVIEWS
"A silly melodrama." *New York Herald Tribune*, September 8, 1953

"[A] story . . . studiously contrived and farfetched." *New York Times*, September 8, 1953

"The trouble with Dwight Taylor's script . . . is that very little character interest emerges and that the outcome is telegraphed with the effectiveness of Western Union." *Newsweek*, September 21, 1953

REVIEWS for Jean Peters:
"Misses Crain and Peters are both decorative and competent." *Hollywood Reporter*, September 8, 1953

"Misses Crain and Peters are okay in their roles." *Variety*, September 9, 1953

"Jean Peters is convincing as Vicki." *Christian Science Monitor*, October 13, 1953

ADDITIONAL REVIEWS and ARTICLES:
Chicago Daily Tribune, December 26, 1952, p. A5; *New York Daily News*, December 26, 1952, p. 41; *Hollywood Reporter*, January 30, 1953, p. 2; *Hollywood Reporter*, February 10, 1953, p. 2; *Variety*, February 25, 1953, p. 9; *Hollywood Reporter*, March 6, 1953, p. 22; *Hollywood Reporter*, March 25, 1953, p. 6; *Hollywood Reporter*, March 27, 1953, p. 11; *Hollywood Reporter*, April 8, 1953, p. 2; *Harrison's Reports*, July 25, 1953, p 146; *Hollywood Reporter*, August 12, 1953, p. 8; *Daily Variety*, September 8, 1953, p. 3; *New York Daily News*, September 8, 1953, p. 5; *Motion Picture Daily*, September 9, 1953, p. 4; *Film Daily*, September 10, 53, p. 6; *Motion Picture Herald*, September 12, 1953, p. 1989; *Boxoffice*, September 19, 1953; *Boston Globe*, October 13, 1953; *Today's Cinema*, October 21, 1953, p. 14; *Kinematograph Weekly* (UK), October 22, 1953,

p. 19; *Los Angeles Times*, October 24, 1953, p. 10; *Hollywood Reporter*, October 27, 1953, p. 3; *Variety*, October 28, 1953, p. 11; *Screenland*, November 1953, p. 14; *Film Bulletin*, November 2, 1953, pp. 22–23; *Pix*, November 28, 1953, pp. 42–43; *Monthly Film Bulletin* (UK), December 1953, p. 179; *Picturegoer* (UK), December 5, 1953, p. 19; *Picture Show* (UK), December 12, 1953; *Daily Variety*, November 16, 1955; *Hollywood Reporter*, November 16, 1955, p. 9

FILM NOTES: *Vicki* was a remake of the 20th Century Fox film *I Wake Up Screaming* (1941). Jean Peters performs two songs: "I Know Why" and "How Many Times Do I Have to Tell You?"

Three Coins in the Fountain

20th Century Fox Film Corporation
USA Technicolor CinemaScope 102 minutes
Premiered in New York City, May 20, 1954

CREDITS: *Producer*: Sol C. Siegel; *Director*: Jean Negulesco; *Screenwriter*: John Patrick; based on the novel *Coins in the Fountain* by John H. Secondari; *Director of Photography*: Milton Krasner; *Art Direction*: Lyle Wheeler; John De Cuir; *Art Department*: Italo Tomassi; *Film Editor*: William Reynolds; *Set Decorations:* Walter M. Scott; Paul S. Fox; *Wardrobe Direction*: Charles LeMaire; *Costumes*: Dorothy Jeakins; *Sound*: Eugene Grossman; Roger Heman; *Music*: Victor Young; *Orchestra*: Edward B. Powell; Ken Darby; Sidney Cutner; Leo Shuken; *Vocal Director*: Ken Darby; *Makeup*: Ben Nye; *Assistant Director*: Gaston Glass; *Technical Advisor*: Giuseppe Lenzi; *Color Consultant*: Leonard Doss; *Songs*: "Three Coins in the Fountain"; music and lyrics by Jule Styne and Sammy Cahn; sung by Frank Sinatra; "Anema e Core"; music by Salve D'Esposito; lyrics by Tito Manlio; "Nanni"; music and lyrics by Franco Silvestri; "O Ciucciariello"; music by Nino Oliviero; lyrics by Roberto Murolo

CAST: Clifton Webb (John Frederick Shadwell), Dorothy McGuire (Miss Frances), Jean Peters (Anita Hutchins), Louis Jourdan (Prince Dino di Cessi), Maggie McNamara (Maria Williams), Rossano Brazzi (Giorgio Bianchi), Howard St. John (Burgoyne), Kathryn Givney (Mrs. Burgoyne), Cathleen Nesbitt (Principessa), Vincent Padula (Dr. Martinelli), Marco Siletti (Bartender), Alberto Morin (Waiter), Dino Bolognese (Headwaiter), Tony De Marco (Waiter in Venice), Jack Mattis (Consulate Clerk), Willard Waterman (Mr. Hoyt), Zachary Yaconelli (Theatrical Ticket Agent), Celia Lovsky (Baroness), Larry Arnold (Waiter in Select Restaurant), Renata Vanni (Anna),

Maurice Brierre (Pepe; Shadwell's Butler), Grazia Narciso (Louisa; the Maid), Gino Corrado (Butler), Charles La Torre (Chauffeur), Merry Anders (Girl), Norma Varden (Woman at Cocktail Party)

PLOT: Maria Williams arrives in Rome to work as a secretary for an American business firm and to replace Anita Hutchins, who has decided to return to the United States. Both girls share an apartment with Miss Frances, who has been working in Rome for the past fifteen years as a secretary to John Shadwell, a debonair, middle-aged American author known for his impeccable taste and caustic wit and for whom Miss Frances has unrequited affection. It emerges that Anita's decision to return to the US is motivated by the fact that she is in love with Giorgio Bianchi, a young Italian translator employed by her firm. However, company rules do not permit her to go out with local employees. The couple's defiance of this rule costs Giorgio his job. Anita quits her position and decides to marry him, but their plans come to naught because he does not earn enough to properly support himself. Meanwhile, Maria becomes romantically involved with Prince Dino di Cessi, a handsome but notorious playboy-prince whose efforts to take advantage of her are frustrated by Miss Frances. Maria, however, sets out on a shrewd campaign to win Prince Dino's heart, and before long, he asks her to become his bride. She then confesses the deceits she has employed to win his love and loses him as a result. In the meantime, Miss Frances, anticipating that her friends are about to be married, decides to leave Shadwell lest she remain an old maid. This awakens Shadwell's love for her, and he asks her to become his wife. Their plans also hit a snag when he learns from his doctor that he has just one year to live. He tries to get out of the marriage proposal through a flimsy excuse, but Miss Shadwell sees through it and convinces him that they should remain together come what may. At the same time, she tells him of Maria and Anita's romantic problems. Using his influence, he sees to it that Giorgio is reinstated in his job and that Prince Dino makes up with Maria. It all ends with the three couples meeting and embracing at the Trevi Fountain, where each of the girls had made a wish at the start of the story.

REVIEWS:
"[*Three Coins in the Fountain*] is at the same time light-hearted and tender-hearted in its appeal to youth and femininity. Seldom has sure boxoffice been combined so skillfully with skilled picturemaking." *Hollywood Reporter*, May 12, 1954

"A handsomely colored romance. . . . *Three Coins in the Fountain* is quite clearly a film in which the locale comes first. However, the nonsense of its fable crumbles nicely within the picture frame." *New York Times*, May 21, 1954

"A three-tiered love story . . . summer . . . Rome . . . colour . . . and Cinema-Scope. What could you ask? The answer: a lot more. . . . [F]ar too many trite romantic clichés slow up the work." *Picturegoer* (UK), July 17, 1954

REVIEWS for Jean Peters:
"Miss Peters has voluptuous appeal. She's also quite charming in the sequence involving her introduction to Brazzi's farmer parents." *Variety*, May 12, 1954

"Now that she has stopped playing lady pirates, Miss Peters reveals herself as a sultry, warm-blooded creature in her clinches with Rossano Brazzi." *New York Herald Tribune*, May 21, 1954

"Jean Peters appears worried rather than intense." *Monthly Film Bulletin* (UK), August 1954

ADDITIONAL REVIEWS and ARTICLES:
Hollywood Reporter, March 2 1953, p. 2; *Hollywood Reporter*, March 26, 1953, p. 2; *Hollywood Reporter*, July 16, 1953, p. 6; *Hollywood Reporter*, July 23, 1953, p. 3; *Hollywood Reporter*, August 6, 1953, p. 4; *Hollywood Reporter*, August 7, 1953, p. 10; *Hollywood Reporter*, August 31, 1953, p. 3; *Hollywood Reporter*, September 18,1953, p. 10; *Hollywood Reporter*, December 15, 1953, p. 3; *Hollywood Reporter*, December 22, 1953, p. 6; *Hollywood Reporter*, January 6, 1954, p. 3; *Hollywood Reporter*, January 11, 1954, p. 5; *Variety*, February 24, 1954; *Variety*, March 4, 1954; *Picturegoer* (UK), April 3, 1954; *Hollywood Reporter*, May 12, 1954, p. 3; *Film Daily*, May 12, 1954, p. 6; *Motion Picture Herald*, May 15, 1954, p. 2293; *Boxoffice*, May 15, 1954, p. 30; *Harrison's Reports*, May 15, 1954; *New York Times*, May 16, 1954, p. 9; *Boxoffice*, May 22, 1954; *Cue*, May 22, 1954, p. 15; *Christian Science Monitor*, Boston May 25, 1954, p. 4; *Los Angeles Times*, May 27, 1954; *New Yorker*, May 29, 1954, p. 52; *America*, May 29, 1954, p. 259; *Films in Review*, June-July 1954; *Life*, June 7, 1954, p. 151; *Newsweek*, May 31, 1954; *Time*, May 31, 1954; *Commonweal*, June 4, 1954, p. 223; *Saturday Review*, June 5, 1954, p 27; *Today's Cinema* (UK), June 23, 1954, p. 30; *Picturegoer* (UK), July 17, 1954, p. 18; *The Evening Standard* (UK), August 19, 1954; *The Star* (UK), August 20, 1954; *The Spectator* (UK), August 20, 1954, p. 221; *Daily Mail* (UK), August 20,

1954; *Financial Times* (UK), August 22, 1954: *The Observer*, August 22, 1954; *Photoplay*, August 1954, p. 14; *Screenland*, August 1954, p. 13; *The Sunday Express*, August 22, 1954; *The Times* (UK), August 23, 1954, p. 10; *The Tatler* (UK), September 1, 1954, p. 372; *Cahiers du Cinéma* (France), October 1954, p. 46; *Films and Filming* (UK), October 1954, p. 29; *Arts* (France), October 27, 1954; *Radio Cinema Télévision* (France), December 1954; *Hollywood Reporter*, March 8, 1955, p. 1; *Film Score Monthly*, July-August 2005, p. 57

AWARDS and HONORS:
Venice Film Festival; Italy 1954: Nominated: Golden Lion: Jean Negulesco

Academy Awards USA 1955; Nominated: Best Picture; Sol C. Siegel; Win: Best Cinematography; Color; Milton R. Krasner. Best Music; Original Song; "Three Coins in the Fountain," music and lyrics by Jule Styne and Sammy Cahn

Directors Guild of America; USA 1955; Nominated: DG Award; Outstanding Director; Jean Negulesco.

FILM NOTES: The working titles were *We Believe in Love* and *There's No Place Like Rome*. The picture was originally scheduled to be shot in black and white and starring Barbara Stanwyck, Gene Tierney, Vittorio Gassman, and Jeanne Crain. In 1964, Jean Negulesco directed *The Pleasure Seekers*, once again based on John H. Secondari's novel *Coins in the Fountain*.

Apache

A Hecht-Lancaster Presentation, United Artists Corp. Release
USA Technicolor 91 minutes
Premiered in Chicago, June 30, 1954
Premiered in New York City, July 9, 1954

CREDITS: *Director*: Robert Aldrich; *Producer*: Harold Hecht; *Production Manager*: Jack R. Berne; *Screenplay*: James R. Webb, from the novel *Broncho Apache* by Paul I. Wellman; *Assistant Director*: Sid Sidman; *Editorial Supervisor*: Alan Crosland Jr.; *Production Manager*: Jack R. Bernie; *Costume Designer*: Norma; *Set Decorator*: Joseph Kish; *Technicolor Color Consultant*: Leonard Doss; *Special Effects*: Lee Zavitz; *Makeup*: Harry Maret, Robert Schiffer; *Hair Styles*: Lillian Ugrin, Katherine Shea; *Orchestrations*: Maurice De Packh, Ruby Raksin; *Music Editor*: W. Lloyd Young; *Sound Engineer*: Jack Solomon;

Photography: Ernest Laszlo, ASC; *Production Designer*: Nicolai Remisoff; *Music:* David Raksin; *Film Editor*: Edward Mann

CAST: Burt Lancaster (Massai), Jean Peters (Nalinle), John McIntire (Al Sieber), Charles Bronson as Charles Buchinsky (Hondo), John Dehner (Weddle), Paul Guilfoyle (Santos), Ian MacDonald (Clagg), Walter Sande (Lt. Col. Beck), Morris Ankrum (Dawson), Monte Blue (Geronimo), Paul E. Burns (General Store Owner), Lonnie Burr (Indian Boy), John George (Shoeshine Man); Ann Kunde (Townswoman Leaving Trading Post), Rory Mallinson (Citizen Noticing Handcuffs), Mort Mills (Sergeant of the Guard Fort), Dick Rich (Loafing Trooper), Steve Rowland (Teenage Bully in Street), Tony Urchel (Apache), Philip Van Zandt (Inspector), William Wilkerson (Apache)

PLOT: Massai indicates his flaming hatred of the white man trying to break the truce, at which point Geronimo surrenders. Despite the fact that he shoots down the truce flag, Massai is taken prisoner by Al Sieber, the chief of the scouts, and an Indian aide, Hondo, under the eyes of Lt. Col. Beck, the cavalry commander—but not before Massai vows to the Indian maid who loves him, Nalinle, that he will always remain on the warpath. On his journey across the country for imprisonment at St. Augustine, Florida, Massai escapes in the confusion that follows the discharge of an old-fashioned flash gun, which is used to take news pictures of Geronimo. In an adventure-filled trek, Massai makes his way across the country and back to the Apache reservation after encountering a Cherokee Indian whose corn farming in the white men's pattern both impresses and disgusts him. With mixed emotions, he takes with him a gift of seed corn. Back at the reservation, he is betrayed by Santos, Nalinle's peace-at-any-price father, who fears Massai's hot blood might touch off another uprising by the young braves, who already sing of Massai around the fires. In irons once more, Massai is again on his way back to the Florida prison when the Indian agent, Weddle, turns him loose in a plot to murder Massai under the camouflage of an attempted escape. Massai outwits Weddle, gets out of the chains, and leaves the scene armed, mounted, and primed for war. He returns to the reservation to avenge himself on his betrayers, one of whom he believes is Nalinle. On his way, supply dumps go up in flames, an ammunition train is exploded, and the horses are stampeded—all part of Massai's war. In the midst of it, he rides off with Nalinle as his prisoner. They flee to a high mountain valley in the Far West, where Nalinle's devotion to him is proved again and again until his heart relents and they marry each other according to tribal custom. But the army finally tracks them down, and as Nalinle prepares to bear his child on what amounts to a little corn farm he has scratched out of the wilderness with his bare hands, he prepares himself to die a warrior's death as the soldiers close in. As they are about to kill Massai, a newborn baby cries. He stands up and walks in the direction of the cry. No one fires. Massai, the warrior, now farmer and father, has turned to the path of peace.

REVIEWS:
"*Apache* . . . is a superior film of its kind, bringing to the screen an exciting and sensitive story." *Motion Picture Daily*, June 30, 1954

"Punchy action film treating Indians sympathetically." *Variety*, June 30, 1954

"[The] action is a leaden, talky and overly detailed business." *New York Times*, July 10, 1954

REVIEWS for Jean Peters:
"Jean Peters' womanly playing of a loyal and long-suffering Indian girl gives this film a heart appeal that lifts it out of the class of the routine Western." *Hollywood Reporter*, June 30, 1954

"An effective dramatic work is done by Jean Peters as an Apache maiden." *Harrison's Reports*, July 3, 1954

"Miss Peters is commendable in a role that is far from glamorous." *NY Daily News*, July 10, 1953

ADDITIONAL REVIEWS and ARTICLES:
Hollywood Reporter, June 7, 1952; *Hollywood Reporter*, September 29, 1953, p. 2; *Film Bulletin*, October 8, 1953, p. 17; *Hollywood Reporter*, October 16, 1953, p. 11; *Hollywood Reporter*, October 30, 1953, p. 2; *New York Times*, December 27, 1953, p. X7; *Hollywood Reporter*, January 8, 1954; *Hollywood Reporter*, January 15, 1954, p. 7; *New York Times*, February 8, 1954, p. 19; *National Parent-Teacher*, June 1954, p. 38; *Nation Parent-Teacher*, June 1954, p. 38; *Hollywood Reporter*, June 28, 1954, p. 8; *Daily Variety*, June 30, 1954, p. 3; *Farm Journal*, July 1954, p. 92; *Modern Screen*, July 1954, p. 25; *Boxoffice*, July 3, 1954; *Motion Picture Herald*, July 3, 1954, p. 49; *Film Daily*, July 7, 1954, p. 10; *Film Bulletin*, July 11, 1954, p. 8; *The Exhibitor*, July 14, 1954, pp. 3,786–87; *Los Angeles Times*, July 22, 1954, p. A6; *Commonweal*, July 30, 1954, p. 413; *Photoplay*, August 1954, p. 16; *Screenland*, August 1954, p. 14; *Time*, August 9, 1954, p. 84; *Today's Cinema*

(UK), August 11, 1954, p. 10; *Kinematograph Weekly* (UK), August 19, 1954, p. 18; *The Times* (UK), August 30, 1954, p. 5; *Monthly Film Bulletin* (UK), September 1954, p. 126; *New Statesman and Nation*, September 4, 1954, p. 264; *Picturegoer* (UK), September 18, 1954, p. 21; *Picture Show* (UK), September 25, 1954, p. 10; *Hollywood Reporter*, October 1, 1954, p. 1; *Il Corriere della Sera* (Italy), January 22, 1955, p. 4; *Cinémonde* (France), February 2, 1955, p. 12; *Cahiers du Cinéma* (France), March 1955, pp. 45-46; *Positif* (France), November 1955, p. 11; *Positif* (France), May 1956, p. 11; *Variety*, October 23, 1957; *Cinéma* (France), May 1958, p. 40; *Daily Variety*, November 8, 1960; *Image et Son* (France), October 1974, p. 137; *Positif* (France), June 1976, p. 12; The Listener (UK), February 12, 1987, p. 31; *The Listener* (UK), November 24, 1988, p. 36; *Empire* (UK), January 2003, p. 164; *Positif* (France), September 2009, pp. 96-98

FILM NOTES: *Bronco Apache* was the working title.

Broken Lance

20th Century Fox Film Corporation
USA Technicolor CinemaScope 96 minutes
Premiered in New York City, July 29, 1954

CREDITS: *Director*: Edward Dmytryk; *Producer*: Sol C. Siegel; *Screenplay*: Richard Murphy, based on a story by Philip Yordan, *Director of Photography*: Joe MacDonald, ASC; *Special Photographic Effects*: Ray Kellogg; *Film Editor*: Dorothy Spencer, ACE; *Art Direction*: Lyle Wheeler, Maurice Ransford; *Set Decorations*: Walter M. Scott, Stuart Reiss; *Costumes Designer*: Bill Travilla; *Wardrobe Direction*: Charles LeMaire; *Makeup Artist*: Ben Nye; *Hair Styling*: Helen Turpin; *Music*: Leigh Harline; *Music Conductor*: Lionel Newman; *Orchestration*: Edward B. Powell; *Sound*: W. D. Flick, Roger Heman; *Assistant Director*: Henry Weinberger

CAST: Spencer Tracy (Matthew Devereaux), Robert Wagner (Joe Devereaux), Jean Peters (Barbara), Richard Widmark (Ben Devereaux), Katy Jurado (Señora Devereaux), Hugh O'Brian (Mike Devereaux), Eduard Franz (Two Moons), Earl Holliman (Denny Devereaux), E. G. Marshall (Horace, the Governor), Carl Benton Reid (Clem Lawton), Philip Ober (Van Cleve), Robert Burton (MacAndrews), Bob Adler (O'Reilly), Robert Grandin (Capitol Clerk), King Donovan (Clerk), Harry Carter (Prison Guard), Nacho Galindo (Cook), Julian Rivero (Manuel), Edmund Cobb (Court Clerk), Jack Mather (Gateman), John Epper (Ranger), Paul Kruger (Bailiff), James Stone

(Stable Owner), Russell Simpson (Judge), George E. Stone (Paymaster), Arthur Q. Bryan (Man in Capitol Rotunda), Chief Geronimo Kuthlee (Chief), Anthony Marsh (Miner), John Roy (Miner), Norman Stevans (Lawyer)

PLOT: The story opens with Joe Devereaux leaving a crude prison somewhere in the great American Southwest in the 1880s. The next day, Joe rejects the offer of $10,000 by his half-brothers—Ben, Mike, and Danny—to start a new life in Oregon. Joe returns to his home and, as he gazes at his father's portrait, recalls the family history. Matt Devereaux, a powerful, vital man, dominates his family. Joe reports cattle rustlers, and when Matt, Joe and Two Moons, the Indian ranch foreman, intercept them, it is discovered that two of the rustlers are Matt's sons, Mike and Danny. Matt banishes the boys from his domain, but Matt's Indian wife attempts to heal the wound in the family structure. At a party in their great living room, the guests include the governor and his beautiful daughter, Barbara. Joe discovers Barbara, and a romance ensues. The two banished brothers are also present at Joe's invitation, and Matt accepts them rather than creating a social impasse. The party breaks up when it is reported that Matt's cattle are dying from poisoning by waste from a copper mine. Matt and his sons ride out to the mine, and a fight breaks out. The Devereauxs' band is about to retreat when Two Moons and sixty vaqueros ride up. There is a tremendous battle with many men hurt but none killed. Matt is faced with a lawsuit, and when he asks for help from the governor, he is told that he can get it if his son stops courting Barbara. This enrages Matt. In court, the suit is going against him when Joe takes the rap. Earlier, Matt had transferred his holdings to his sons, and while Joe languishes in jail, his brothers attempt to sell more of the Deveraux ranch to the mine operators. Matt, trying to help Joe, pleads with the three for mercy. They defy him, and he suffers an apoplectic stroke. When he tries to ride after them, he falls from his saddle and dies. At the funeral, Joe tosses a lance between Ben and himself, which is the Indian way of proclaiming a blood feud. The story then returns to Joe standing before his father's picture. He takes his father's pistols, but his mother persuades him to forget revenge. On the way to town, he is intercepted by Ben, who attempts to murder him. Two Moons shoots Ben. Later, Barbara and Joe ride up to Matt's grave. The Indian lance still lies there. Joe breaks it, symbolizing the end of the feud.

REVIEWS:
"*Broken Lance* emerges as a powerful and gripping dramatic entertainment."
Harrison's Reports, July 31, 1954

"Despite a quantity of horse-opera clichés and distractingly handsome scenery, the focus is made clear and sometimes intense by a couple of eminently competent craftsmen, Spencer Tracy and Richard Widmark." *Newsweek*, August 16, 1954

"A superficial, glossy, entertaining melodrama." *Monthly Film Bulletin* (UK), November 1954

REVIEWS for Jean Peters:
"Jean Peters is excellent as the strong-willed girl." *Hollywood Reporter*, July 23, 1954

"Jean Peters is the standard Western heroine, the kind that is usually left standing by while the hero kisses the horse. At the beginning of her career, she was rather impressive in her quietness and managed to suggest depth. She is still quiet." *Films and Filming* (UK), October 1954

"Jean Peters, as the [g]overnor's daughter . . . is decorative but hardly the frontier type." *New York Times*, July 30, 1954

ADDITIONAL REVIEWS and ARTICLES:
Hollywood Reporter, November 23, 1953, p. 2; *Hollywood Reporter*, December 1, 1953, p. 1; *Hollywood Reporter*, December 7, 1953, p. 2; *Daily Variety*, December 16, 1953; *Hollywood Reporter*, January 25, 1954, p. 2; *Hollywood Reporter*, February 5, 1954, p. 3; *Hollywood Reporter*, February 11, 1954, p. 6; *Hollywood Reporter*, February 24, 1954, p. 6; *Hollywood Reporter*, March 2, 1954, p. 6; *Hollywood Reporter*, March 5, 1954, p. 1; *Hollywood Reporter*, March 18, 1954, p. 9; *Hollywood Reporter*, April 9, 1954, pp. 5, 8, 11; *New York Times*, May 2, 1954, p. X5; *Hollywood Reporter*, May 14, 1954, p. 5; *Modern Screen*, July 1954, p. 25; *Daily Variety*, July 23, 1954, p. 3; *Film Daily*, July 23, 1954, p. 10; *Motion Picture Daily*, July 23, 1954, p. 6; *Variety*, July 28, 1954, p. 6; *Boxoffice*, July 31, 1954, p. 50; *Motion Picture Herald*, July 31, 1954, p. 89; *Los Angeles Times*, July 31, 1954, p. A3; *Boston Globe*, August 6, 1954, p. 9; *Boxoffice*, August 7, 1954; *Film Bulletin*, August 9, 1954, p. 12; *America*, August 14, 1954, p. 486; *Hollywood Reporter*, August 18, 1954, p. 1; *Time*, August 23, 1954, pp. 72, 75; *Chicago Daily Tribune*, August 27, 1954, p. A10; *Commonweal*, August 27, 1954, p. 513; *Catholic World*, September 1954, p. 464; *Today's Cinema* (UK), September 16, 1954, p. 7; *Kinematograph Weekly* (UK), September 23, 1954, p. 13; *Photoplay*, October 1954, p. 9; *Films in Review*, October 1954, pp. 434–35; *National Parent-Teacher*, October 1954, p. 39; *The Times* (UK), November 14, 1954, p.

11; *The Tatler* (UK), November 24, 1954, p. 72; *Picturegoer* (UK), November 27, 1954, p. 20; *Films and Filming* (UK), December 1954, p. 19; *Picture Show* (UK), December 11, 1954, pp. 8–9; *Il Corriere della Sera* (Italy), February 25, 1955, p. 4; *Cinémonde* (France), March 4, 1955, p. 18; *Mon Film* (France), April 20, 1955, p. 8; *Cinématographe* (France), November 1978, p. 80; *Sight and Sound* (UK), August 1991, p. 60; *Discourse* (UK), Autumn/Winter 1995/96, pp. 23–31

AWARDS and HONORS:
Golden Globes; USA 1955; Winner: Best Film Promoting International Understanding

Academy Awards USA 1955; Winner: Best Writing, Motion Picture Story Philip Yordan; Nominated: Best Actress in a Supporting Role: Katy Jurado

FILM NOTES: Posters and press books indicate that DeLuxe was the color print used; however, Technicolor appears in the film credits as the correct color print.

A Man Called Peter

20th Century Fox Film Corporation
USA Color DeLuxe, CinemaScope 119 minutes
Premiered in New York City, March 31, 1955

CREDITS: *Director*: Henry Koster; *Producer*: Samuel G. Engel; *Screenplay*: Eleanore Griffin, based on the book by Catherine Marshall; *Director of Photography*: Harold Lipstein; *Film Editor*: Robert Simpson; *Art Directors*: Lyle Wheeler, Maurice Ransford; *Set Decorators*: Walter M. Scott, Chester Bayhi; *Special Visual Effects*: Ray Kellogg; *Music*: Alfred Newman; *Sound*: Bernard Freericks, Harry M. Leonard; *Wardrobe Direction*: Charles LeMaire; *Costume Designer*: Renié; *Makeup Artist*: Ben Nye; *Vocal Supervision*: Ken Darby; *Orchestrations*: Edward B. Powell; *Color Consultant*: Leonard Doss; *Assistant Director*: David Silver

CAST: Richard Todd (Peter Marshall), Jean Peters (Catherine Wood Marshall), Marjorie Rambeau (Miss Fowler), Jill Esmond (Mrs. Findlay), Les Tremayne (Senator Harvey), Robert Burton (Mr. Peyton), Gladys Hurlbut (Mrs. Peyton), Richard Garrick (Col. Whiting), Gloria Gordon (Barbara), Billy Chapin (Peter John Marshall), Jacqueline Cox (Diana), John Pike (David), Brian Franklin (Young Peter), Sally Corner (Mrs. Whiting, Voltaire

Perkins Senator Wiley), Edward Earle (Senator Prescott), Marietta Canty
(Emma), Peter Votrian (Peter Marshall, age seven and fourteen), Rickey
Kelman (Peter age five), Louis Torres Jr. (Peter age six), Agnes Bartholomew
(Grandmother), Arthur Tovey (Usher), Mimi Hutson (College Girl), Janet
Stewart (College Girl), Sam McDaniel (Maitre d'), Dorothy Neumann (Miss
Crilly), Oliver Hartwell (Janitor), Doris Lloyd (Miss Hopkins), William For-
rest (Seminary President), Barbara Morrison (Miss Standish), Betty Caul-
field (June Whitney), Ann Davis (Ruby Coleman), Carlyle Mitchell (Dr.
Milton Black), Emmett Lynn (Mr. Briscoe), Bill Walker (Butler), Charles
Evans (President of Senate), Larry Kent (Chaplain at Naval Academy), Ruth
Clifford (Nurse), Ben Wright (Mr. Findlay)

PLOT: Peter Marshall is born with a love of the sea and has early aspira-
tions to become a sailor. The son of poor but deeply religious parents,
Peter grows up into a young man of vigor and outstanding character. As he
crosses a moor on a dark night, he suddenly stops and calls, "Who is it?"
but proceeds and trips. He puts his hand ahead of him into nothingness:
he has fallen on the brink of an abandoned quarry. On his knees, he looks
upward and exclaims: "So it was YOU who called me." When Peter returns
home, he tells his mother that God has called him to the ministry and is
sending him to America. From that day forward, Peter considers himself to
be completely in the hands of God, or The Chief, as he calls Him. Things
are difficult in America at first, and Peter fears he has misunderstood The
Chief. But by a series of near miracles, he finds himself in a theological
seminary and then as a remarkably successful young preacher. As a pastor
of Westminster Presbyterian Church in Atlanta, Peter's services appeal
greatly to young people, among them Catherine Wood, a student at nearby
Agnes Scott College. She adores him from a distance, as do many other
young women, but he is only casually aware of her. Church work throws
them together, and his awareness increases but remains impersonal. Suddenly, The Chief reveals to Peter the miracle of love. They are married, and
Peter is called to the pastorate of New York Avenue Presbyterian Church
in Washington, Abraham Lincoln's place of worship. Peter has certain
problems, of course, but his religious concept and the beauty with which
he expresses it attract thousands to the church and brings increasing
acclaim to its minister. A boy, whom they christen Peter John, is born to
the Marshalls. After Pearl Harbor, Peter extends his ministry to the military
and his duties are vastly increased. Catherine comes down with tubercu-
losis and is confined to her bed for months. Peter is beside himself and
feels he may have offended The Chief. Increasingly embittered, Catherine

finally resigns herself to God's will. And suddenly, she is well! The strain on Peter takes its toll, and he suffers a heart attack at the pulpit in 1946. He recovers but spurns the doctor's advice and the advice of his family and friends to take things easier. He believes that whether he lives or dies is wholly in the hands of The Chief, and he continues to labor strenuously in His service. Against all advice, he accepts the post of chaplain of the US Senate, where his trenchant prayers bring him a national reputation. But it is all too much, and in 1949, he is stricken with another, this time fatal, heart attack at the age of forty-six. For a protracted season, Catherine seeks some explanation for the untimely death of this good young man. One day, it comes to her that the answer lies in Peter's final words to her: "See you, darling. See you in the morning."

REVIEWS:
"Tender, yet forthright." *Variety*, March 23, 1955

"The film version of *A Man Called Peter* meets its challenges commendably. It is certainly a popular rather than a deeply significant picture." *Christian Science Monitor*, April 5, 1955

"Sentimental. Wordy. Its 'slippers and fireside' approach to the religious theme may strike you as too cozy." *Picturegoer* (UK), May 7, 1955

REVIEWS for Jean Peters:
"Superlative also would be required to describe the work of Jean Peters." *Hollywood Reporter*, March 23, 1955

"Jean Peters plays Catherine Marshall in a wholesome, ladylike way." *New York Times*, April 1, 1955

"Jean Peters gives a warm performance." *New York Herald Tribune*, April 1, 1955

ADDITIONAL REVIEWS and ARTICLES:
Daily Variety, December 3, 1952; *Los Angeles Times*, January 1953, p. 22; *Hollywood Reporter*, September 15, 1953, p. 1; *Daily Variety*, November 19, 1953; *Hollywood Reporter*, November 19, 1953, p. 8; *Daily Variety*, December 7, 1953; *Hollywood Reporter*, December 7, 1953, pp. 2, 11; *Hollywood Reporter*, March 22, 1954, p. 2; *Hollywood Reporter*, May 21, 1954, p. 3; *Hollywood Reporter*, August 4, 1954, p. 2; *Hollywood Reporter*, August 26, 1954, p. 2; *Hollywood*

Reporter, September 1, 1954, p. 2; *Picturegoer* (UK), September 18, 1954, p. 10; *Hollywood Reporter*, September 23, 1954, p. 2; *Hollywood Reporter*, October 5, 1954, p. 7; *Hollywood Reporter*, October 11, 1954, p. 2; *Hollywood Reporter*, October 12, 1954 p. 3; *Hollywood Reporter*, October 14, 1954 p. 4; *Hollywood Reporter*, October 22, 1954, pp. 6, 7; *Hollywood Reporter*, October 27, 1954, p. 4; *Hollywood Reporter*, October 28, 1954, p. 2; *Hollywood Reporter*, November 9, 1954, pp. 2, 6, 9; *Hollywood Reporter*, November 10, 1954, p. 2; *Hollywood Reporter*, November 12, 1954, p. 2; *Hollywood Reporter*, November 18, 1954, p. 8; *Hollywood Reporter*, November 22, 1954, p. 2; *Hollywood Reporter*, November 24, 1954, p. 2; *Hollywood Reporter*, December 1, 1954, pp. 6, 9; *Hollywood Reporter*, December 9, 1954, pp. 9, 13; *Hollywood Reporter*, December 20, 1954, p. 2; *Hollywood Reporter*, February 15, 1955, p. 5; *Look*, March 1956, pp. 27–28; *Motion Picture Herald*, March 1955, p. 377; *Hollywood Reporter*, March 2, 1955, p. 11; *Hollywood Reporter*, March 15, 1955, pp. 2, 5; *Hollywood Reporter*, March 17, 1955, p. 3; *Daily Variety*, March 23, 1955. p. 3; *Film Daily*, March 23, 1955, p. 6; *Motion Picture Daily*, March 23, 1955, pp. 1, 6; *Boxoffice*, March 26, 1955; *Harrison's Reports*, March 26, 1955, p. 50; *New York Daily News*, March 27, 1955, p. 2; *New York Herald Tribune*, March 27, 1955, p. D3; *Hollywood Reporter*, March 29, 1955, p. 2; *Hollywood Reporter*, March 30, 1955, p. 2; *Hollywood Reporter*, March 30, 1955, p. 5; *Kinematograph Weekly* (UK), March 31, 1955, p. 23; *Today's Cinema* (UK), March 31, 1955, p. 7; *Hollywood Reporter*, April 1, 1955, p. 3; *Films in Review*, April 1955, p. 187; *New York Daily News*, April 1, 1955, p. 2; *Redbook*, April 1955, p. 6; *Screenland*, April 1955, p. 72; *Library Journal*, April 1, 1955, p. 775; *American Magazine*, April 1955, p. 16; *Los Angeles Times*, April 2, 1955, p. 15; *Independent Film Journal*, April 2, 1955, p 16; *Saturday Review*, April 2, 1955, p. 32; *Life*, April 4, 1955, pp. 115–20; *Newsweek*, April 4, 1955 p. 60; *Film Bulletin*, April 4, 1955, p. 20; *Hollywood Reporter*, April 5, 1955 p. 8; *The Exhibitor*, April 6, 1955, p. 3944; *Chicago Daily Tribune*, April 8, 1955, p. A7; *Commonweal*, April 8, 1955, pp. 14–15; *America*, April 9, 1955, p. 55; *New York Times*, April 10, 1955 sec. II p. 1; *Time*, April 11, 1955, p. 110; *Hollywood Reporter*, April 14, 1955 p. 1; *New Yorker*, April 16, 1955, p. 146; *New York Times*, April 17, 1955 sec. II p. 5; *The Times* (UK), April 22, 1955, p. 17; *Film Culture*, May-June 1955, pp. 24–25; *Woman's Home Companion*, May 1955, pp. 18–19; *Monthly Film Bulletin* (UK), May 1955, p. 71; *Catholic World*, May 1955, pp. 141–42; *National Parent-Teacher*, May 1955, p. 38; *Hollywood Reporter*, May 6, 1955, p. 1; *Hollywood Citizen-News*, May 19, 1955; *Modern Screen*, June 1955, p. 14; *Films and Filming* (UK), June 1955, p. 22; *Hollywood Reporter*, June 10, 1955, p. 1; *Hollywood Reporter*, December 14, 1955, pp. 1, 4; *Hollywood Reporter*, February 2, 1956, p. 3; *Picturegoer Film Annual* (UK), 1957–58 pp. 106–7; *Films of the Golden Age*, Spring 2002, pp. 8–9; *Classic Images*, August 2005, pp. 30–31

AWARDS and HONORS:
Academy Awards USA 1956: Nominated: Best Cinematography, Color:
Harold Lipstein

Directors Guild of America, USA 1956: Nominated: Outstanding Directorial
Achievement in Motion Pictures: Henry Koster

FILM NOTES: Simultaneous world premieres of the film were held on
March 31, 1955, in Glasgow, New York, and London.

TELEVISION MOVIES

Winesburg, Ohio

Hollywood Television Theatre
USA Color 90 minutes
PBS Network March 5, 1973

CREDITS: *Director*: Ralph Senensky; *Producer*: Norman Lloyd; *Associate Producer*: George Turpin; *Associate Director*: Zane Radney; *Teleplay*: Christopher
Sergel based on a novel by Sherwood Anderson; *Art Direction*: Michael
Baugh; *Music*: Robert Prince; *Costumes*: Noel Taylor; *Lighting Designer*:
Danny Franks; *Audio*: Tom Ancel; *Stage Manager*: Mike Stanislavsky

CAST: Jean Peters (Elizabeth Willard), Joseph Bottoms (George Willard),
William Windom (Dr. Reefy), Albert Salmi (Tom Willard), Norman Foster
(Old Pete), Gary Barton (Art), Curt Conway (Will Henderson), Dabbs Greer
(Parcival), Chip Hand (Seth), George Winter (Turk), Laurette Spang (Helen
White), Don Hammer (Ed Crowley), Alvin Hammer (Salesman), Pitt Herbert
(Mr. Wilson), Arlene Stuart (Mrs. Wilson)

PLOT: Elizabeth Willard is a frail, sickly mother living in Winesburg, Ohio,
where she was once a reigning beauty. She tries to get George, her talented
young son, to leave the town that has suffocated her dreams and led her to
an empty life. But Tom, Elizabeth's husband, who runs a depressing hotel
in town, wants the boy, who is a promising writer, to stay and help out.

REVIEWS:

"An easy play to watch and it stands on its own melodramatic merits, but it has little to do with what Sherwood Anderson wrote in his 1919 tales." *Washington Post*, March 5, 1973

"A compelling story." *Hartford Courant*, March 5, 1973

REVIEWS for Jean Peters:
"The production . . . is outstanding, underscored by a sensitive and moving performance by Miss Peters." *Hollywood Reporter*, March 5, 1973

"Miss Peters retains her sweetness and beauty but lacks the inner fire to bring out the tumult in Elizabeth Willard's soul." *Boston Globe*, March 5, 1973

"The actress is adequate, but her performance is a surface one. It's a blunt performance with lines delivered on time, but character revelation is lost as she rigidly moves through three acts." *New York Daily News*, March 5, 1973

ADDITIONAL REVIEWS and ARTICLES:
The Morning Call, March 2, 1973, p. 38; *The Pittsburgh Press*, March 2, 1973, p. 42; *Courier Post*, March 3, 1973, p. 3; *TV Guide*, March 3, 1973, pp. 25–26; *Boston Globe*, March 4, 1973, p. 17; *Chicago Tribune TV Guide*, March 4, 1973, p. 5; *Courier Post*, March 5, 1973, p. 13; *Milwaukee Journal*, March 4, 1973, p. 4; *New York Sunday News*, March 4, 1973, p. 17; *Philadelphia Daily News*, March 5, 1973, p. 42; *Los Angeles Times*, March 5, 1973, p. F13; *Los Angeles Herald-Examiner*, March 18, 1973, p. C3; *Ladies' Home Journal*, March 1973, pp. 70, 72

TELEVISION MINISERIES

The Moneychangers

Paramount Television—NBC
USA Color 320 minutes
NBC Network December 4, 1976

CREDITS: *Director*: Boris Sagal; *Producers*: Ross Hunter, Jacques Mapes; *Associate Producer*: Marvin Miller; *Teleplay*: Dean Riesner, Stanford Whitmore, based on a novel by Arthur Hailey; *Music*: Henry Mancini; *Cinematography*: Joseph F. Biroc; *Editing*; Richard Bracken; *Casting*: Mildred Gusse; *Art Direction*: Jack De Shields; *Set Decorations*: George Gaines; *Costumes*: Guy C. Verhille; *Makeup*: Joe DiBella, Ron Snyder; *Hair Stylist*: Kathryn Blondell,

Dorothy Byrne; *Production Manager*: Joseph M. Ellis; *Assistant Director*: Mel Efros; *Sound*: Bud Alper, Frank White, Harold E. Wooley; *Special Effects*: Joseph P. Mercurio, Edwin Tillman; *Music Editor*: James E. O'Keefe

CAST: Kirk Douglas (Alex Vandervoort), Christopher Plummer (Roscoe Heyward), Timothy Bottoms (Miles Eastin), Susan Flannery (Margot Bracken), Anne Baxter (Edwina Dorsey), Percy Rodrigues (Nolan Wainwright), Ralph Bellamy (Jerome Patterton), Joan Collins (Avril Devereaux), Robert Loggia (Tony Bear), Marisa Pavan (Celia Vandervoort), Jean Peters (Beatrice Heyward), Hayden Rorke (Lewis Dorsey), James Shigeta (Wizard Wong), Amy Levitt (Juanita Nunez), Patrick O'Neal (Harold Austin), Lorne Greene (George Quartermain), Helen Hayes (Dr. McCartney), Roger Bowen (Fergus Gatwick), Leonardo Cimino (Ben Rosselli), Douglas Fowley (Danny Kerrigan), Basil Hoffman (Stanley Inchbeck), Lincoln Kilpatrick (Deacon Euphrates), Harry Lewis (George Sperrie), Woodrow Parfrey (Mr. Tottenhoe), Michael Shannon (Lew Endicott), Stan Shaw (John Dinkerwell), Joseph R. Sicari (Julius LaRocca), Chick Vennera (Humphy Lopez), Virginia Grey (Miss Callahan)

PLOT: A power struggle between Alex Vandervoort and Roscoe Heyward for the presidency of a vast banking empire brings the two ambitious executives into a conflict that impacts the lives of those around them.

REVIEWS:
"If 'rich banker, poor banker' is what you are looking for in the way of easy entertainment, certainly this one offers its own brand of super-soap-opera panache." *Christian Science Monitor*, December 2, 1976

"[The] cast is good enough to make most of this nonsense bearable." *New York Times*, December 3, 1976

"The cast of mostly familiar names is pro, the scripting is slick if simple, resulting in a fairly entertaining potboiler." *Variety*, December 8, 1976

REVIEWS for Jean Peters:
"Jean Peters was as beautiful as ever as the spendthrift wife of an ambitious man." *Hollywood Reporter*, December 6, 1976

"Two veteran actresses, Anne Baxter and Jean Peters are unusually impressive in their roles." *Pittsburgh Post-Gazette*, December 3, 1976

ADDITIONAL REVIEWS and ARTICLES:
Variety, March 12, 1975, p. 44; *New York Daily News*, February 16, 1976, p. 57; *NY*, June 22, 1976, p. 40; *Los Angeles Times*, June 24, 1976, p. E18; *Hollywood Reporter*, June 28, 1976, p. 4; *Hollywood Reporter*, July 1, 1976, p. 15; *Variety*, August 18, 1976, p. 2; *Time*, September 6, 1976, p. 71; *Variety*, September 22, 1976, p. 2; *New York Daily News*, December 2, 1976, p. 156; *New York Post*, December 2, 1976, p. 62; *Democrat and Chronicle*, December 5, 1976, p. 5; *Los Angeles Times*, December 10, 1976, p. G7; *New York Times*, December 12, 1976, p. D33; *New York Sunday News*, December 12, 1976, p. TV 1; *New York Times*, December 22, 1976, p. 59; *Hollywood Reporter*, July 27, 1977, p. 1; *Variety*, July 27, 1977, p. 1; *Films in Review*, November 1977, p. 555; *Time Out London* (UK), January 20, 1978, p. 15; *The Sun* (UK), January 26, 1978; *TV Times* (UK), January 1978, pp. 2–3; *Il Corriere della Sera* (Italy), June 1, 1979, p. 23

AWARDS and HONORS:
Primetime Emmy, USA 1976; Winner: Outstanding Lead Actor in a Limited Series: Christopher Plummer
Nominated: Outstanding Achievement in Graphic Design and Title Sequences: Phill Norman. Nominated: Outstanding Cinematography in Entertainment Programming for a Series: Joseph F. Biroc (for part I). Nominated: Outstanding Lead Actress in a Limited Series: Susan Flannery. Nominated: Outstanding Limited Series: Ross Hunter, Jacques Mapes

NOTES: *The Moneychangers* aired in four ninety-minute segments as part of NBC's Big Event. *Arthur Hailey's The Moneychangers* was the alternative title.

Peter and Paul

Universal Television-Procter & Gamble
USA Color 198 minutes
CBS Network April 20, 1981

CREDITS: *Director*: Robert Day; *Producer*: Stan Hough; *Teleplay*: Christopher Knopf; *Story*: Stan Hough; *Director of Photography*: Richard C. Glouner, ASC; *Film Editor*: Houseley Stevenson; *Production Designer*: George Renne; *Costume Designer*: Nino Novarese; *Costumes*: Lambert Marks, Hugo Pena; *Music*: Allyn Ferguson; *Art Director*: Marylene Aravantino; *Set Decorators*: Joseph Stones, Joseph Chevalier; *Makeup*: Albert Jeyte, James Kail; *Sound*: Bryan Marshall, David Pearson; *Casting*: Phil Benjamin, Weston Drury Jr., George Katakouzinos; *Assistant Directors*: James Gardner, Mark Schilz; *Unit Production Managers*: George Bisk, Dimitris Dimitriadis, John C. Chulay

CAST: Anthony Hopkins (Paul), Robert Foxworth (Peter), Eddie Albert (Festus), Raymond Burr (Herod Agrippa I), José Ferrer (Gamaliel), Jon Finch (Luke), David Gwillim (Mark), Herbert Lom (Barnabas), Jean Peters (Priscilla), Julian Fellowes (Nero), Shanit Keter (Daphne), Denis Lill (James I), John Rhys-Davies (Silas), Gareth Thomas (Julius), Clive Arrindell (Timothy), Kenneth Colley (Theodotus), Vernon Dobtcheff (Herod's High Priest), Donald Douglas (Burrus), Valentine Dyall (Seneca), James Faulkner (Menachem), Paul Herzberg (Herod Agrippa II), Emrys James (Ananias), Olga Karlatos (Bernice), Harold Kasket (Pisidian High Priest), Stanley Lebor (Naaman), Despina Tomazina (Peter's Wife), Yannis Voglis (John), John Gabriel (Bald Man), Howard Goorney (1st Minister), Michael Griffiths (2nd Minister), Kevork Malikyan (Sapai), Adrian Mann (Mark, as a Boy), Nicholas Savalis (James II), Robert Day (Scribe)

PLOT: The story recounts the works of Peter, the rock of the Church, and Paul of Tarsus, the first missionary to the Gentiles. Their journey of faith is chronicled from Christ's Crucifixion until they sacrifice their own lives for their beliefs three epochal decades later.

REVIEWS:
"Mr. Knopf has failed to dramatize what are truly fascinating arguments and developments. The action is always coming to a standstill." *New York Times*, April 10, 1981

"A huge, lush affair . . . the cast is enormous with several notable performances." *Los Angeles Times*, April 10, 1981

"[The] production is interesting intellectually and . . . challenging, but it does not have the grandeur of the now classic *Jesus of Nazareth*." *New York Daily News*, April 10, 1981

REVIEWS for Jean Peters:
"Jean Peters, wife of producer Stan Hough, makes the role as memorable as the lines allow." *Newsday*, April 12, 1981

ADDITIONAL REVIEWS and ARTICLES:
Screen International (UK), December 20, 1980, p. 4; *Wall Street Journal*, April 6, 1981, p. 26; *Time*, April 6, 1981, p. 76; *New York Post*, April 10, 1981, p. 94; *TV Guide,* April 11, 1981, pp. 13–15; *New York Sunday News*, April 12, 1981, *TV Week*, p. 4; *New York Times*, April 12, 1981, *The Guide*, p. 3; *Village Voice*, April

22, 1981, p. 56; *Films in Review*, December 1981, p. 633; *Daily Mail* (UK), March 22, 1983, p. 21; *Daily Mirror* (UK), March 22, 1983, p. 17; *Daily Telegraph* (UK), March 22, 1983, p. 13; *The Times* (UK), March 22, 1983, p. 15; *Scotsman* (UK), March 26, 1983, p. 3; *Broadcast* (UK), April 4, 1983, p. 21; *Chicago Sunday Times*, April 12, 1981, *TV Prevue*, p. 1; *The News Journal*, April 12, 1981, p. 90; *Variety*, November 28, 1984, pp. 52–53

AWARDS and HONORS:
Primetime Emmy Awards USA 1981, Winner: Outstanding Achievement in Makeup: Albert Jeyte, James Kail
Nominated: Outstanding Costume Design for a Special: Vittorio Nino Novarese

NOTES: *Peter and Paul* aired in two 99-minute parts. *The Acts of Peter and Paul* was the original working title.

TELEVISION SERIES

Murder, She Wrote

"Wearing of the Green"
Season 5 Episode 6
USA Color 47 minutes
CBS Network November 27, 1988

CREDITS: *Director*: Seymour Robbie; *Producer*: Robert E. Swanson; *Executive Producer*: Peter S. Fischer; *Supervising Producer*: Robert F. O'Neill; *Associate Producer*: Anthony J. Magro; *Writer*: Peter S. Fischer, based on the characters created by Richard Levinson and William Link; *Story Editor*: Chris Manheim; *Director of Photography*: John Elsenbach; *Music*: Richard Markowitz; *Theme Music*: John Addison; *Film Editor*: Joe Morrissey; *Set Decorator*: Robert Wingo; *Costumes*: Robert Eli Bodford Jr., Nick Mezzanotti, Debi Orrico; *Casting*: Rob Stephenson

CAST: Angela Lansbury (Jessica Fletcher), Lucie Arnaz (Det. Bess Stacey), Jean Peters (Siobhan O'Dea), Barbara Bosson (Diane Raymond), Michael Constantine (Laszlo Dolby), Erin Gray (Andrea Dean), Patty McCormack (Det. Kathleen Chadwick), John McMartin (Hudson Blackthorn), David Naughton (Ken Parrish), David S. Sheiner (Leo Selkirk), Barry Dennen

(Sheldon Persky), Wayne Heffley (Security Guard), David Sage (Stavros), Thomas Bellin (Superintendent), Harry Moses (Policeman)

PLOT: Sleuthing writer Jessica Fletcher is in New York researching her new book. While visiting the vaults of Blackthorn & Sons jewelry store, a priceless tiara is stolen. A subsequent murder of a gem dealer leads Jessica through a puzzling maze involving a reclusive legendary former actress and a news reporter accused of murder.

REVIEWS and ARTICLES:
Los Angeles Times, August 17, 1989, p. IV 12; *Hollywood Reporter*, September 29, 1988; *Kansas City Star*, October 24, 1988, p. 26

OTHER TELEVISION APPEARANCES

The Arthur Murray Party, NBC-TV Network, August 24, 1954, B&W, 30 mins. As advertised in the *Cincinnati Enquirer*, Jean Peters is one of the guests, along with actress Gene Tierney, singer Johnnie Ray, comedian Jackie Miles, and choreographer Jonathan Lucas.

Dinah!, CBS-TV Network, May 29, 1979, color 90 mins.
Dinah Shore's guests are singer-actress Diahann Carroll, actresses Jean Peters, Jane Powell, Debbie Reynolds, Jane Russell, and fashion designer Bill Travilla. They discuss what glamour is.

NOTE: Some sources incorrectly report Jean Peters as a guest on *Dinah!* in the episode aired on March 8, 1979.

ARCHIVE FOOTAGE

Cinéma Cinemas, "Fuller à la table," France, Antenne 2 (1982)
Director Samuel Fuller analyzes the first scenes of *Pickup on South Street* featuring Jean Peters.

Marilyn Monroe: Beyond the Legend, USA, Cinemax (April 19, 1986)
A documentary about Marilyn Monroe. Jean Peters appears in a scene from *Niagara*.

Hollywood Mavericks, USA (September 7, 1990)
A documentary presented by The American Film Institute focusing on seventeen maverick directors. Jean Peters appears in a scene from *Pickup on South Street*.

Century of Cinema, "A Personal Journey with Martin Scorsese through American Movies," UK-USA (March 21, 1995)
A documentary exploring director Martin Scorsese's obsession with films from the 1940s and 1950s. Jean Peters appears in a scene from *Pickup on South Street*.

American Cinema, *Film Noir*, USA PBS (1995)
A documentary about American film noir. Jean Peters appears in a scene from *Pickup on South Street*.

Biography: *Marilyn Monroe: The Mortal Goddess*, USA A&E (September 29, 1995)
In this exploration of the life and career of Marilyn Monroe, Jean Peters appears in a clip from *Niagara*.

20th Century Fox: The First 50 Years, USA AMC (January 21, 1997)
A documentary about 20th Century Fox. Jean Peters appears in a scene from *Niagara*.

Biography: *Richard Widmark: Strength of Character*, USA A&E (June 29, 2000)
The life and the career of Richard Widmark. Jean Peters appears in a clip from *Pickup on South Street*.

The 73rd Annual Academy Awards USA ABC (March 25, 2001)
In memoriam, showing a brief moment from *Pickup on South Street*.

The Men Who Made the Movies: Samuel Fuller, USA TCM (July 2, 2001)
Samuel Fuller discusses his career as a filmmaker. Jean Peters appears in a few clips from *Pickup on South Street*.

Biography: *Marlon Brando: The Agony of Genius*, USA A&E (September 23, 2005)
The life and the career of Marlon Brando. Jean Peters appears in a few clips from *Viva Zapata!*

Spisok Korabley (*Catalog of Ships*), Russia (April 22, 2008)
A documentary about ships. Jean Peters appears in a brief clip from *Anne of the Indies*.

Compression: *As Young as You Feel*, de Harmon Jones, France (June 2016)
The entire film *As Young as You Feel* is played in fast-forward mode in just three minutes and twenty-four seconds without any sound.

RADIO BROADCASTS

Mail Call
"Episode 226," Armed Forces Radio Service, December 18, 1946

Words with Music
"A Night Piece" read by Jean Peters, Armed Forces Radio Service (1946)
Dreamy organ music reveries intertwined with a poetry reading.

Lux Radio Theater: *Captain from Castile*, CBS, February 2, 1949
Jean Peters plays the role of Catana Pérez. Cornel Wilde takes Tyrone Power's picture role. Actors Raymond Burr and Gerald Mohr portray the characters played on the screen by Lee J. Cobb and Cesar Romero.

Screen Guild Players: *Deep Waters*, NBC February 17, 1949
Dana Andrews, Jean Peters, and Dean Stockwell reprise their screen roles (not to be confused with a *Lux Radio Theater* broadcast of *Deep Waters* aired on CBS, December 9, 1949, starring Donna Reed in place of Jean Peters).

Lux Radio Theater: *Love That Brute*, CBS, October 9, 1950
Jean Peters and Paul Douglas re-create their screen roles.

Tusher in Hollywood, KMPC, March 9, 1952
Hollywood's commentator William Tusher interviews Jean Peters.

Spotlight Playhouse Presents: *Family Theater: Genius from Hoboken*
MNS, May 7, 1952. Jean Peters is the hostess for the broadcast.

Lux Radio Theater: *Viva Zapata!* CBS, November 3, 1952
Jean Peters plays the role of Josefa Zapata, while Charlton Heston takes Marlon Brando's movie role.

Bob Hope Radio Show, NBC, December 15, 16, 17, 18, and 19, 1952
Jean Peters is the "Lady Editor of the Week."

Lux Radio Theater: Wait 'Till the Sun Shines, Nellie, CBS, May 4, 1953
Jean Peters once again plays Nellie Jordan Halper, a role limited to the first act (except for a brief appearance in Act 3).

Lux Radio Theater: Lure of the Wilderness, CBS, May 25, 1953
Jean Peters and Jeffrey Hunter reprise their film roles of Laurie Harper and Ben Tyler.

Lux Radio Theater: The Day the Earth Stood Still, CBS, January 4, 1954
Jean Peters plays the role of Helen Benson, performed on the screen by Patricia Neal.

Hollywood Star Introductions to *Three Coins in the Fountain*, 20th Century Fox, May 1954
A publicity broadcast aired by several broadcast channels before playing commercial recordings of *Three Coins in the Fountain*.
Cut 1—Clifton Webb; Cut 2—Dorothy McGuire; Cut 3—Jean Peters.

Public service announcement for LA County Museum of Art films, Los Angeles County Museum of Art (LACMA), September 1973.
Jean Peters announced the 20th Century Fox film series at LACMA.

PROJECTS WITH JEAN PETERS'S NAME ATTACHED AS ACTRESS

Scudda-Hay, Scudda Hoo, 20th Century Fox (1946).
Jean Peters tested for the role of a young farm girl. June Haver won the part.

I Wonder Who's Kissing Her Now, 20th Century Fox (1946)
Jean Peters was originally cast to make her film debut in this picture, but she refused the part because it required her to look ugly.

Julie, 20th Century Fox (1947)
The *Los Angeles Times* (5/6/47) reported that John Payne, Clifton Webb, and Jean Peters would star in this picture, which was shot two years later as *Dancing in the Dark* (1950). Betsy Drake replaced Peters as the leading lady.

By the Night Star, 20th Century Fox (1947)
Syndicated newspapers (7/14/47) reported that George Montgomery and
Jean Peters were cast as the leads in *By the Night Star*. The picture was
never made.

Apartment for Peggy, 20th Century Fox (1947)
Columnist Sidney Skolsky announced that Jean Peters was the favorite for
the leading actress role in this picture opposite William Holden. Jeanne
Crain was cast eventually.

Call Me Mister, 20th Century Fox (1947)
The *New York Daily News* (11/11/47) reported that Jean Peters was added to
the star-studded cast of this film based on a Broadway play. The picture
was made four years later, starring Betty Grable and Dan Dailey.

White Fang, 20th Century Fox (1947)
Jean Peters was supposed to play opposite Mark Stevens in a remake of
Jack London's popular novel. The picture was never made.

Yellow Sky, 20th Century Fox (1948)
Jean Peters was reported to play the female lead. She turned it down
because she disliked the role. Anne Baxter replaced her.

The Street with No Name, 20th Century Fox (1948)
The *Hollywood Reporter* (7/18/47) announced that Jean Peters would have a
major role in this picture directed by William Keighley. Barbara Lawrence
was the final choice.

The Heller, 20th Century Fox (1948)
According to the *Hollywood Reporter* (2/18/48), Jean Peters was cast to play
the title role in this story about a young girl on the verge of delinquency.
The picture was never made.

Portrait of Jennie, Vanguard Films (1948)
According to modern sources, Jean Peters was considered for the role of
Jeannie Appleton.

Cabin in the Sky, 20th Century Fox (1949)
Some sources reported that director Lloyd Bacon wanted Peters to play a
major role in this never-produced film.

Sand, 20th Century Fox (1949)
According to the *Hollywood Reporter* (3/25/48), Jean Peters was signed for the female lead in this picture based on a Will James story. She refused that part, and Coleen Gray was cast instead.

Magnolia Alley (1949)
The *Los Angeles Evening Citizen News* (3/2/49) reported that Jean Peters was in discussion to join Jessie Royce Landis on stage in *Magnolia Alley*, George Batson's play that opened on Broadway in April 1949. Julie Harris actually played the role.

Wildcat, 20th Century Fox (1949)
The *Mirror News* (4/9/49) reported that 20th Century Fox intended to cast Jean Peters in *Wildcat*, a story set in the American Old Fields starring Richard Widmark. The project remained unrealized.

Mr. Belvedere Goes to College, 20th Century Fox (1949)
According to documents in the 20th Century Fox Records of the Legal Department at the UCLA Arts-Special Collections Library, Jean Peters was originally scheduled to play the role of Ellen Baker. Shirley Temple was eventually cast.

Samson and Delilah, Paramount (1949)
Jean Peters was one of the many actresses considered for the title role.

The Australian Story, 20th Century Fox (3/21/49)
Peters was rumored to be cast as the female lead in this film that was released in 1952 as *Kangaroo* starring Peter Lawford and Maureen O'Hara.

Triumph to the Morn, 20th Century Fox (2/9/50)
According to the *Hollywood Reporter* (3/25/48), Jean Peters was set to join Cornel Wilde and Richard Basehart in Mexico to be part of the production. Linda Darnell replaced Peters. The picture was retitled *Two Flags West*.

Bloodhounds of Broadway, 20th Century Fox (1952)
The *Los Angeles Examiner* (4/12/51) reported that Victor Mature and Jean Peters were set to costar with Mitzi Gaynor in this picture. Only Gaynor appeared in it.

Fire Devils, aka *Red Skies of Montana*, 20th Century Fox (1951)

In August 1951, Sheilah Graham wrote in her syndicated column that Jean Peters, Dana Andrews, and Richard Widmark would star in this "terrific story." A month later, preproduction began, and Victor Mature, Jean Peters, and John Lund were announced as the final cast choices. According to *Variety* (5/9/51), due to injuries suffered by Mature in a motorcycle accident along with the likelihood of bad weather, the production was "put off till spring." The project was eventually abandoned. Later, the screenplay was revised, and Peters's role was assigned to Constance Smith, and Mature and Lund were replaced with Richard Widmark and Jeffrey Hunter.

Way of a Gaucho, 20th Century Fox (1952)
The *Hollywood Reporter* (8/20/19) noted that Jean Peters was cast as Teresa. Later, the actress had to withdraw from the picture due to health reasons. Gene Tierney replaced her.

Hand Across the Sea, 20th Century Fox (1951)
According to the *Hollywood Reporter* (10/15/51), Darryl Zanuck bought this original story and assigned it to producer Stanley Rubin. Michael Rennie and Jean Peters were set for top roles.

Powder River, 20th Century Fox (1953)
The *Los Angeles Evening News* (4/24/52) reported that Jean Peters was signed by Fox to play a schoolteacher in *Powder River* opposite Cameron Mitchell and Rory Calhoun. Corinne Calvet was the final choice.

The River of No Return, 20th Century Fox (1954)
In 1952, the *Los Angeles Evening News* (5/17/52) reported that Jean Peters had a good chance of starring in this film opposite Dale Robertson. However, Marilyn Monroe and Robert Mitchum were the final choices.

The Circle, 20th Century Fox (1952)
Hedda Hopper announced (9/11/52) that producer Sol Siegel was ready to produce a Western suspense story. Wanda Tuchok was tailoring the script for Rory Calhoun and Jean Peters. The picture was never made.

How to Marry a Millionaire, 20th Century Fox (1953)
Director Jean Negulesco considered casting Jean Peters in one of the three female leading roles.

Twelve Miles Reef, 20th Century Fox (1953)

According to *The Hollywood Reporter* (3/5/53), Jean Peters was supposed to join the cast of this film, later retitled *Beneath the 12-Mile Reef* and starring Terry Moore and Robert Wagner. However, shooting overlapped with *Three Coins in the Fountain*, to which Peters had already committed.

The Fancy Dancer: A Play (1953)
The *New York Herald Tribune* (10/31/53) reported that Jean Peters and Juan Hernandez had been offered roles in this play written by Davis Lord. The production was never set up.

Sequel of Anne of the Indies, 20th Century Fox (1953)
The British magazine *Picturegoer* (12/29/53) reported that Fox was planning a sequel to *Anne of the Indies* starring Peters once again in the title role. The picture was never made.

Tarantula, Universal International Pictures (1953)
Producer Edward Small wanted to borrow Jean Peters from 20th Century Fox to star in this film. The project was postponed and later produced by William Alland in 1955.

The Egyptian, 20th Century Fox (1954)
Jean Peters, Marlon Brando, and Kirk Douglas were the original cast members and were all replaced for different reasons before the film went into production.

The Garden of Evil, 20th Century Fox (1954)
In December 1953, *20th Century Fox Dynamo* publication announced that Richard Widmark would play an American soldier of fortune opposite Jean Peters in *The Garden of Evil*. The part was eventually assigned to Susan Hayward.

Siege at Red River, 20th Century Fox (1954)
Jean Peters tested for the main female role that was later assigned to Joanne Dru.

Woman's World, 20th Century Fox (1954)
According to studio publicity, Peters fell ill with the flu, and Fox replaced her with Arlene Dahl.

Lewis and Clark, Paramount (1954)

According to the *Hollywood Reporter* (5/21/54), Paramount was interested in casting Jean Peters as the female lead along with Fred McMurray and Charlton Heston. The picture was later renamed *Far Horizons*.

The Bottom of the Bottle, 20th Century Fox (1955)
The *Hollywood Reporter* (8/31/55) stated that Jean Peters, Van Johnson, and Joseph Cotten were in the cast of *The Wrong Man* (formerly *The Bottom of the Bottle*). Ruth Roman replaced Peters, and the title reverted to its original.

The View from Pompey's Head, 20th Century Fox (1955)
Photoplay reported that Peters was briefly suspended after turning down this film.

The Ten Commandments, MGM (1956)
According to Cecil B. DeMille's biographer, Jean Peters was considered for the role of Lilia, the slave girl, in *The Ten Commandments*. Debra Paget was the final choice.

The Last Wagon, 20th Century Fox (1956)
According to the *Hollywood Reporter* (4/6/56), Jean Peters was rumored to be replacing Joan Collins, but the role was assigned to Felicia Farr.

Kiss Them for Me, 20th Century Fox (1957)
According to the *Los Angeles Times* (2/16/57), producer Jerry Wald was trying to persuade Peters to star in this picture opposite Cary Grant. Suzy Parker was the producer's final choice.

Designing Woman, MGM (1957)
Jean Peters was considered for the female lead.

The Gift of Love, 20th Century Fox (1958)
Director Jean Negulesco considered casting Peters as the female lead.

The Best of Everything, 20th Century Fox (1959)
In her syndicated column, Hedda Hopper announced that Jean Peters was in talks with director Jean Negulesco to join the cast. Eventually, Peters turned down the offer.

Anatomy of a Murder, Columbia Pictures (1959)

According to the *Hollywood Reporter* (3/4/59), Jean Peters was considered, along with fifteen other actresses, to replace Lana Turner in this Otto Preminger film.

MAGAZINE COVERS

Screen Romances, November 1947
This Year of Films (UK), 1947
Movie Show, February 1948
Movie News (Singapore), December 1948
Cavalcade (UK), April 23, 1949
Parade Boston Sunday Post, November 13, 1949
Photoplayer Magazine (Australia), April 1, 1950
NY Sunday Mirror, May 14, 1950
Movie Life (Australia), October 2, 1950
Photoplay (UK), February 1952
NY Post Weekend Magazine, February 10, 1952
Picturegoer (UK), February 16, 1952
Picture Show (UK), February 16, 1952
Picture Show (UK), April 26, 1952
Quick, June 9, 1952
Parade Long Island Sunday Press, July 27, 1952
Picturegoer (UK), January 31, 1953
Red Star Weekly (UK), April 25, 1953
Picturegoer (UK), July 18, 1953
Picturegoer (UK), April 3, 1954
Chicago Tribune Magazine, July 11, 1954
Picture Show (UK), December 11, 1954
NY Sunday News, May 1, 1955
Picture Show (UK), May 14, 1955
Pix (Australia), June 18, 1955

SELECTED BIBLIOGRAPHY

BOOKS

Barlett, Donald L., and James B. Steele. *Empire: The Life, Legend and Madness of Howard Hughes*. New York: Norton, 1979.

Barlett, Donald L., and James B. Steele. *Howard Hughes: His Life and Madness*. New York: Norton, 2004.

Behlmer, Rudy. *Memo from Darryl F. Zanuck. The Golden Years of 20th Century Fox*. New York: Grove Press, 1994.

Brady, John. *The Craft of the Screenwriter*. New York: Simon & Schuster, 1981.

Brando, Marlon. *Songs My Mother Taught Me*. New York: Random House, 1994.

Brown, Peter Harry, and Pat H. Broeske. *Howard Hughes: The Untold Story*. New York: Warner Books, 1997.

Burroughs Hannsberry, Karen. *Femme Noir: Bad Girls of Film*. Jefferson, NC: McFarland & Co., 2009.

Buskin, Richard. *Blonde Heat: The Sizzling Career of Marilyn Monroe*. New York: Billboard Books, 2001.

Cameron, Ian, and Elizabeth Cameron. *Broads*. London: Studio Vista, 1969.

Capua, Michelangelo. *Jean Negulesco: The Life and Films*. Jefferson, NC: McFarland & Co., 2017.

Dewey, Donald. *Lee J. Cobb: Characters of an Actor*. Lanham, MD: Rowman & Littlefield Publishers, 2014.

Dietrich, Noah, and Thomas Bob Dietrich. *Howard, the Amazing Mr. Hughes*. Greenwich, CT: Coronet, 1972.

Dmytryk, Edward. *It's a Hell of a Life but Not a Bad Living*. New York: New York Times Books, 1978.

Dunne, Philip. *Take Two: A Life in Movie and Politics*. New York: Limelight Editions, 1992.

Franceschina, John. *Hermes Pan: The Man Who Danced with Fred Astaire*. Oxford: Oxford University Press, 2012.

Fuller, Samuel. *A Third Face: My Tale of Writing, Fighting, and Filmmaking*. New York: Applause, 2002.

Hack, Richard. *Hughes, the Private Diaries, Memos and Letters*. Waterville, ME: Thorndike Press, 2001.

Higham, Charles. *Brando: The Unauthorized Biography*. New York: New American Library, 1988.

Higham, Charles. *Howard Hughes: The Secret Life*. New York: Putnam, 1993.

Higham, Charles, and Joel Greenberg. *The Celluloid Muse: Hollywood Directors Speak*. London: Angus & Robertson, 1969.

Kazan, Elia. *A Life*. New York: Knopf, 1988.

Keats, John. *Hughes*. London: MacGibbon & Kee, 1967.

Kranzpiller, Peter. *Jean Peters*. Vogt, Germany: Verlag fur Filmliteratur Peter Kranzpiller, 2008.

Lamparski, Richard. *Whatever Became of? . . . Ninth Series*. New York: Crown, 1984.

Landis, Jessie Royce. *You Won't Be So Pretty*. London: W. H. Allen, 1954.

Mathison, Richard. *His Weird and Wanton Ways: The Secret Life of Howard Hughes*. London: Hale, 1978.

McGilligan, Pat. *Backstory 2: Interviews with Screenwriters of the 1940s and 1950s*. Berkeley: University of California Press, 1991.

Miller, Eugene L., and Edwin T. Arnold. *Robert Aldrich: Interviews*. Jackson: University Press of Mississippi, 2004.

Minne, Olivier. *Louis Jourdan: Le Dernier French Lover d'Hollywood*. Paris: Séguier, 2017.

Moore, Terry. *The Beauty and the Billionaire*. New York: Pocket Books, 1984.

Negulesco, Jean. *Things I Did . . . and Things I Think I Did*. New York: Linden Press/Simon & Schuster, 1984.

Porter, Darwin. *Brando Unzipped*. New York: Blood Moon Production, 2004.

Porter, Darwin. *Howard Hughes: Hell's Angel*. New York: Blood Moon, 2005.

Slatzer, Robert F. *The Life and Curious Death of Marilyn Monroe*. London: W. H. Allen, 1975.

Strait, Raymond. *Mrs. Howard Hughes*. Los Angeles: Holloway House Publishing, 1970.

Thompson, Frank. *Henry King Director: From Silent to 'Scope*. Los Angeles: Directors Guild of America, 1995.

Todd, Richard. *In Camera: An Autobiography Continued*. London: Hutchinson, 1989.

Victor, Adam. *Marilyn Encyclopedia*. Woodstock, NY: The Overlook Press, 1999.

Wagner, Robert. *Pieces of My Heart. A Life*. London: Hutchinson, 2008.

Weaver, Tom. *Science Fiction and Fantasy Film Flashback*. Jefferson, NC: McFarland & Co., 1998.

Whiting, Charles. *American Hero: The Life and Death of Audie Murphy*. York, UK: Eskdale Publishing, 2000.

Young, Jeff. *Kazan: The Master Director Discusses His Films*. New York: Newmarket Press, 1999.

NEWSPAPERS AND PERIODICALS

Anderson, Jack. "Hughes' Personal Life Suffered." *San Angelo Standard-Times*, April 14, 1976.

Awbrey, Stuart. "Last of Nellie Is Filmed in Hollywood." *Hutchinson News*, October 8, 1951.

Beck, Marilyn. "Mrs. Howard Hughes Rejoins the World." *Sunday Examiner*, February 25, 1973.

Berg, Louis. "Jean Hits the Top." *New York Herald Tribune*, June 6, 1954.

Brown, Peter Harry. "Howard's End." *Vanity Fair*, April 1996.

Browning, Norma Lee. "The Magic Made Her Come Back." *Chicago Tribune TV Week*, March 4, 1973.

Campbell, John. "On the Range with Broken Lance." *New York Times*, May 2, 1954.

Carroll, Harrison. "Behind the Scenes in Hollywood." *Lancaster Eagle-Gazette*, August 5, 1949.

Cassa, Anthony. "Pete, the Reluctant Movie Star." *Hollywood Studio Magazine*, September 1980.

Churchill, Reba, and Bonnie Churchill. "Better Than Red Apples." *Silver Screen*, December 1947.

Clary, Patricia. "Hollywood Film Shop." *Bakersfield Californian*, January 3, 1951.

Cohen, Harold V. "The New Film." *Pittsburgh Post-Gazette*, July 2, 1951.

Connolly, Mike. "Rambling Reporter." *Hollywood Reporter*, May 14, 1952.

Connolly, Mike. "Rambling Reporter." *Hollywood Reporter*, September 3, 1953.

Crosby, Joan. "A 17-Year Hiatus for Jean Peters." *TV Scout Entertainment News and Features*, February 26, 1973.

Demaris, Ovid. "Howard Hughes. We See You! We See You!" *Esquire*, March 1969.

Gardella, Kay. "Hughes' Ex-Wife Makes TV Debut." *Sunday News*, March 4, 1973.

Gebhart, Myrtle. "Farm Girl Is Promising Film Star." *Boston Sunday Post*, June 15, 1947

Graham, Sheilah. "Whatta Gal!" *St. Louis Globe-Democrat*, April 28, 1947.

Graham, Sheilah. "Chasing Howard Hughes." *Ladies' Home Journal*, August 1974.

Guernsey, Otis L., Jr. "On the Screen." *New York Herald Tribune*, August 10, 1951.

Haber, Joyce. "Hughes, Jean Talk." *Victoria Advocate*, January 22, 1972.

Hall, Gladys. "Exploding the Myth of the Mysterious Jean Peters." *Photoplay*, October 1954.

Handsaker, Gene. "Hollywood." *Times Munster*, February 12, 1951.

Harris, Eleanor. "The Girl Who Didn't Go Hollywood." *Collier's*, November 5, 1949.

Holland, Jack. "Cinderella from Ohio." *Screenland*, October 1947.

Holsopple, Barbara. "Jean Peters Returns to Acting in Winesburg, Ohio." *Pittsburgh Press*, March 2, 1973.

Hopper, Hedda. "Study in Contradiction—That's Jean Peters' Life." *Los Angeles Times*, March 25, 1951.

Hopper, Hedda. "Jean Peters Wanted to Be a School Marm." *Hartford Courant*, March 25, 1951.

Hopper, Hedda. "Looking at Hollywood with Hedda Hopper." *Chicago Sunday Tribune*, March 25, 1951.

Hopper, Hedda. "Widmark to Play Ex-Con." *Salt Lake Tribune*, December 4, 1951.

Hopper, Hedda. "Hollywood's New Sex-Boat." *Photoplay*, July 1952.

Hopper, Hedda. "Hollywood's Mystery Girl." *Photoplay*, March 1953.

Hopper, Hedda. "Actress Jean Peters Weds Oil Man." *New York Daily News*, May 30, 1954.

Hopper, Hedda. "Hollywood's Gorgeous Jean." *Chicago Tribune Magazine*, July 11, 1954.

Howell, Cindy. "Jean Peters Returns to Acting in Winesburg, Ohio." *Des Moines Register & Tribune*, March 4, 1973.

Johnson, Erskine. "In Hollywood." *Fitchburg Sentinel*, January 30, 1952.

Johnson, Erskine. "Lost Horizon Sequel Planned." *Rhinelander Daily News*, February 27, 1952.

Johnson, Erskine. "You'll Remember." *Binghamton Press*, October 29, 1953.

Johnson, Erskine. "In Hollywood. Jean Peters Falls Victim to LA Smog." *Fitchburg Sentinel*, October 1954.

King, Henry. "Try and Stop Me!" *Modern Screen*, December 1947.

Lane, Lydia. "Surmounting the Materialism." *Los Angeles Times*, December 10, 1976.

Lyons, D. L. "America's Richest Wife." *Ladies' Home Journal*, November 1968.

Lyons, D. L. "The Liberation of Mrs. Howard Hughes." *Ladies' Home Journal*, March 1971.

Lyons, D. L. "Jean Peters: Howard Hughes' Ex-Wife Speaks Out." *Ladies' Home Journal*, March 1973.

Mann, Arnold. "Top of the Line Design." *Emmy Magazine*, March/April 1984.

Meyer, Jim. "Jean Peters." *Films in Review*, March 1964.

Millier, Arthur. "Unknown 20-Year-Old Wins Prize Screen Role." *Los Angeles Times*, November 10, 1946.

Muir, Florabel. "Hughes Secretly Signs Jean Peters as a Bride." *New York Daily News*, March 16, 1957.

Parsons, Louella. "In Hollywood with Jean Peters." *Los Angeles Examiner*, October 12, 1947.

P. D. "Wagner Learns to Love." *Picturegoer*, September 11, 1954.

Peters, Jean. "He Kissed Me!" *Movieland*, November 1947.

Peters, Jean. "No More Wardrobe Blues." *Screen Stars*, April 1951.

Peters, Jean. "The Role I Liked the Best." *The Saturday Evening Post*, September 27, 1952.

Peters, Jean. "Wardrobe Mistress." *Screen Stars*, October 1952.

Peters, Jean. "What I Like About Bob Wagner." *Movie Life*, 1953.

Peters, Jean. "Jean Peters Gives . . . Rules for Roommates." *Baltimore Sun*, April 12, 1953.

Peters, Mary E. "She Never Left Home." *Modern Screen*, June 1949.

Phillips, Dee. "Is Being Sexy Enough?" *Screenland*, August 1951.

Price, Mark J. "Actress Jean Peters Dies of Leukemia." *Akron Beacon Journal*, October 20, 2000.

Redelings, Lowell E. "Hollywood Scene." *Los Angeles Hollywood Citizen News*, December 13, 1946.

Redelings, Lowell E. "Hollywood Scene." *Los Angeles Evening Citizen News*, June 24, 1949.

Redelings, Lowell E. "Hollywood Scene." *Los Angeles Evening Citizen News*, September 21, 1951.

Redelings, Lowell E. "Hollywood Scene." *Los Angeles Evening Citizen News*, April 9, 1953.

Roosevelt, Edith K. "Long Tresses Seen Key to Caresses." *Salt Lake Tribune*, July 7, 1952.

Schallert, Edwin. "Jean Peters, Weary of Ragged Roles Wants Finery in Films." *Los Angeles Times*, March 2, 1952.

Scott, John L. "Change to Svelte Becomes Jean Peters." *Los Angeles Times*, April 24, 1949.

Scott, Vernon. "Secluded Life Not for Howard Hughes' Mate." *Pittsburgh Press*, December 12, 1969.

Scott, Vernon. "Jean Peters Returns to Work, But Still Likes Housewife Role." *Bridgeport Post*, October 17, 1976.

Scott, Vernon. "Jean Peters in Mini-Series." *Lubbock Avalanche-Journal*, November 21, 1976.

Silden, Isobel. "It's No Crime When Yesterday's Stars Get into 'Murder.'" *Los Angeles Times*, August 17, 1989.

Slatzer, Robert. "Jean Peters: 1926–2000." *Classic Image*, December 2000.

Slocum, Beth. "Isolations Haunts Jean Peters in Ohio." *Milwaukee Journal*, March 4, 1973.

Smith, Cecil. "Jean Peters Back After 18 Years." *Los Angeles Times*, March 5, 1977.

Theisen, Earl. "Jean Peters in Rome." *Look*, August 24, 1953.

Thomas, Bob. "Jean Peters Turns Down Sexy Buildup, Goes Against Trend." *Sedalia Democrat*, October 5, 1952.

Toby, Henry. "Italy Finds a New Heart-Throb." *Picturegoer*, March 5, 1955.

Wagner, Joyce. "Actress in a New Role After Years as Wife of Recluse." *Kansas City Star TV*, March 4, 1973.

Wallace, Inez. "Lure of the Wilderness." *Cleveland Plain Dealer Pictorial Magazine*, September 1952.

Wallace, Rosalie. "Halfway to Heaven." *Photoplay*, November 1948.

White, Constance. "Love is in the News." *Photoplay*, July 1954.

Wilkerson, William R. "Tradeviews." *Hollywood Reporter*, December 3, 1947.

Wilson, Earl. "It Happened Last Night." *New York Post*, January 19, 1970.

Witbeck, Charles. "TV Keynotes: Winesburg Revisited." *Morning Call*, March 2, 1973.

Worden, Frederick. "Why I've No Time for Love!" *Screenland*, February 1954.

INDEX

ABOUT THE AUTHOR

Michelangelo Capua is the author of several biographies of Hollywood film stars and filmmakers. He lives in London.